W9-BXR-924

THIS BOOK BELONGS TO:
Ann & Bill Kessler

Books by Harvey Swados

Out Went the Candle

On the Line

False Coin

Nights in the Gardens of Brooklyn

Years of Conscience: The Muckrakers

A Radical's America

A Radical's America

Harvey Swados

little, brown and company · boston · toronto

A Radical's America

an atlantic monthly press book

LIBRARY OF CONGRESS CATALOG CARD NO. 62-9540

FIRST EDITION

ACKNOWLEDGMENTS

Pieces in this book first appeared in *Antioch Review, Anvil and Student Partisan, Atlantic Monthly, Chrysalis, Dissent, Esquire, Mademoiselle, Menorah Journal, Monthly Review, The Nation, New World Writing, Noble Savage, Partisan Review, Saturday Review,* and *Western Review.*

ATLANTIC-LITTLE, BROWN BOOKS
ARE PUBLISHED BY
LITTLE, BROWN AND COMPANY
IN ASSOCIATION WITH
THE ATLANTIC MONTHLY PRESS

Published simultaneously in Canada
by Little, Brown & Company (Canada) Limited

PRINTED IN THE UNITED STATES OF AMERICA

There ought to be, behind the door of every happy, contented man, someone standing with a hammer, continuously reminding him with a tap that there are unhappy people.

— Anton Chekhov

Introduction

For the first time, I find myself faced with the necessity of explaining something I have written. Supposedly it is the novelist who shivers most nakedly in the cold light of self-revelation, forever trapped by the button he himself has pressed; but I have always found that my fiction, for better or worse, wore its own disguises and thus absolved me of the necessity of apologizing for its appearance. In a sense, my stories and novels, once published, were no longer mine. The essays that follow, however, remain defiantly and stubbornly mine – perhaps that is why they seem to cry out for some explanation for their being placed between covers.

When I ask myself, Why this book?, I begin by recalling my willful refusal of requests that I "do" a book on labor. The reasons for this resistance have slowly become clearer to me, and their enumeration may give the reader some idea of what this book is *not* about.

First, it was troubling to be asked to say more than I had already said in a book of fiction called *On the Line,* since I detected an implication that fiction does not tell a truth analogous to and maybe superior to many other truths. Second, I resented being labeled in the casual American way as an expert on labor when I was in fact no such thing and had no desire to become an expert on any problem. Third, while I was fascinated by problems of work and labor, they did not seem to me to be "worth" a book – and I become more and more persuaded that for a writer it is the book that counts, not the short story, not the article, but the finished book which he himself has conceived. Fourth, I was at least as fascinated by other manifestations of American life and liveliness – by the question of "popularity" in books, movies, all manner of things; by the position of women in our civilization; by the sedulous avoidance of serious problems in our political debates, discussions and campaigns. All of these matters and more I had already been writing about for years, one sometimes leading to another, one sometimes growing out of a story or novel in progress or a conversation or argument I had gotten into.

So it seemed logical that if there was to be a book at all, it had better be a book which would include all of these worth saving, in reasonable proportions. There arose the logical question: Why me? What did I have to say about my America that would be worth the time of others to read, not as fiction, but as blunt statement or apology or polemic? The novelist needs no more excuse for his existence than the magician or the juggler; the essayist, however, and specifically the essayist who disclaims *expertise* in any field other than storytelling (and even that will inevitably be questioned), must establish his claim on the reader's patience. My claim is my identity:

1. I am a novelist. We Americans have had self-educated novelists and college-professor novelists, reactionary novelists and Communist novelists. With the exception of Henry James, none of them to my knowledge has achieved in his nonfiction the suavity and finesse of the European man of letters, of the Thomas Mann of *Essays of Three Decades*. By comparison, our essays in nonfiction have been jagged, tentative, unsure – and yet enormously exciting. Mann's contemporary, the Fitzgerald of *The Crackup*, the notebooks, the letters, can tell and teach more about the craft of writing than any other novelist or critic since the splendidly magisterial essays of James. In our own day, there is more about what it means to be a Negro in this world in James Baldwin's books of essays, *Notes of a Native Son* and *Nobody Knows My Name*, than in any other single place outside of a novel; there is a whole new range of insights into our literary heritage in Wright Morris's under-discussed essays *The Territory Ahead;* there is fuel for a roaring bonfire of argument in Norman Mailer's perhaps over-discussed essays in *Advertisements for Myself*. These novelists (and such others as James T. Farrell and Jessamyn West, in her fascinating *To See the Dream*) have displayed qualities of mind that have made them worth listening to, no matter what they talk about; I hope to be counted among their company.

2. I am a middle-class man of the mid-century, born and brought up in a middle-sized American city, graduated from a Middle Western state university, with a wife, three children, a

house, and an automobile. Although I have worked in factories of various kinds, have shipped out to sea, and have been associated with radical movements, I consider myself basically middle-class in temper and outlook. Like most Americans, I am of the city but not for it, for the countryside but not of it (despite the fact that I live in it in preference to the city). Certain segments of American society are as foreign to me as the warring Congolese tribes: the very rich, the migrant workers, café society. If I have not written of them it has not been because I lacked curiosity, but rather because the opportunity to learn about them has not come my way any more than it has come the way of most middle-class Americans. My own Buffalo boyhood and predominantly white-collar adulthood have been for the most part as typical as my experiences in World War II, which I got through, like the majority of my generation, without shooting at anyone or being specifically shot at. But I saw ships go up around me, houses disappear, children die, all in that impersonal mechanics of destruction which we have been learning so well in this century, and it was in that war that I, like many others, really learned the meaning of boredom and of fear.

3. I am a Jew. My claim that this is another element of my typicality in mid-century America should not be taken as whimsicality. In my grandparents' time, at the beginning of this century, the Jew was thought of as two kinds of person, each of them "un-American" if not "anti-American": first, as a mysterious and frightening money-changer, akin to the Wall Street titans but not of them; second, as a clannish, poverty-stricken, crime-ridden, disease-infected, unassimilable foreign element (the magazines of the period included solemn discussions of whether, since there were so many Jewish pimps, procurers, muggers, and pickpockets, there was not something inherently criminal in the Jewish character). Now, little more than half a century later, not only would such formulations be unthinkable (except in the hate sheets); not only has the Jew been replaced by the Negro and then by the Puerto Rican as bottom dog and supposedly congenital criminal; but the Jewish workingman has all but disappeared, and the suburban Jew has emerged in his place as the middle-class man par excellence, in a country that prides itself on being solidly middle-class.

But this transformation of peddler and proletarian into P.T.A. member has not (not yet, anyway) completely submerged traditional Jewish dedication to learning, to culture, to education, and to solidarity with the oppressed. It is not accidental that the Navy officer who forced a national debate about the American educational system should have been a Jewish immigrant (that his notions are eccentric and reactionary need not be argued here). No more is it accidental that *avant-garde* painting should have been all but dominated in the past decade by Jews, or that the editorial board of a magazine entitled *Dissent* should be predominantly Jewish.

Furthermore, at a time when America is at long last, if reluctantly, renouncing the isolationism which was an inevitable consequence of eighteenth-century geography and nineteenth-century flight from Europe, it is the twentieth-century American Jew who feels most strongly his blood ties to the old continent. It was *our* aunts, uncles, grandparents, cousins whose annihilation forcibly recalled to us, more strongly than to any other Americans, a sense of the size and shape of the world.

And here at home, it is the Jew, the urban man in a land now only one quarter rural, who (even if he never lays claim to the connection) knows the urban Negro as well as a white can know him – not with the pathetically false knowledge of the patronizing Southerner, but as customer and counterpart, as the man who has supplanted him in the East Side slum, as the man who endures what the Jew's father and grandfather endured.

There is no plea for the Jew as best American. If there are any such, they are more likely the handful of practicing Christians who mean business about the most important matters in the world, peace and racial integration – and indeed, McCarthy's Cohn and Schine, and the Rosenbergs and their executioner, Judge Kaufman, are as representative of the decade as Catholic layman Bill Buckley or Protestant layman Nelson Rockefeller. It is rather a recognition that in our country the Jew has moved from a marginal position to one of centrality. In the next generation it may very well be the Negro, the tenth American, who will come to be regarded by many of his fellow citizens – and by many around the world – not necessarily as Presidential timber (that old Jewish gag is already much too old, even for Irish politicians) but as the most typical American.

4. I am a socialist. I think it incumbent upon me to distinguish this from either a liberal or a Stalinist bias; perhaps in the course of making the distinction I may also succeed in establishing what I hold to be true but have never before attempted to articulate: that a socialist attitude is at least as firmly in the American grain as a liberal or an absolutist stance. As intellectuals are increasingly polarized, with the *nouveau riche* among them drawn to the Washington orbit, the *nouveau* radicals first to Belgrade, now to Peking and Havana, there seem to be fewer and fewer able to withstand the magnetic attraction of power and prestige at the one pole or of absolute self-righteousness at the other.

Those few among the latter who are still attempting to sell us Moscow as the wave of the future ought to be made to commit to memory the July 1960 speech of Nikita Khrushchev to the Soviet Union's writers and artists. "It is only through the firm leadership of the Communist Party," he told them, "that Soviet writers, artists and musicians . . . are finding creative inspiration."

In this perverse parody of a noble doctrine, Khrushchev decreed that "In a Socialist society, development of literature and art does not take place spontaneously and anarchically, but is regularly directed by the party." The fist emerges: "They may ask what right did we have to settle matters in that fashion. We answer: according to the rights of leadership . . . Perhaps it may sound rude, but in my opinion it is better to grab a man by the ear and drag him from the abyss than to let him fall into it."

For one of my convictions the voice of the absolutist bully is no more the voice of socialism than are those of the self-righteous terrorists, the neo-Stalinist Chinese chieftains dragooning a continent into industrialism, or the Cubans who appropriate the word to describe a social order in which unions are handed over to the Communist cabal, in which promised elections are first postponed and then abrogated, in which the crowd in the square shouting up the Maximum Leader is told that its euphoric chanting represents the democratic validation of a development program. Perhaps the final irony is that those of us who supported the Cuban Revolution against the Batista sadists and their American cohorts should now be accused by the *nouveau* radicals of wanting Cuban children to go hungry and unschooled because we cannot close our eyes to the deformation of that revolution under the pressure of an all but unbridled American imperialism.

No, I cannot accept the appropriation of mankind's most precious aspirations by these people. No more can I accept the intellectual and moral bankruptcy of those who vastly overbalance them in this country: the professors and liberals who utilize the perversions of socialism as an excuse to capitulate to the bottomless hypocrisy of American capitalism. The fact that this polarization takes place does not mean for me that either pole has any real claim to stewardship of the American dream. In August 1960 I wrote the following lines for a symposium in *Liberation* on the Kennedy-Nixon campaign:

> The argument is already being advanced that it would be more worthwhile to vote for Kennedy because (a) Johnson as Vice President will be harmless; (b) Adlai Stevenson will be given a job; (c) there are important liberal intellectuals like Schlesinger, Galbraith, Cox, etc., in the Kennedy camp; (d) nothing could be worse than Nixon in the White House. I am not impressed by this reasoning, which seems nothing more than the usual speciousness which invariably precedes liberal cries of betrayal.

In less than the allotted Hundred Days, the betrayal duly took place. At home, the continuing attempt to placate the implacable Southern reactionaries who dominate the Congress meant that millions of underpaid laboring people, mostly Negroes, and among them the "thousands of exploited laundry workers — so often cited in the campaign speeches of John F. Kennedy — were sold down the Potomac." So James Wechsler told the liberals of Americans for Democratic Action, in confused convention assembled, even while they were being asked to support a program of billions for a mad race to the moon and a madder digging of holes ("shelters") in the earth. Abroad, Cuba was cynically assaulted in the most shameless maneuver in modern American history. And not one of the liberal intellectuals who had flocked to the fraudulent banner of the New Frontier had the guts to retrieve his honor or his self-respect by resigning or otherwise dissociating himself from the arrogant idiocy of his Administration's invasion attempt.

It may be countered that, since this is a position which would be regarded by most Americans as eccentric, if not subversive, one cannot simultaneously claim it to be representative of any central aspect of the American tradition. But the American people have not been given an honest choice for a long time now. If they were to be given such a choice I believe that their openness and generosity of spirit would reassert itself; for they are being snowed as deliberately, and very possibly as ruthlessly and efficiently, as are the peoples of any Communist country. "We have been so vastly regimented," said Mr. Justice William O. Douglas in May 1960, "that almost overnight opinion is shaped to fit a synthetic image." To my mind this brainwashing is the most terrible indictment that can be made not only of Communism but of contemporary capitalism as well:

"'I wish I had the guts to tell the American people what the CIA is doing in Southeast Asia.' The speaker," wrote Paul A. DuBrul, Managing Editor of *New America,* "was a correspondent for a top American network, recently in the States for a short vacation. He and his listener knew that he wouldn't tell the American people, however, at least not until another debacle of the caliber of the U-2 and Cuban incidents takes place . . ."

The six o'clock news on TV features a "man in the street" interview on the Cuban situation. Only one man speaks critically of American behavior: the camera lingers long and lovingly on the newspaper he carries under his arm – the *Worker.* "You see, Daddy? You see?" cries the serious-minded schoolboy triumphantly to his father.

The same schoolboy turns to *World Week,* the "National Magazine of Social Studies and International Affairs" distributed throughout American schools, to read a description of the American White Paper on Cuba, and is confirmed in what he has already seen on TV: "The State Department," he reads, "might have added that Castro had uprooted a friendship between Cuba and the U. S. stretching back to 1898, the year Cuba won its freedom from Spain." Not one word, nothing, on what the U. S. had done to uproot the "friendship."

His younger brother, who can make his way through the headlines, is already being indoctrinated by the mechanism of organized distraction through horror and hatred. "Mommy, what are tots?" he asks, pointing to the newspaper which features on page one: MOTHER HURLS TOTS INTO RAVINE. He returns from school to demand in bewilderment: "Isn't Grandpa Russian? They say the Russians are the bad ones."

The children happen to be mine, but they could be anyone's. The irresponsible appropriation of the pervasive, inescapable mass media, of the popular arts, of the schools themselves for the systematic inculcation of a prefabricated attitude in which smugness is married to sadism – this is nothing less than a crime against humanity. The brutal, self-satisfied words of Nikita Khrushchev echo plangently in one's ear: "They may ask what right did we have to settle matters in that fashion. We answer: according to the rights of leadership."

The rulers of America too have arrogated unto themselves the right not simply to lead but to "settle matters" by imposing upon us a bipartisan foreign policy, a bipartisan popular culture, a bipartisan information-propaganda grid, a bipartisan self-congratulation, a bipartisan cant. This is not the America of Thoreau, of Emerson, of Emily Dickinson, any more than it is the America of Golden Rule Jones, of John P. Altgeld, of Jane Addams; and I hereby reassert that those of us who persist in saying No to a society built on worship of the buck for the things and people it can buy, those of us who persist in dreaming of a society built on mutual aid and mutual respect, have just as much right to consider ourselves as representative of an essential corpuscular element in the American bloodstream as do the Luces, the Nixons, the Kennedys, and all those who, in appropriating for themselves even the rhetoric of our common dream, have turned it into a nightmare.

No doubt some will insist that I mislabel myself, that one cannot be at the same time a skeptic and a socialist, that one cannot say No and Yes from the same throat, and that if America were visited by almost any variety of socialism, from "tiptoe" to "total," I should be as outraged as I now am by the shrill and malevolent vacuity of American capitalism today.

This may be. It is one reason why, although I am a political man, I am a novelist, not a politician, and shall never join any party nor run for mayor of any place. If he is not inconsistent, the novelist is nothing – and I intend to cherish my inconsistencies as I do my children.

This is also why, as I said at the outset, I have resisted all efforts to make of me a systematic thinker, or even to make of this a systematic book. The pages that follow were written at various times over the last decade from a variety of concerns and in various moods; the temper that informs them and, I hope, unites them, I have just tried to isolate and describe.

As for myself, I regard this book in a sense as a balancing of my accounts in order that I may confront new problems, now that I have turned forty. If I have attempted to maintain a tension between skepticism and idealism, I have also attempted to secure some kind of personal connection between the writing of these essays about my America and the creation of fiction. In the process my kinship has been with those writers who imply, even when they treat of trouble and terror, that the world could be better, just as my commitment has been to those human beings who believe – despite every awful evidence to the contrary – that the world *must* be better. It is to them that I dedicate this book, in comradeship and homage.

Harvey Swados
San Francisco
June 1961

Contents

1.

The Jungle Revisited

On the first of July, 1960, an era came to an end. It was hardly marked by historians, even by those hasty historians who write for the newspapers; but on that day the federal humane-slaughter law went into effect, and the nation became a little less hectic. Probably the sudden quiet was noticed by almost no one but the workers in the slaughterhouses, where cattle and pigs, calves and lambs had been shoved, screaming, squealing, grunting, howling in fear and terror, to be shackled, clubbed, stabbed, slashed and hacked into edible portions for the dinner tables of America.

The insensate shrieking of the terror-stricken beasts, ringing through the old brick walls of the Chicago stockyards, which could still be heard until the new law of 1960 brought unconsciousness followed by painless death, was in a sense the final echo of those dreadful days that you read about in *The Jungle*. For the visitor to the Chicago stockyards of today who carried in his mind an image of the stockyards of *The Jungle* (which Upton Sinclair wrote in 1905, "sometimes blinded by his own tears," as he says himself) would observe at once that the scene was changed almost – but not quite – beyond recognition.

For one thing, Chicago is no longer the "hog butcher of the world." As automobiles are now being put together not just in Detroit, but in California, Wisconsin and New Jersey, so are pigs being killed in great new slaughterhouses in Wichita, Des Moines, Omaha. Those packing houses still in Chicago are by comparison small and even old-fashioned, half-forgotten by the teeming millions of

America's second city, who depend for their livelihoods on other, newer enterprises. The stockyards remain, vast buying and selling marts, as a tumble-down, noisy, noisome relic of an earlier day, but they too will disappear when the redevelopers have their way and housing projects spring up on soil fertilized by many millions of doomed animals. Then indeed the era about which Sinclair wrote with such passion will have passed into history.

In the meantime, the curious visitor can still follow the pigs as they trot, nose to tail, through the pens of a Chicago packer to their death and their destination on the breakfast table. He will observe, after his initial surprise at the comparative smallness of the entire operation, that 90 per cent of the people involved in the killing and cutting at a typical plant are Negroes. Almost all of the Lithuanians, Poles, Croatians and Slavs who fill the pages of *The Jungle* have moved on to other employment. No longer immigrants, no longer victimized as greenhorns by unscrupulous loansharks, foremen, and rental agents, they have scrambled up and out, leaving the room at the bottom of the heap to the Negroes.

Not only is the killer, alone with death in his high-walled, blood-soaked cell, still "a great burly Negro" as he was sixty years ago; his less-well-paid fellow workers are too, for the most part. They still work in a building marked by great shifts in temperature, from the close and airless to the great freezer storage rooms; they are still surrounded by blood and stench, entrails and excrements, death and dissection.

But the conditions of their work are happily better than those described in *The Jungle*. Protected against discrimination and the grosser forms of exploitation by their union, the United Packing House Workers of America, they work and live better than their forerunners – just as the animals now die better than their forebears. Seasonal employment, the scourge of all laboring people, from the auto workers of Detroit to the sugar workers of Cuba, has been all but overcome in the packing industry, thanks to improved methods of raising, feeding, and shipping; and unemployment insurance helps to take up the slack when work does fall off. Electric saws have replaced the axes of the "splitters" and "cleaver men," and no one need work at a dangerous or exhausting rate of speed. Killing and cutting are sometimes done at the same plant by the same people, who thus learn a variety of operations and vary their day with different jobs of work. Women workers need hardly fear that demands will be made on their bodies in order that they may continue to sell the power in their hands and backs. Children are debarred from laboring alongside their elders, who make enough to be able to dream that when their offspring come of age, they will be doing something else, something better.

For, while this is a good job, working in a packing house, it is only relatively a good job. It is good for someone whose parents were tenant farmers and never had the chance for more than a year or two of school, never made enough to buy a car or decent furniture, or occasional entertainment, never had the hope of looking forward to a better future for their children. It is so good that workers of such a background will come to feel a vested interest in it – it is *their* job; they have earned it by virtue of steadiness and skill and loyalty – and will fight hard to hold on to it against the incursions of scabs, as one meat packer discovered in a recent strike. But it is not a good job to most Americans. It cannot be challenging or fascinating or glamorous or lucrative to anyone much more sophisticated than a sharecropper, willing to trade away the dusty cabin for the city flat and the noisy, bloody job that bespeaks change and opportunity. Inevitably these people too will come to understand, even from looking at movies and picture magazines, that what they are doing to earn a living is not generally considered worthy of a modern, sensitized human being, no matter how much union security and how much government supervision – and then the whole cycle will start again. Either new strata of hitherto submerged populations will move in to replace the Negroes, as the Negroes moved in on Upton Sinclair's Lithuanians (and as the Puerto Ricans took over the bottom-dog jobs formerly held only by Negroes in New York City), or the character of production will have to change radically, to make the atmosphere palatable and attractive to ambitious young people.

Because the truth seems to be that the meat-packing industry in Chicago has not kept pace technologically with many other industries. The workers, as we have said, look different from the way they must have to Sinclair – they no longer have the appearance of creatures moving through a living nightmare; but aside from the humane slaughter, the improved cleanliness, the better light, the careful government supervision, the electric saws, and the umbrella of their union, what they *do* does not seem to have changed so remarkably in these last sixty years. With *The Jungle* fresh in your mind, you could still tour a Chicago packing house today and have a reasonably good idea of the process of production.

It is worth noting that the packing-house industry was perhaps the first in the country to adopt modern mass-production methods. At any rate, Henry Ford was much impressed by its use of the conveyer-belt system to move carcasses before stationary workmen who could attack them with their tools, performing the same set of operations repetitively; thus the disassembling of animals served as the inspiration for the assembling of automobiles, while the utilization of "everything but the squeal" may perhaps have served as the inspiration for Ford's celebrated penurious techniques in the design, production, and sales of the Model T.

But the conveyer belt and the stationary workman in the packing house were dependent on a gravity operation: the beast had to be hoisted up as high as possible in order that his innards – skin, blood, intestines, and the rest – could be funneled and channeled down from floor to floor. Hence the high old buildings, which seem now so hopelessly obsolescent in an architectural economy whose landscape is increasingly punctuated with the dashes and hyphens of long, low industrial plants housing one-level continuous-flow mechanized and automated operations; and which, even with their occasional, up-to-date, made-in-Germany sausage-stuffing machines, still have the look of movie sets for a somewhat expurgated and mildly modernized version of *The Jungle.*

Is that, however, why we persist in reading this book? Surely if we want only to find out "what it was like" or "what it is like now" or to make a mental connection between the two, we could turn as readily to any substantial reference work. Just as surely, this book does not continue to live because of its unique literary values or esthetic virtues.

It must be nearly forty years now since Van Wyck Brooks blasted Upton Sinclair for coming to the writing of novels from the wrong set of preconceptions. And nothing that has happened in the world of fiction since then has served to weaken Brooks's case. It was his contention that it is folly, and the death of art, for the would-be novelist to think that he can only write with full effectiveness about lumberjacks by becoming one himself, and living in the woods for years on end. Such misunderstanding of the author's role can only create one more bad lumberjack and one more bad novelist. The novelist must maintain a certain reserve, a certain distance from his characters, in order to see them and know them most fully; otherwise he will inevitably collapse into the stammering sentimentalism of the overinvolved.

Certainly the subsequent developments in American fiction have in general sustained the Brooks thesis. The false identification of writer with class in the proletarian novel of the Thirties, or of writer with uniform in the war novel of the Forties, issued largely in nothing more than flatulent overvaluing of human beings as types or models. Those novels which, in turn, have stood out from the ruck have been the products of writers whose primary devotion was not to their class or their credo but to their craft.

Besides, the more we examine a work like *The Jungle,* the more difficult it is to defend its specifically literary merits – and the more it becomes obligatory for the commentator to make a pious listing of Sinclair's inadequacies and exaggerations. Very well. No one could deny that the style of the book is undistinguished, at best. No one could deny that he drags out the agony and piles horror upon horror until we want to cry, "Stop! Enough! No more!" No one could deny that structurally it is a broken-backed book, with most of the intensity concentrated in the first two thirds, which are concerned with the struggle of the immigrants to sustain themselves in Packingtown, and most of the propaganda concentrated in the last third, after the dissolution of Jurgis Rudkus's family and during his conversion to socialism.

If what the reader wants is a fictional rendering of the psychological effect of prolonged association with the killing of helpless animals, then he should read the unforgettable story by Pierre Gascar, "The House of Blood." This tale, which deals with the life of a little boy apprenticed to a sadistic provincial French butcher, is to be found in Gascar's *Beasts and Men* and is in its own way definitive. If what the reader seeks is an allegorical revelation of some of the overtones of the endless parade of cattle to the abattoir, he must read James Agee's stunning story "A Mother's Tale," which begins like a bedtime story, complete with talking beasts, and becomes a Christian parable as it grows to encompass a world of millions marching meekly to death camps.

Still, I should assert that there are certain human values which do not find complete expression in either of these stories, and for which one must turn to a book like *The Jungle*. And so, as I would hope that the educated person reads all three, I must now say what it is about this book that does make us persist in reading it.

For me it is the furious passion with which Upton Sinclair here apotheosizes the sweat and agony of an essential generation of Americans, an entire generation without which this country could not possibly have achieved what it has. If he had done nothing more, Sinclair would have justified – as one way of functioning – the method not of immolation in the working class but of observation and creation, which has gone so far out of fashion in recent years among Western novelists. We need not go through his entire enormous *oeuvre*, so much of it cranky or banal, to sustain such a statement about *The Jungle*, any more than we should feel compelled to justify all of Zola's immense output in order to come to a similar conclusion about *Germinal:* Both books were the product of men who proceeded, notebook in hand, to research a new territory, and then retired to write, not in tranquillity but in the heat of anger and hope about the price paid by countless thousands to build what is known as a civilization.

Zola's brutalized coal miners of northern France and Sinclair's immigrants of Chicago's Packingtown can nevermore be fully forgotten. They take their place in history as the cruelly used builders of the modern era, along with all the other untold millions who gave up their lives on the altar of production in the strange and terrible rites of the new industrial age.

This was not exactly what Sinclair had in mind. Judging from his own testimony, as well as from the internal evidence of the book itself, he (and many of his contemporaries, like Jack London) thought of *The Jungle* as a tract that would help win many converts to the ideas of socialism and to the growing Socialist Party. No doubt it did – at least the years following its serial publication in the mass-circulation Socialist weekly *Appeal to Reason* were the period of maximum growth and influence of American Socialism – but over the generations the book's impact has been quite different. In fact, as a result of the disgust and outrage that swept not only this country but virtually the entire world, once it became clear that *The Jungle* was not simply the invention of an overheated mind, remedial reform legislation was enacted which did much to halt the revolutionary upsurge that Sinclair had been hoping to implement.

Indeed, when I came to reread *The Jungle* I found that I had forgotten quite completely the lengthy propagandistic passages with which the last portion of the book is so replete, but that I had retained from boyhood an ineradicable memory of the wretchedness of the residents of Packingtown and of the horror of the industry in which they slaved. It is my impression that this is a common experience, and my guess that no one who reads *The Jungle* will ever be able to erase from his memory its opening chapters.

No writer, not even the most ardent propagandist, can predict the consequences once he sets his pen to paper. If Socialist agitation in the United States was to some degree blunted by the passage of such legislation as the Pure Food and Drug Act, in large part immediately inspired by the reaction of Theodore Roosevelt and others to *The Jungle*, the ultimate effect of this book on many thousands of minds cannot now be measured — nor will it ever be measurable.

It seems to me precisely now, as this country emerges from the mindless euphoria that has gripped it for at least a decade, that *The Jungle* must renew its hold on the imaginations of an entirely new generation of readers. For a time, Americans of the vast broad middle range appeared hypnotized by the advertising mentality into believing not only that we had it made, but that the American standard of living had been achieved at the cost of certain human expenditures which were at worst a trifle distressing and at best glamorous, in a liberal-patriotic kind of way. The sacrifice of millions of lives, of millions of proud and hopeful and bravely pioneering spirits, to the accumulation of capital, even though it took place within the memory of many Americans still alive, and even though it still continues in certain backward areas of American society, became something hardly to be believed, to be relegated to obscurity, to be mentioned, if at all, only jocularly—as with the abominable exploitation of women and children in factories, fields, and sweatshops.

But now we are entering a new time. We sense uneasily that we do not have it made, that with a war-economy prosperity have come new and staggering problems, and that there is a vast suffering world beyond our national boundaries, struggling in a variety of ways to accumulate capital and thus to move as we have moved up into the twentieth century. We sense too that, throughout this world, no matter how the capital is accumulated and no matter whether it be in the Western sector, in the Communist zones, or in the burgeoning new nations of the formerly colonial areas, it is being done at a stupendous cost in human suffering. There is a close parallel between the payment in hunger, blood, and agony of the peoples of the underdeveloped world and that extracted from the immigrant builders of the American empire. It is a parallel that we will neglect only at our own peril; it is one that should fill us with humility and compassion for all who must strain like beasts of the field to bring the world to the next epoch; it is one that *The Jungle* will help to sustain in the forefront of our consciousness, which is where it belongs. To the extent that it fulfills this function, this book will persist as a force in the spiritual and social lives of a new and, it is to be hoped, a responsible generation of readers.

The Atlantic Monthly, December 1961

The Reform Journalism of the Muckrakers

Something exhilarating happened to American journalism at the beginning of the twentieth century. For a brief period – a decade, roughly from 1902 to 1912 – an extraordinarily keen group of editors and publishers made common cause with some of the nation's outstanding novelists, poets, historians, lawyers, economists, and researchers. The cause, which changed the course of our history, was the exposure of the underside of American capitalism.

Ever since the Civil War, there had been plenty of editors and writers willing and eager to inculcate a credulous public with legends of wealth accumulated solely by thrift and canniness, of progress achieved thanks to completely unregulated free enterprise, and of the natural inferiority of the lower orders: Ambrose Bierce argued against the socialists that slums and child labor ought not to be combated because they were the inevitable lot of those too stupid and shiftless to raise themselves and their offspring from the heap. But a new wind blew in with the new century, reintroducing two qualities which had for too long been relegated to the wings of the American scene: honesty and compassion.

Honesty was now defined not merely as "discretion" or "balance" but as unflinching determination to bring to light the reality behind the convenient myths about the rulers of America, regardless of whether the rulers' power lay in the political machine, in the corporate cannibalism tagged as the trust, or even in the pulpit. Compassion was now defined not merely as "charity" or "sympathy" but as outraged identification with the friendless and the voiceless at the bottom of society, regardless of whether they were illiterate croppers, sweated newcomers, aggrieved laborers, or terrorized Negroes.

During this vigorous decade, honesty in pushing the investigation of corporate and governmental corruption to its nethermost reaches and in arriving at the ultimate logical conclusions was not mislabeled treason, subversion, *lèse-majesté* or cynicism. Nor was compassion for the suffering of the exploited millions — as ruthlessly sacrificed in the frenzy to industrialize as the masses of any contemporary Communist ex-colony — mistaken for sentimentality or confounded with the "square."

In fact it was the Square Deal's father who also fathered the name which has identified these journalists from that day to this. On April 14, 1906, in the midst of the labors of this unusual band, Teddy Roosevelt unloosed an attack on them, taking as his text a passage from *Pilgrim's Progress:* ". . . the Man with the Muckrake, the man who could look no way but downward with the muckrake in his hand, who was offered a celestial crown for his muckrake, but would neither look up nor regard the crown he was offered, but continued to rake to himself the filth of the floor."

The Presidential attack, sanctimonious and largely unjustified though it was, created a permanent label, one which has entered the language as has the more recent "egghead"; but it did not succeed in slowing the momentum of such men as Charles Edward Russell, Ray Stannard Baker, Lincoln Steffens, Finley Peter Dunne, and Upton Sinclair. That did not take place until the end of the Taft Administration, when B. H. Hampton, last of the great muckraking publishers, awoke one day in 1911 to find that financial control of *Hampton's,* haven for writers displaced from other journals, had been maneuvered out of his hands and that the magazine was going to be scuttled — apparently by underground agreement of some of the financial interests which had been plagued by its revelations.

Historians differ as to whether muckraking was bought out and killed off, or whether – regardless of what happened to *Hampton's* – it would in any case have died with the ebbing of the Roosevelt era. Certainly some of the muckrakers themselves, tired, disillusioned, or disoriented by American participation in World War I, directed their energies into other channels: one became a corporation executive, another a chronicler of romances, a third a biographer, a fourth a professional reactionary.

But just as certainly, during the first decade of this century, these writers showed themselves at their best; and they, together with the editors and publishers who were bold and idealistic enough to commission and to print their exposés, showed America at its periodic best. There is something to be said for the notion that our country recuperates from its greedy decades almost like a repentant drunkard recovering from a debauch by trying to examine the causes of his drinking bout and by making earnest resolutions to sin no more. The difference between the nation and the drunkard may lie in the fact that, in its moods of sober self-criticism, the nation really does redress many of the wrongs, really does help those who cannot help themselves, and does thereby renew its world image as a state concerned not solely, or even primarily, with self-aggrandizement but, much more importantly, with dignity, freedom, and decent self-respect.

This is not to say that the national mood during these intervals of thoughtful stocktaking is always one of unalloyed benevolence, any more than were the pages of the muckraking magazines purely rationalistic or invariably redolent of Christian brotherhood. Just as the New Deal years were also the years of the Silver Shirts, the Liberty League, and the German-American Bund, so can one find in the pages of the muckraking magazines reams of nonsensical food-faddism and, worse, occasional articles about semibarbaric Negroes or aggressively acquisitive Hebrews which should have been beneath the contempt of any self-respecting editor; and it is perfectly true that a humane, passionately reform-minded editor like B. O. Flower could wax as eloquent in the pages of the *Arena* over the virtues of spiritualism or Christian Science as over those of civic reform or public ownership. But we speak here of an over-all tone, a mood, and it is surely beyond dispute that in those years such periodicals as *Hampton's*, *Pearson's*, *Cosmopolitan*, and *McClure's*, to say nothing of *Collier's* or the *Arena*, reflected in their major concerns everything that has been traditionally largest and noblest in the American spirit.

That may very well explain the twofold reaction to Theodore Roosevelt's epithet on the part of the journalists whom he attacked. If Gustavus Myers and Ida Tarbell were appalled at this parodying of their scholarly researches, others – Upton Sinclair and Charles Edward Russell among them – responded to the challenge by accepting the label and insisting on wearing it with pride, as a proof of the force with which their work was striking home.

Now the Muckrake Men I know [*insisted Upton Sinclair in the* Independent *in 1908*] are all men of personally clean lives and generous hearts; there is not one of them who would not have been something noble, if he had felt free to choose. Of those who come immediately to my mind, one would have been a metaphysician, another would have been a professor of ethics, three at least would have been poets, and one would have founded a new religion. Instead of that they are Muckrake Men . . . not because they love corruption, but simply because they hate it with an intensity which forbids them to think about anything else while corruption sits enthroned . . .

As a rule, the Muckrake Man began his career with no theories, as a simple observer of facts known to every person at all "on the inside" of business and politics. But he followed the facts, and the facts always led him to one conclusion; until finally he discovered to his consternation that he was enlisted in a revolt against capitalism.

He is the forerunner of a revolution; and, like every revolutionist, he takes his chances of victory and defeat. If it is defeat that comes; if the iron heel wins out in the end – why, then, the Muckrake Man will remain for all time a scandal-monger and an assassin of character. If on the other hand, he succeeds in his efforts to make the people believe what "everybody knows" – then he will be recognized in future as a benefactor of his race.

History would seem to justify those who gloried in T.R.'s diatribe; for, decades later, the surviving journalists of the era vied in asserting pride of rank in the muckraking elite and in reading others out of it. This was to be true even of those (a majority of the original group) whose political philosophy had shifted over the years: Mark Sullivan, become a spokesman for conservative Republicanism, was to insist in his later years that he, and not Lincoln Steffens, had fired the opening gun of the muckrakers' crusade. One hardly presses his claim to charter membership in a group which he cannot regard as representative of what is best in the national character.

It should not be thought that the muckrakers sprang full-blown from the brows of a handful of editors, any more than that their spirit was swept from the scene once and for all by the storm clouds of the First World War. Their fervor, their passionate denunciation of corporate aggrandizement at the expense of the individual American, their belief in the boundless possibilities of a better nation, instinct in every line they wrote – all these are to be found in Henry Demarest Lloyd's *Wealth Against Commonwealth,* which was published in 1894.

The men and women who do the work of the world [*asserted Lloyd in his opening chapter*] have the right to the floor. Everywhere they are rising to "a point of information." They want to know how our labor and the gifts of nature are being ordered by those whom our ideals and consent have made Captains of Industry over us; how it is that we, who profess the religion of the Golden Rule and the political economy of service for service, come to divide our partial existence for the many who are the fountains of these powers and pleasures. This book is an attempt to help the people answer these questions. It has been quarried out of official records, and it is a venture in realism in the world of realities. Decisions of courts and of special tribunals like the Interstate Commerce Commission, verdicts of juries in civil and criminal cases, reports of committees of the State Legislatures and of Congress, oath-sworn testimony given in legal proceedings and in official inquiries, corrected by rebutting testimony and by cross-examination — such are the sources of information.

Indeed, the only thing wrong with this powerful book, from a journalistic standpoint at least, was that it was too far in advance of its time, for it anticipated in every area the main lines of attack of the muckrakers; to a modern reader its method and its commitment are all but indistinguishable from those of the muckrakers, and if it was less widely absorbed than their work, this can only be attributed to the fact that the public was "not ready" for it — which may be another way of saying that it was not made readily available as an article of mass consumption.

A decade later, however, the public was ready. Or again, we may put this another way by saying that the revelations of the muckrakers were made easily available to the public by a mass medium, the cheap popular magazine. If it is worth noting that the traditional American periodicals — whether scholarly, historical, literary, or simply upper-class in general — played little part in the tumultuous activity of the decade, despite the fact that some of their most valued contributors blossomed as muckrakers in other journals, it is even more important to emphasize the mass circulation of those other journals. A low-price magazine which could vault to a circulation of nearly half a million in a country with, at the turn of the century, little better than a third its present population, and with a substantial proportion of newly arrived immigrants and native illiterates, was obviously saying something of value to millions of Americans. When we multiply this by the total number of magazines whose circulations were zooming upwards because they were encouraging and publishing the muckraking writers; when we remind ourselves that there were at the time no true picture magazines, no television, no radio, no movies, we begin to sense that we are here witnessing the birth of the modern mass media. (The parallel – but distinct – development of yellow journalism is one which cannot be examined here.) Isn't it worth pondering, the fact that the mass magazine was born of this arousal of the American conscience by a band of bold editors making common cause with novelists, poets, and littérateurs?

In his brilliant early book *The Golden Day*, Lewis Mumford makes what seems to me a most telling argument against overvaluing the ultimate impact of the muckrakers. "In attack, in criticism," he says, "they did able work; but when it came to offering a genuine alternative, their picture became a negative one: industry without millionaires, cities without graft, art without luxury, love without sordid calculation. They were ready to upset every aspect of modern industrial society except the fragmentary culture which had brought it into existence."

Mr. Mumford goes on to point out a truth which the thirty-five years since he first committed it to paper have only strengthened – that capitalism itself *can* provide what it was attacked for not providing, and that the real indictment of it lies elsewhere:

> The essential poverty of America was a qualitative poverty, one which cut through the divisions of rich and poor; and it has been this sort of poverty which has prevented us from projecting in the imagination a more excellent society. Life was more complicated in America but not more significant; life was richer in material goods but not in creative energies. These eager and relentless journalists were unaware of the necessity for establishing different kinds of goods than the existing ones; they had no notion of other values, other modes, other forms of activity than those practiced by the society around them.

Anyone who reads the literature, not the journalism, produced by the muckrakers, must be persuaded of the justness of Mr. Mumford's reproach. Those reformers who, like Brand Whitlock, invested all their indignation, as well as all their creative energy, not in journalism but in novel writing, produced books which, despite the polite references to them by American historians, are all but unreadable today. Those who divided their energies between poetry and muckraking – Edwin Markham, Ernest Crosby, Charles Edward Russell – produced poetry which is now hardly recalled even by specialists in the period. Those who were both storytellers and muckrakers, from novelists like Frank Norris and Owen Wister and David Graham Phillips (who did an occasional muckraking piece), to writers of the volcanic energy of Jack London or Upton Sinclair (who regarded both their fiction and their polemics as performing equivalent functions), produced rows of books which, even at their best, are simply not worthy of comparison with the great imaginative works of other epochs.

Writing in *Cosmopolitan,* in 1906, Upton Sinclair, still flushed with the fantastic success of *The Jungle,* spelled out the reasons why the opening chapters of that bombshell of a book were (and still are) so explosively charged; at the same time he unconsciously exposed the roots of an esthetic misconception that was to strangulate not only his own later fiction, but also much of the work of Sherwood Anderson and of the proletarian writers of the 1930's:

In many respects I had *Uncle Tom's Cabin* in mind as a model of what I wished to do . . . But now there is a stirring of life within the masses themselves. The proletarian writer is beginning to find a voice, and also an audience and a means of support. And he does not find the life of his fellows a fascinating opportunity for feats of artistry; he finds it a nightmare inferno, a thing whose one conceivable excellence is that it drives men to rebellion and to mutual aid in escaping. The proletarian writer is a writer with a purpose; he thinks no more of "art for art's sake" than a man on a sinking ship thinks of painting a beautiful picture in the cabin; he thinks of getting ashore, and of getting his brothers and comrades ashore – and then there will be time enough for art . . . So far as I myself am concerned, the well-springs of joy and beauty have been dried up in me – the flowers no longer sing to me as they used to, nor the sunrise, nor the stars; I have become like a soldier upon a hard campaign – I am thinking only of the enemy. The experiences of my life have been such that I cannot think of them without turning sick; there is no way that I can face the thought of them at all, save as being practice for the writing of *The Jungle*. I see that it was necessary that some one should have had such experiences, in order that it might be impossible for any man to have them again.

Regardless of whether the novelist blocked his own development by imagining himself a soldier rather than an artist, or whether he simply lacked the necessary imaginative gifts from the very outset, the unhappy fact remains that the literary efforts of the muckrakers were not on a par with their journalistic labors.

But what of these labors? Can one go along with Lewis Mumford when he concludes that: "For all the effect that these painstaking pictures had in lifting the worker onto a more active plane of manhood, one would willingly trade the whole literature for a handful of good songs . . ."?

The best answer is to be found in the course of America's social progress in the twentieth century, so profoundly influenced for the better by these writers themselves. Seldom, if ever, has the craft of journalism more responsibly served the individual conscience and the national interest. The ardent American notion of a free society, freely inclusive, freely elected, and mutually helpful, had been cynically shoved aside in the closing decades of the nineteenth century. If it was revivified in the early years of the new century, to the benefit of every American who has come of age since then, that must be credited in substantial measure to the ringing voices of the muckrakers, recalling their fellow citizens to an honest understanding of their responsibilities and their potentialities in a democratic society.

There remains the question of whether these high-minded men and women could really have accomplished greater things had they foresworn journalism, could really have become the poets and philosophers that Upton Sinclair knew them truly to be, had they concentrated on belles-lettres. Judging from what they actually produced, it would seem highly doubtful. In truth, it would seem more logical to conclude that in these magazine articles and books, written under pressure and often with a directly propagandistic motive, they were writing at the top of their bent and expressing the very best that was in them.

In our time the rules of the game have apparently changed, but the questions continue to be asked. Is it possible for the young writer to find his way to the large American audience, not by producing pap or worse, but by telling the people strikingly and excitingly what "everybody knows"? Can he do this even while he works in private at shaping his dreams for the possible pleasure of a happy few?

The latter question can be answered only by the individual artist in the living out of his own life; for some it will be yes, for others no. But the former question is a public question, and one that should be considered publicly. If there is a parallel between the decade that opened the first half of the century and that which opened the second, it is not between the magazines of both eras; it is between the mass media peculiar to each. Clearly, television, radio, the movies, are to the great American public now what the cheap magazines were then. If we are to understand the muckrake phenomenon in terms of our own time, and also to consider the possibility of re-establishing connection between the writer as a publicly useful man and the concerned (not merely consuming) public, then we ought to try to imagine what it would be like if today's novelists and poets were suddenly to assume leading roles in television, at the invitation of and with the enthusiastic co-operation of the masters of the medium. We ought to try to imagine what it would be like if this collaboration were to exclude the advertisers and their agents from active participation in programming, and were to aim solely at confronting the viewing public evening in and evening out, forcefully and passionately, with words and pictures of the

American scene, with tributes to the heroic and assaults on the venal, the cowardly, the exploiting.

Such a conjoining of public-spirited and intellectual forces would provide us with a modern equivalent of what happened during the decade of conscience. This is not the place to consider whether the obvious barriers to such a conjoining would be too formidable to be surmounted, or whether our native resourcefulness can muster the ingenuity to brush them aside once there is established a consensus that the writer and the mass medium ought to unite for the benefit of the populace at large. Such problems will have to be confronted by the new generation in the light of the old American experience; if it rediscovers the muckrakers, it may find in them not only the light, but the heat as well.

Introduction to *Years of Conscience: The Muckrakers* (Meridian Books, 1962)

Footnote: By comparison with the muckrakers, our current crop of journalists seems to have been born timid, tired, or disillusioned. The most effective work today, limited as it is, is being done by the television journalists, a frustrated group of capable men perfectly aware that they function as public-service window dressing for an industry single-mindedly devoted to the worship and propagation of mass idiocy. As for the magazines and newspapers, they have rendered gratuitous before the fact a White House charge that they trifled with the national security by telling the American people too much. When President Theodore Roosevelt branded the journalists of his day as filth grubbers, they responded, as I have noted above, by redoubling their efforts. When President Kennedy brands the journalists of our day as irresponsible, they hasten to demonstrate their "responsibility." The *Saturday Evening Post* proudly publishes photographs, which it had previously patriotically suppressed, of guerrillas training for the Cuban invasion; the Miami *Herald*, which like other Florida newspapers had suppressed news of Cuban exiles training and recruiting in violation of our laws, continues to hold back news of post-invasion adventurers exercising in the area. The *Herald*, it says, "feeling that the story is within the sensitive area of national policy, withheld publication until after the matter was aired in Washington . . ."

The Miners: Men Without Work

The miners have been called in the past the backbone of the American labor movement. Never yet broken in to the abject life of the workers in the industrial cities, they have still a tradition of resistance and a habit of joint action.
– *Edmund Wilson, "Frank Keeney's Coal Diggers"*

St. Michael, Pennsylvania

It is a strange thing to come to a town and find it full of grown men. They stroll the narrow, shabby streets, chat at the corners, lean against the peeling pillars of the town saloon, the St. Michael Hotel & Restaurant, and they look more like movie actors than real human beings, because something is wrong.

Then you ask for one of them by name, in this town where it is obvious that everyone knows everyone else, and you get the reply, "Oh, he'll be along any minute. Today's sign-up day." And it is borne in upon you that these men are subsisting on unemployment insurance checks, that this is a community where practically all of the able-bodied men have been out of work for many months. Where are the children? In school, although most of these people are older and no longer have small children. Where are the teen-agers? Looking for work, moved away, trying their luck elsewhere. Where are the women? Working, many of them – which is a story in itself.

St. Michael is a company town (of the Berwind-White Coal Mining Company) tucked into one of the many folds of the mountains of western Pennsylvania. It is as American as any town you could want, by any standards you could name. But the menfolk are practically all out of work, and have been ever since the 24th of April, 1958, when Maryland Shaft #1 closed down. This may be why there is not much travel agency business for Caribbean cruises. In its own way, however, it is a tourist attraction, or would be if tourists could ever find their way to it over the winding, rutted, poorly marked roads that tie it to all the other little mining communities of the region: for it was here thousands drowned in the Johnstown Flood. Today the old boathouse, then used by wealthy summer residents from Johnstown and Pittsburgh, stands high and dry on the St. Michael hillside – now a weather-beaten saloon, it is one of the four hangouts for the miners of St. Michael, who are proud of the tragic story of the area, just as they are proud of the tragic history of their calling.

Six hundred and fifty of these men were working at Maryland #1 when the company started to mechanize. The number was gradually reduced to four hundred; then, after two layoffs and six months of part-time operation, there came a day which none of the miners had believed could really come, even though there had been signs, hints, warnings. The mine shut down.

It is not practically relevant whether the closing was a result of there being too much coal or too many men. What matters is what is happening to the people. Later on we shall return to the larger issues of increased productivity resulting from mechanization and concomitant shifts in fuel usage. For now let us stay with the men.

It was only a couple of years ago that the coal dust problem was so bad in St. Michael that a civic committee was formed to cope with it. "I was used to not recognizing my husband, to say nothing of the other men who'd come out of the mine and wave to me," says one miner's wife. "But the coal dust got so bad that it lay over the town like a pall. Everything was covered with it, and we got worried, not just about silicosis down in the mines, but about what it was going to do to all of us right out on the streets."

The dust too was a by-product of mechanization, a result of the automatic miners chewing away furiously hundreds of feet under the earth, and the company informed the committee that there was no point in investing the large sum that would be necessary to abate the nuisance, since it was already losing money on every carload of coal being taken from Maryland #1. All too soon thereafter the mine closed down, and the dust stopped sifting through the streets. The committee was disbanded. . . .

Most of the miners have been used to seasonal operations, working winters and taking off summers, and for quite a long time they assumed that this was to be just another layoff. But then the summer was over, fill-in jobs elsewhere in the area did not seem to be available, and the company took out its expensive automatic equipment and moved some of it down to Maryland Shaft #2, half a dozen miles away at Wilmore. At that point the miners and their families began to face up to the reality of their prospects, and habits began to change. The first item to stop moving at the general store was dog food. After the dog food gathered dust, it was the bottled baby food in the little glass jars that stayed on the shelves. A while after that, the shopkeeper himself gave up and locked his doors forever.

The saloons are still going in St. Michael's Hotel, the Workers' Educational & Social Club, the American Legion Hall, and the old boathouse, but many of the whisky drinkers have switched to beer, many of the beer drinkers have switched to Squirt, and even more do not show up at all nowadays in the saloons.

"I used to spend between forty and fifty dollars every two weeks in the saloons," says one miner. "Now I never go any more. It's one thing to be a good fellow when you have it – it's a little different when you have no job."

The town barber, a horn-rimmed young man in a starched white shirt who is on the school board and looks startlingly middle-class in a community that is overwhelmingly working-class, stares at his cigar and muses over his beer at the Legion bar: "I bear no resentment to the miners who don't come in any more to have me cut their hair. I guess if I'd been out of work as long as they have, I'd ask my wife to cut my hair too."

Some of the miners have managed to get jobs elsewhere. Hampered by the fact that their skills – and such intangible assets as courage, fortitude, *esprit de corps* and insouciance in the face of continuous danger – are not readily transferable to other trades, they have been absorbed only in lower-paying jobs. Those who came from other communities and only boarded in St. Michael have gone home. A few have gotten into the steel mills, but not many. A few more have gotten construction work and jobs with the State Highway Department, but again not many; the men point to the million-dollar addition to the high school plant now going up, with only seven miners among the construction crew, and they claim that it is impossible to get such a job without "politics." A number of the miners are now working, often for a third or less than what they used to earn, as orderlies in hospitals and institutions, and as janitors and stockmen in big stores. Some have tried to relocate – at least one man has been back and forth to California twice, tracking down rumors of steady employment there – only to return to home grounds when jobs haven't materialized.

Practically everyone, they say, would come rushing back to St. Michael if Maryland #1 were to reopen, even those few who have gotten good-paying jobs elsewhere (a man with seniority is allowed up to three weeks to reapply for his job). Mining is something that gets in a man's blood, and a coal mine is a man's world in a way that a department store or a mental hospital can never be.

It is truly ironic that a substantial proportion of these men, who pride themselves on their ability to live with danger, to work hard, fight hard, drink hard, love hard, are now learning housework and taking over the woman's role in the family.

What happened was terribly simple. When it became apparent that the mine was not going to reopen, the men signed up for unemployment insurance and their wives began to look for work. Committees were set up — as they have been, hopefully, sometimes pathetically, in similarly depressed areas in Kentucky, West Virginia, Illinois, and Michigan — to see what could be done about bringing in new businesses that could provide employment. The ones that did come to the western Pennsylvania area were those that could benefit not only from tax rebates, low rents, cheap utilities, and other enticements, but also from a substantial pool of people hungry for work — almost any kind of work at almost any kind of wage. Now there are in the area a scattering of small garment factories (brassières, shirts, shirtwaists, children's wear) all employing not men but women to bend over their sewing machines.

So the women go out to work in the new factories at minimum wages and the men stay home, running the washing machines and the vacuum cleaners, doing the shopping and the dusting, often babysitting, occasionally cooking and scrubbing. There are variations. Some wives hire themselves out as cleaning women to middle-class homes in other towns while their husbands serve as cleaning women at home. There are rebellions too. One husband sits in the saloon waiting for his wife to finish her shift and come after him at midnight, which she does, standing in the doorway in her pedal-pushers, her arms folded, smiling tiredly but firmly until he shoves back his chair, finishes his beer, and walks her home. He insists on playing his role as a man even if he cannot do his work as a man, and one can only guess as to whether his wife loves him any less than do those women whose husbands have taken to drowsing in front of the TV after they have finished the dishes and await their wives' return from the factory. But these are for the most part younger women; it is hard for a woman in her fifties to keep up with the production pace in a factory, and a number of them have had to give it up and reluctantly rejoin their husbands on the rockers or the porch steps.

What else does a man do besides keep house and rock, and hang around the saloon, after he has been out of work for fourteen months? One miner says, "I've been going from town to town, city to city, every place within a hundred miles of here, looking for work. I know it's a wild-goose chase. I'm too old. My own boy is thirty-two, or maybe thirty-three, with three kids of his own, and *he* can't find work. One or two places where he could have had work as a carpenter, he couldn't get a journeyman's card in the union. So what chance do I stand? Just the same, I keep trying – it keeps me occupied."

Those men who have given up looking, or are working sporadically here and there, now and then, put in a lot of time hunting and fishing in the neighborhood. The miners of this area are as fanatical a lot of fishermen as you will find anywhere in the United States; and they also like to come home with deer, pheasant, and sometimes even bear. This is not the least of the ties that bind these jobless men to their home place. There are others, which have to be understood if the men and their problems are to be fully understood.

The miners of St. Michael have banded together and purchased (with money borrowed from their local union) the huge old home of the former mine superintendent, on a bluff overlooking the valley, and have christened it "The Sportsmen's Club." Here, in addition to over sixty acres of wooded recreation and picnic grounds and a *boccie* court, they have a big screened-in run that they built themselves, to hold more than five hundred baby pheasants, which they acquired from the state conservation authorities and will release for hunting when they are grown. The Sportsmen's Club is one more social center that is their very own, in addition to the Legion Hall and the Workers' Educational & Social Club, down the street from each other and from the St. Michael Hotel. Most of the big social events are held in the Legion Hall, which is decorated with blowup photographs of the local boys — all with Slavic or Croatian names — who have played football at the great state universities, some of them in the Rose Bowl. (The football scholarship is not a joke in St. Michael: it is a very practical way for miners' sons to get a college education and so move on and out into another world.)

It doesn't take much of an excuse to throw a party either; and whether it is a testimonial for a local hero, or a blowout with the hundred dollars the company gives when the mine operates for a year without a fatal accident (not too often, unfortunately), a sheep is roasted, a pig is spitted, the liquor flows, and, as one miner who has the scars to prove it says, "You get twenty-six miners together and you have twenty-seven fights." The oratory is as pungent as the food. "You women," the toastmaster is fondly remembered as having said to the wives last Christmas, "went and voted for Eisenhower. Well, now you've all got jobs!" Lithuanian slugs it out with Ukrainian; Pole battles with Welshman; and they all stick together against owners, outsiders, and union bureaucrats.

Over at the Workers' Educational & Social Club (also refurbished and enlarged with a loan from the union local) there are, in addition to the bar and the miniature bowling alleys, a meeting hall, kitchens, a library, and a parlor, where those miners are laid out who choose to die and be buried without the consolation — or interference — of organized religion.

This is a very special kind of life, and a miner knows what he is missing when he tries his luck in the cities or the suburbs.

"More than one of our boys has gone off to Pittsburgh or Cleveland and come back because he couldn't stand those cement lawns."

"In a big city, you have to pick a fight with a stranger.

Here in St. Michael, you can fight with your friends."

"Seriously, here we all know each other, we're clannish, we stick together, we help each other out. It's a good place to live."

It's also a cheap place to live. The company houses, put up during the depression, are comfortable and have pleasant yards, even if their plumbing is simple and the roads around them are sooty and potholed; they rent for from $9.00 to $14.25 a month. When you consider too that water and sewage are provided directly from the mine's pumps at a nominal price, as is 25-cycle electricity (even with the mine shut down), you can understand why $25.00 a day is a first-class wage for a miner in a company town, even if the mine only has orders enough to run three or four days a week. Naturally mine families are reluctant to trade in all this – in addition to fish and game and the produce of all the farms that checkerboard the mining country – for the inflation of the metropolis and the suburb.

There is an even more compelling economic reason for the unemployed miners of St. Michael not wanting to leave the industry or the community. According to the United Mine Workers' contracts, a miner must have worked for twenty years out of the last thirty in order to be eligible for a $100-a-month pension at the age of sixty. You can't live, much less support a family, on that sum, but when it is added to social security, savings and life insurance, it can make the difference between a comfortable old age and a miserable one. Seniority leading up to pension eligibility, however, cannot be transferred from one company to another, or even from one mine of a company to another, unless there is such a shortage of miners that you can move onto a panel and directly into another mine without going to the bottom of the list.

Thus if you are forty-eight years old and have worked in the mines for thirty years, you are not going to receive any pension at all unless you can get in two more years before you reach the age of sixty. It is hard to believe that somehow, sometime during the next dozen years, you will not be able to get in two more years in the mines to qualify for the pension. There are a lot of these borderline men, desperately hanging on — much more desperately than the younger men who have seen their pension hopes go glimmering and who are ready to sell out and move away, even though they discover that their possessions too have become as worthless as their retirement plans, with their 25-cycle electric stoves and television sets quite unsalable in a community which may never again use the mine's power lines. And of course there are quite a few men safely past fifty, who have the twenty years under their belts, and now have nothing to worry about beyond surviving and supporting their families in one way or another for the next decade, until they reach pension age.

Meanwhile, unemployment insurance is running out.

As these lines are written, most of the miners of St. Michael have six more checks (of about $30) coming to them. When these lines are read, the checks will have stopped. What then?

"After the last check," says one of the younger men, "comes the revolution."

Well, maybe. But probably not. In order to hazard some sort of guess as to what lies in store for these hundreds of Americans, and for many more thousands like them, from Illinois to West Virginia, we shall have to leave St. Michael for a moment and consider the problem of coal nationally.

For the past decade the coal miner has been squeezed from two directions: by mechanization and by the introduction of increasingly popular substitute fuels. While output per man per day has almost doubled in that decade (from 6.26 tons per day in 1948 to 11.3 tons per day in 1958), the number of men employed in the mines has been more than halved, from 441,631 to 218,600. And as a result not only of slumps but of competition from gas (whose production has increased 365 per cent in the last fifteen years) and fuel oils, coal production has receded from a peak of over 600 million tons in 1947 to less than 500 million tons.

The railroads, once major consumers of coal, have now practically converted to diesels; household heating, formerly fueled with the coal-stoked furnace, has lately converted so largely to gas or oil that anthracite mining — confined to three Pennsylvania counties — is all but moribund; when we speak of coal nowadays, for all ordinary purposes we are speaking of bituminous.

It is electricity (in addition to steel, stationary at about 100 million tons) that is expected to take up the slack. With the production of energy from mineral fuels and water power already doubled in the last twenty years, it is now forecast that coal production will have to increase by 50 per cent to meet the expanded energy demands of 1975. Does this mean that more men will be needed to mine coal, or even that most of the currently unemployed miners will be put back to work? One would have to be a professional optimist (or a union official) to think so.

For one thing, the development of alternative sources of energy has not ended. Atomic power may not be economic at present; that does not mean that it never will be. For another, the inexorable development of mechanization has not yet come to a halt, even though it is true that it is nearing the saturation point: mechanical mining machines which can mine up to eight tons of coal per minute, and other new equipment, now cut about 85 per cent of all underground coal production. The development has been truly fantastic, as extreme perhaps as in any other industry. It would seem a logical inference that those mines which for one reason or another are not susceptible of economic mechanization will have to give way to those which are.

We need hardly be surprised that the National Coal Association is both proud of its adventure in mechanization and enthusiastic about the prospects for coal. But it does seem a trifle unusual — particularly in a period of mass unemployment in the industry—that the United Mine Workers should refuse to yield precedence to the operators in their eagerness to welcome the man-displacing machine and their Rotarian optimism about coal's future.

Indeed, the visitor to the Mine Workers' somber and dignified headquarters in Washington is bombarded by the union's research men with data and statistics arrayed to buttress what is obviously the John L. Lewis line: mechanization benefits the miner, and new uses for electric power will vastly increase the need for coal in the years ahead. One thing is sure: no one can charge Mr. Lewis with being soft on featherbedding. His aides are anxious to demonstrate that the union has gone along wholeheartedly with mechanization. (In 1930 10 per cent of coal production was mechanically loaded, in 1956 85.4 per cent; in 1930 8.3 per cent was mechanically cleaned, in 1956 61 per cent; and by now nearly nine tenths of all mined coal is mechanically cut.) True, facts are mixed with foolishness, as in current efforts to beat the drums not only for heat pumps and coal by wire, but also for electric automobiles and coal-fired home furnaces. And Mr. Lewis's propagandizing for technical progress seems to stop short when it comes to projects like the St. Lawrence Seaway, the economic development of atomic energy, and the mechanization of competing fuel industries.

Nevertheless the figures pour forth from the Research and Marketing Department of the UMW. It is only when the visitor asks for a figure on the number of coal miners out of work as a result of mechanization and competition of other fuels that silence suddenly descends.

The conversation is shifted to the 65,000 men on pension. But no, the visitor insists, that is not what he meant—it is rather the men of working age in the union who are not now working. Finally, with extreme reluctance, there comes an estimate of perhaps 50,000 men.

And what is to become of these men?

Once again there is great enthusiasm expressed for electric power, the increasing amounts of coal it will demand, and the great proved reserves of coal – estimated at 1900 years' worth – waiting to be dug. But by the unemployed miners?

Probably not. The price of progress. Some must fall by the wayside as others progress. It's a cruel world.

Several inferences seem inescapable. First, that the union's estimated figure on unemployment, about which it seems to prefer not to speak, is very likely as deflated as its membership figure is inflated. (On the same visit, actual working members in anthracite were estimated at 30,000–40,000, and in bituminous at around 300,000 full- and part-time miners. Both figures bear no relation to those released by the U. S. Bureau of Mines or by the Bureau of Labor Statistics, and would seem to be based less on reality than on the growing need to prevent the UMW from being tabbed as numerically a second- or third-class union.)

Second, that Mr. Lewis has more or less decided to cut his losses, concentrate on consolidating the solid gains of a steadily shrinking membership – while maintaining the façade of an enormous organization – and trust to time and mortality to resolve once and for all the problem of the unemployed workers in the coal fields, and so erase them from the agenda of the union and from the public conscience as well. Certainly Mr. Lewis has not recently been devoting himself as passionately to pressing the case of the displaced miners as he has to furthering such concerns of the operators as aiding the career of one of the most conservative and sanctimonious men in public life: "Senators of long service," observed Marquis Childs in a recent syndicated newspaper column, "are saying they have never experienced such pressures as are being applied to bring about the confirmation of Admiral Lewis L. Strauss as Secretary of Commerce. The pressures come from a wide range of sources, indicating an extensive and thoroughly prepared campaign. Several Senators have had telephone calls from John L. Lewis . . . Lewis' theme is that Strauss, as Secretary of Commerce, would be helpful to the coal interests. . . ."

One long-time critic of the Lewis leadership in Washington is particularly bitter in his condemnation of the failure of the UMW (which he estimates at little more than 160,000 actual members) to take positive measures to protect the interests of the unemployed. With labor displacement in the coal industry greater per thousand employed than in any other industry, no program has yet been proposed for the vegetating displaced miners. He attributes this in part to the fact that 90 per cent of the union's executive board are appointees, in part to the fact that the delegates who attend the union's quadrennial conventions are *working* miners, with no substantial grievances if they are getting from three to five days' work a week, and with the laid-off and the pensioners unrepresented. At the last convention, a delegate who arose to discuss the plight of the unemployed and to suggest that perhaps the shorter work-week might be explored as one way to spread the work among the membership was very coolly received by his fellow delegates, and then was verbally torn to pieces by a buckshot charge of oratory from John L. Lewis himself.

Not only is seniority meaningless in an aging industry; in effect, this critic observes, the UMW is being subsidized in areas like western Pennsylvania by the garment unions, with their lower wage rates.

It would be unfair, however, to assume that the UMW is doing nothing at all for the welfare of its unemployed members. The Washington headquarters is at pains to point out that the UMW is co-operating with "area development organizations" wherever they are being set up by local businessmen and chambers of commerce in the hope of attracting new industry (including, presumably, more garment factories) to blighted areas. It is also campaigning for revision of mine safety regulations – which at present apply only to operations employing at least fifteen miners – so that they will include all working miners, even those in the most marginal strip mines; it points with justified indignation to the fact that these little operations are by far the most dangerous, with only 2 per cent of coal production accounting for 25 per cent of all fatalities in the industry.

What does this matter of safety have to do with unemployment? A lot. In an area which we have not discussed so far, the coal-mining country of Kentucky, West Virginia, and Tennessee, the operators had leased the land in which they drilled their mines from local people who had owned it for generations. As the mines were worked out, or were proved unsuitable for mechanized operation, the operators pulled out and turned the land, and the mines, back to the men from whom they had leased it and who had often been working for them. These men too have been existing on unemployment insurance and government surplus food. Since the mines are on their land, a good many of them have gone back to digging on their own, trying to pull out enough leftover coal to eke out a living.

In a way, it is as if unemployed steelworkers or auto workers were to club together to turn out steel or automobiles in competition with the big corporations. In this peculiarly American form of free enterprise one man can have as many as ninety-two mines on his property, with each mine being picked at by from two to four men scattered along the worked-out mountainside. Naturally their productivity is terribly low, as low as two tons per man, and since they are at the mercy of the brokers to whom they must sell for whatever they can get, they very often wind up with a couple of dollars for a day's dangerous and backbreaking work.

These are the men, digging away in the dogholes, as they are called, who are not covered by mine safety regulations, and whom you may read about from time to time in little newspaper items. (Last spring an entire family of nine men was entombed in a doghole.) If the UMW is successful, the dogholes will have to be certified by inspectors before they can be worked. And what will happen to the men, who will at least be prevented from taking so many chances in hacking away with pick and shovel at the only thing they know how to do? Their strange senseless heroism in the year 1959 can perhaps be seen as analogous to the bravery of soldiers struggling on in a lost war which cannot possibly benefit them, their families, or their heirs – to say nothing of the entire social order of which they are a part.

The office of District 2 of the UMW, which includes the miners of St. Michael, is located in the county seat of Ebensburg, Pa., about seventeen winding miles from St. Michael. It has taken over an old mansion in the better part of town and it is staffed by Lewis appointees. One would think, as one gets closer to the workers themselves than Washington, D. C., that one would find a greater awareness of their problems and a deeper searching for possible answers.

A visitor walks into the District Office and asks why so many men are being laid off in the district. Because they were unfortunate enough to be stuck in uneconomic low-seam mines which do not adapt to mechanization as well as the mines of District 5 or West Virginia. But even with a 6 per cent increase in tonnage nationally, men are being laid off everywhere. Then what is the answer?

"I don't really know."

Once again, there is the story of efforts to attract new industry, with its usually turning out to be light industry, employing women. As for the men in District 2 who are still working, with the exception of the captive (steel company-owned) mines, working hard to stockpile metallurgical coal in expectation of a steel strike, they are averaging three days a week, and glad to have jobs, with the prospect of occasionally picking up a fourth or fifth day of work. The fact is simply that with three days of work the operators take out all the coal they can sell: which is one more reason for the cutbacks.

What about the men who aren't working?

"They don't come in here, so we don't get any complaints at the office. We're not in touch with them."

And what will happen when the unemployment insurance runs out?

"I don't know how they'll get along."

The truth is that no one really does know. The barber of St. Michael may be as close to the truth as anyone when he observes that the men were so stunned by the closing of the mine that they are still in a state of shock, and unable to face the reality that they may never again be able to work at their chosen trade.

Until you go down the pit, it is difficult to sense how much mining can mean to a man, or how strange and unlikely it can seem that you are not going to work when others near you are working. The men who work at Wilmore, in Maryland Shaft #2, are friends and neighbors of the St. Michael men; they have worked together in the past, and they still hunt and fish together. But the men at Wilmore are still working, proud—as the miners of St. Michael are proud—of the fact that they take out the finest coal in the country. At dawn, with the rising sun on their backs, they straggle into the big grimy locker room and strip to the skin, depositing their street clothing in wire baskets, which they then haul to the high ceiling and secure with long double chains.

The impression is strong that the men have packed away their humor and lightheartedness with their street clothes; at any rate, they seem brooding and thoughtful as they foregather in their dark neck-to-ankle working outfits, adjusting the lamps on their helmets and the big batteries that power them from the wide belts at their waists. They wait in quiet patience for the elevator that will take them down to the other world. Here danger begins.

As you descend the seemingly endless shaft, you are assured that the speed of the elevator is regulated by law to a fraction of that when equipment is being lowered or coal raised, and that if the chain cable should go, metal dogs will snap out and lock themselves into the timbers that line either side of the concrete shaft. Nevertheless men have died in the elevator; not long ago an engineer's miscalculation drove them into the ground so hard that they bounced out of the cage, their bones snapping like matches.

Down in the mine, the men clamber aboard the hooked-together cars pulled by electric locomotives, and clatter off to their separate work centers, starting down the main heading and then cutting off on the various spurs that dart away into the darkness like so many veins. You travel for perhaps a mile, then get off at the end of the line and plod along in a bent-necked stoop until you come to an extensible belt conveyer. Here you hitch a ride, stretching flat on your belly on the rattling leather belt-line. The increasing roar of heavy machinery tells you that you have arrived at the mechanical loader, and you move on crab-wise, the glow of your lamp picking a path through the thick cloud of coal dust as you squat forward on your haunches.

You are at the face of the mine. You come alongside the mechanical miner, and you rest on your knees, watching the great continuous mining machine chewing its way into the coal seam with a remorseless roar. There is only the monstrous machine, and a handful of men. One of them shouts, "How far to go?" and the answer comes back: "Twenty feet."

You bend forward to cry into the superintendent's ear. "How long will it take to break through those twenty feet into the next chamber?"

"About forty-five minutes."

"How long would it have taken the men, without the machine?"

He answers laconically, his face already black and preoccupied as he squirts chewing tobacco. "Three shifts."

The slate roof sags, and the men swiftly use the machine to hoist a timber hydraulically into place before they press on. In this world without light and without women, the men are quick, daring, decisive. Formerly they could hear the roof starting to give so that they could quickly install timber props or run for safety; now the roar of the machine drowns out the little telltale sounds, and they must watch even more carefully. The dust, too, that used to rise all the hundreds of feet to the surface and rain down on the streets of St. Michael is a thousand times thicker from the slashing machine than it used to be when the men attacked the seam themselves; you can taste the silicosis in the air as the thick particles parch your nasal passages and clog your lungs. Roof falls have been many and serious in this particular mine. They are a delay and a serious annoyance to the supervision, a challenge to the men, who must crawl about the too-low passages like dwarfs or hunchbacks, shoring up the timbers and building cribs to protect the right of way.

Back on the surface the dirty coal rises in smoking carloads to the tipple. There you follow its course as it is cleaned, washed, sorted, through the towers high above the ground, and there too it seems impossible that the attack on the bowels of the earth will ever stop. How can a man who has been a part of it, who still lives within sight, sound, and smell of the consuming drama, believe that he will not again be permitted to be an actor in it?

In the saloons, the saying goes, the miners love more women than they ever did above ground, and dig more coal than they ever did below ground. At St. Michael, they brag about their narrow escapes, and about their friends' past heroism, as well as about the quality of their coal and the quantity of it they have taken from the mine. And they wonder whether they will ever do it again. In the meantime, they wonder about the meantime.

"In 1922," the president of the local says, "I lived

through the winter in a tent on top of that hill with my family. My father was out for eighteen months and we had nothing to live on, nothing. I can tell you one thing: we'll never go back to 1922 again."

"My family will never go hungry," another man says. He stares down into his glass of draught beer, and then looks up defiantly. "Not as long as I've got a rifle and two shotguns at home, they'll never go hungry. Maybe it's not a nice thing to say, but it's how I feel."

Others say the same, but it does not look as though it will come to that. When unemployment insurance runs out, the miners will be eligible to go on DPA (Department of Public Assistance). They will have to sign over their property to the State of Pennsylvania, and give up their insurance, but they will be allowed to keep their cars — as long as they demonstrate that they are using them to look for work.

They will do it, an old militant of the area believes, because they will have no alternative. They will cash in their policies and turn over their property in return for the dole and the opportunity to go on as they are now, waiting and hoping, some waiting for the pension, others just for their social security. They will continue to eat mollygrub, the federal government food-surplus parcels so weighted with rice that, as one man remarks wryly, "You can get slant-eyed from eating so much of it."

"I am not disillusioned," the old radical insists. "But I am very tired. Even now, with the checks running out, they are apathetic, and willing to go on DPA. Yet if there were some leadership . . . Right now the officers of at least ten locals would come out for nationalization of the mines. With leadership, many more of the 184 locals certainly would. You heard them curse the old parties — they are looking and waiting for new leadership, and it doesn't seem to be forthcoming."

Even recognition of their problems does not seem to be forthcoming. It would seem axiomatic that the future of the miner is tied up with the future of the whole economy, and that any progress for the labor movement – as for the rest of us – will have to come through political action. The UMW vision of a new coal miner, mobile, no longer tied to the company town, living in a suburb and driving forty miles to work in a mechanized mine where he will be a technician operating a piece of machinery – this may not only be the ultimate reality, it may already be coming to pass. But surely we must think hard about what values of the declining generation will be transferred to a young man who will go into the mines not because it is as thrilling or challenging as going to sea or riveting a skyscraper, but simply because it is a job that, although dirty and tiresome, has a good wage scale and a better pension plan; and about what his relations will be with his fellow workers, whom he will not fish with, fight with, or drink with, but will see merely as anonymous black faces below the earth and anonymous white faces on the suburban-bound highways above the earth.

Only a romantic fool, and an ignorant one at that, would bewail the loss of backbreaking, tortuous, dangerous, poisonous drudgery, and its replacement by impersonally effective machinery. But the loss of fraternity, solidarity, and the comradeship of courageous accomplishment – these are all too precious and rare in the moral landscape of America, and if we allow their transmitters to rot and fade, we commit an act even more criminal than the spoliation of the physical landscape for personal gain.

Dissent, Autumn 1959

Footnote, 1961: Since the above was written, Congress has improved the quality of the mollygrub handed out to the unemployed miners, and appropriated some money for retraining and relocation in depressed areas. Mr. Lewis, too, has gone into retirement. There is no word, however, that his fate has paralleled that of the aged members of his union, who discovered not long ago that their pensions would have to be reduced; the continuing decline of employment in the industry has meant smaller payments into their pension and welfare fund.

West Coast Waterfront: End of an Era

One of the first things to strike an outsider about San Francisco is the respect and esteem in which longshoremen are held by the rest of the community. They are good credit risks; they are homeowners (yes, some have swimming pools); they are pillars of society; Negro members are deacons and elders of their churches and are regarded in their neighborhoods as doctors used to be by the newly fledged Jewish communities. I cannot think of another part of the country in which, thanks in large part to their union, laborers are so well regarded and are in turn so proud of their work and their affiliation.

One reason why these workers – and the International Longshoremen's and Warehousemen's Union, it must be added – are so well regarded and themselves have so much self-respect is that the union has substantially complete control over the labor force (so that worker loyalty is always to the union rather than to any employer who buys his services through the hiring hall), and control too over the way in which the work is done. Everybody on the West Coast knows that these workers have had a pretty good life, and a pretty clean union (this is not the place to probe such minor sores as the alleged job-selling activities of certain union-elected dispatchers at the hiring halls). Contractual negotiations have been carried on not merely in public, but in a "goldfish bowl," with workers free to observe while Union President Harry Bridges, surely one of the most adroit, sharp-tongued, and agile-witted maneuverers in the entire labor movement, spars with the Pacific Maritime Association's J. Paul St. Sure, the most universally respected management negotiator on the Coast (and very possibly in the nation). His political heresies aside, Bridges has been incorruptible and has spoken always for the ranks, acutely sensitive to their voice.

However, contrary to popular opinion, the ILWU is not a mass-membership industrial union. In fact, its entire longshore membership (exclusive of Hawaii) is little more than fifteen thousand. And of these, a number are ships' clerks. The actual number of working longshoremen is therefore very small indeed. Nor is the ILWU, as many believe, a Communist-dominated union. In fact, the Communist Party in Harry Bridges's own Local 10 (San Francisco) now consists of one aging stalwart, who turns to with his little bundle of newspapers and leaflets, and a handful of his followers. The CP is a foundering hulk on the waterfront, of no use to anyone as either vote bloc or whipping boy. Still meaningful, however, are the existence of a substantial number of sophisticated workingmen in the union, most of whom received their political education in or around the CP, and also the undimmed passion of Harry Bridges for the Soviet Union and Communist China, though he no longer needs the Communist Party.

Now a five-year contract, which has received international attention, has been signed between the ILWU and the Pacific Maritime Association. This latter is no monolithic organization of ruthless waterfront employers. It was born out of the employers' defeat in the 1934 general strike, and exists now solely as a bargaining agent with the maritime unions; internally its members are apparently as torn with dissension and wholehearted mutual contempt as any labor union, and member employers have been known to make backdoor arrangements with particular unions in order to beat out competitor companies.

With the ratification of the contract, excited newspaper

reporters and publicity men have been telling us, February 1, 1961, marked a new day in the history of men and machines, a day which was "historic" and "epoch-making," in that, by mutual agreement, employers and workers were exchanging the introduction of labor-saving equipment for the establishment of a fund to provide for early retirement, no layoffs, and a guaranteed minimum workweek. The contract is officially titled an "Agreement on Mechanization and Modernization." It has been described, I think inaccurately, as an "automation" or a "mechanization" agreement. Such an interpretation has been fostered by both union officialdom and employers in their publicity handouts, with the result that newspapers have been running leads like that of the San Francisco *Examiner* of last October 25: "Harry Bridges' outcast longshore union showed the Nation's labor organizations yesterday how to live and prosper with automation." In fact, both parties are quite frank, in private discussion, in referring to the contract as a twenty-nine-million-dollar bribe to buy back certain working conditions that have been in force for a generation.

In order to understand the terms of this deal, its relation to the real problem of mechanization/automation, and what effect it will have on the working lives of the thousands of members of the union, we are going to have to go back and spell out some of the conditions that existed prior to the new contract – conditions that made West Coast longshoring the most attractive way of life for a casual laborer in the United States, if not in the entire world.

As a result of the truly historic 1934 strike, the longshoremen won a jointly operated hiring hall, which freed them from serflike dependence on the caprice of individual employers or bosses. They also won a set of conditions relating to the job itself, which were easily enforceable by a militant democratic union, particularly one strongly influenced by professional revolutionists – conditions which came to be accepted as a way of life by the flood of new recruits to the waterfront during the boom days of World War II (in the San Francisco Bay area, mostly Negroes from the Deep South; in the Port of Los Angeles area, mostly Latins from the Southwest and from Mexico).

One of these work conditions, which is not often talked or written about but which strikes me as both civilized and unique, has been the longshoreman's relative freedom of choice as to which days in the week he will take off. The mechanics of this were worked out by the men themselves and were democratically defined by union rules for both "gang" men and "plug" men. This arrangement was made possible first by the fact that the industry works around the clock and through the week, depending on the number of ships in port, and second by the existence of a pool of casuals always available for work.

When he got to work, the longshoreman who worked less difficult cargoes – light case goods, containers, unitized loads – could often look forward to rest periods equal to 25 to 40 per cent of his work day, depending on whether he was discharging or loading. The men viewed this as justifiable, because they were never compensated in wages for the unpaid hours necessarily spent at the hiring hall every day or in time off for the necessarily continuous work on more difficult cargoes.

At work the sling-load limit was set at 2100 pounds, which meant that large or unwieldy or dangerous loads would be broken – "skimmed" – into two or more manageable loads within the weight limit, thereby spreading the work equitably and making it possible for those laboring in the hold to work off a four-wheeler. The longshoreman who worked in the port of San Pedro knew finally that his fairly continuous employment was assured by multiple handling, a jurisdictional form of featherbedding which delimited teamster from longshore work and specified that under certain circumstances a cargo load would have to be moved from pallet boards to the skin of the dock, put together and taken apart one or two extra times between its removal from the ship and transport from the dock by truck.

Aside from this last practice, retained almost solely at San Pedro and almost universally conceded by the longshoremen themselves to be ultimately indefensible make-work, these have been generally the conditions of the working life of the West Coast longshoreman. They have given him substantial and unique control over what might be called the process of production on the docks (that is, the movement of cargo), and they have now been amended or altered for a *quid pro quo* of twenty-nine million dollars, by membership vote of PMA and by referendum among over eleven thousand voting longshoremen and clerks.

Where does mechanization come into the picture? In four words: the employers shall be allowed to "utilize labor-saving devices."

But this does not mean that hitherto no such devices had been introduced in the maritime transportation industry. It means, quite simply, that, from here on out, such devices will be manned by the minimum number of longshoremen needed to carry out the operation, rather than by contractually specified six- or eight-man gangs. In short, while it has already been profitable for certain of the larger shipping companies to mechanize their ships and their port facilities even while they had to pay men to serve as "witnesses" (the term is Harry Bridges's), it will now be much more profitable under the new contract for those companies that can afford the capital investment to proceed with mechanization and thus compete more advantageously with foreign operators. To this extent, and to this extent only, is the new contract a "mechanization" agreement.

There are an infinite number of gradations of mechanization taking place on the waterfront ("automation" as such is not really at issue, since what is being replaced is not brain power but back power), from the blowing or pumping of sugar, like oil, into ships' holds, to such seemingly petty (to the outsider!) refinements in unitizing cargoes as mounting fuel drums, strapped in units of three, on a board at their place of manufacture, rather than having them handled and stowed singly on the waterfront. The most impressive of these conversions to date has no doubt been Matson's transformation of the SS *Hawaiian Citizen* into a fully containerized vessel, together with a parallel transformation of the yards and cranes in the ports of San Francisco, Los Angeles, and Honolulu.

When you climb aboard the *Hawaiian Citizen* you are no longer entering the swaying world of the seafaring man. It has become an ingeniously designed mobile warehouse, floating between the states of Hawaii and California and rapidly filled and emptied at either end. Cargo is packed in huge twenty-four-foot aluminum cubes, which are picked up by a monstrous four-legged device known as "Christine" (because it looks bisexual, or asexual) and coupled to yard tractors driven by ILWU men who used to drive fork-lifts and jitneys. The tractors haul them to an enormous gantry crane, which picks them up and deposits them in the hold, where they fit, one atop the other, like the blocks of a Chinese puzzle. What is more, a two-way cycle is constantly in operation: as a load is placed in the ship, another load is removed from it; the entire ship can be emptied and reloaded in a fraction of the time required by traditional methods.

On the day that I watched the loading of the *Hawaiian Citizen,* during the waning hours of the old contract, several of the "witnesses" were snoozing and chatting just aft of the number two hatch. They will no longer be there, on the company payroll, under the terms of the new agreement — but this is hardly the most striking aspect of this mechanized vessel. After all, at workplaces with cost-plus contracts all over the country, from Anchorage to Miami, a small percentage of men are sleeping on the job, whether they are workers curled up in a dark corner or executives with their feet up on the desk. Since I do not have to meet a payroll, I am so far from feeling that there is anything shocking about this that I incline to the belief that maybe we would all live longer if there were more of it.

What is shocking, though, is the cold gray impersonality of the containerized shipping operation represented by the *Hawaiian Citizen.* Not only will nobody be sleeping—nobody will be daydreaming, or arguing politics, or even getting a personal kick out of the cargo that he pats after he stows it properly in the hold. For anyone who, like myself, has ever followed the sea, the *Citizen* is no longer a freighter. The cargo is not visible: it is simply a ranked series of metallic cubes locked into place. One man, alone on his tractor, drives the cube to the gantry; a second man, alone at the controls one hundred fifty feet above the pier apron, picks up the 46,000-pound cube and guides it onto the trolley; a third man, alone at the hatch, wiggles his fingers to indicate that it is being properly lowered into the rack that will hold it rigid until it is discharged in the same way some days later.

It is too early to say whether new challenges will develop which will make working on a fully containerized shipping operation as varied, or as much fun (I use the word advisedly), as more traditional waterfront work. Perhaps; but one wonders. One man described it to me as "ulcerating" work. Another said that it was "cold and inhuman."

In any case, we must be quite clear that this wave of the future is not battering at the docks. Harry Bridges, at sixty, does not envisage anything approaching complete mechanization of the waterfront in his lifetime. Neither do a number of younger men at the executive end. The waterfront is not a coal mine, where you can swiftly calculate whether it will pay to install automatic equipment: if it won't, you shut down the uneconomic mine; if it will, you buy the equipment and throw out the men, and in a decade you have mechanization.

No, the infinite variety of objects shipped, from nails to locomotives, together with the conflicting aims of shippers and the infinite variety of conditions prevailing in various ports, is going to preclude rapid conversion of our merchant fleet to *Hawaiian Citizens* or of our docks to full-scale mechanization for many decades. You can't even blow coffee into a hold the way you can sugar or oil: as of now, there are too many grades of coffee, and too many orders for one bag of this and three bags of that. Besides, shipping is a two-way business. For every Matson Line auto ship, specially designed so that cars can be driven aboard at California (instead of pushed aboard by the traditional eight-man gang), loaded like sardines, and driven off at Hawaii, at such a saving that it pays to send the ship back empty from Hawaii, there are a hundred ships plying between here and the Orient that will be dependent for decades on the individual products of Asia and the individual toil of its thousands of straining dock workers. Mechanization, total mechanization, of our shipping industry – like so many other problems that tax human ingenuity – is going to have to be globally resolved.

What about the meantime? In the meantime Harry Bridges will spend his declining years as leader of a steadily declining work force. His fully registered membership will have job security, an eventual guaranteed minimum work week, and a fairly comfortable and secure old age, with $7,920 coming each man's way after twenty-five years of service, in addition to his pension and social security. In return, he will yield up those conditions for which he fought, not only in 1934 but for a decade and a half thereafter, in a series of over twenty major port strikes. As his social life becomes more and more middle-class in all of its values, so will his union become more and more of a tightly enclosed job-protective association, as Bridges himself conceded to me; and his working life will become less and less spontaneously rhythmic, and more and more rigidly routinized as mechanization creeps in and productivity studies are utilized to standardize output and to housebreak the longshoreman.

One way of looking at it is to say that, in order for the longshoreman to maintain his privileged place in the general community, he is going to have to yield up his privileged place on the waterfront. The first area of freedom that I mentioned, that of deciding for yourself whether you want to work on any given day, will be one of the first to go. Man-hour requirements are going to be substantially reduced, perhaps as much as 35 per cent (they will have to be, if the employers are going to make back that twenty-nine million dollars). In order to make a week's pay, the longshoreman will really have to scuffle. To get his minimum-wage guarantee (the new agreement calls for a floor under earnings, with the minimum tentatively established at thirty-five hours), he will have to accept any work offered – work, like bananas or freezers, that he would formerly have left to the casuals. Of course, it can be argued that what he is getting in exchange is a much more complete security than he ever had before (although most observers are skeptical that the minimum-wage guarantee will ever go into effect, since it will probably be computed annually); nevertheless it remains true that, in the course of obtaining this security, he will be transformed. He will become more like other American workers, whether manual or white-collar: he will go to work more regularly, more steadily, more habitually, he will do what he is told – and in consequence, I suspect, he will come to like it less.

Now whether or not this free hand in management that employers now have, for the first time in a generation, is going to result in severe exploitation of the longshoremen is a question that can only be resolved on the docks in the months ahead (and by PMA, to whom individual employers wishing to introduce changes will have to make application). Several things can be said at the outset, however. First: It should not be taken for granted that all of the work practices which the union has bartered away were simply boondoggling. True, no one can defend the business of insisting that every single little piece of cargo be placed on the skin of the dock, and then picked up again, one at a time – that is, not unless he is arguing for the principle of make-work as an employer contribution to the struggle against rising mass unemployment (a defensible principle, by the way, for a radical union which sees it as a holding action). Nor can anyone defend some of the other practices, such as four hours on and four hours off, when they were abused as a means of goofing off by irresponsibles who had no trade-union background and were not indoctrinated by the ILWU in the honorable traditions of trade unionism. In the most notorious instance, a dead man was carried on a San Pedro walking boss's time sheet for two days before it was discovered that he had died in a brawl in Tia Juana. That these practices have, by and large, been eliminated in recent years is symbolized by the enforcement of a "performance and conformance" clause in the 1959 agreement.

It is also true that many men never abused these practices, but utilized them as part of a natural work rhythm, in the course of which they spelled each other, equalized their burdens, and lightened the load for the older men in the gang; it has to be remembered that, unlike the forest ranger or the lighthouse keeper, the longshoreman is engaged in a highly co-operative enterprise, one in which the goof-off artist as much as the eager beaver can not only disrupt the work rhythm but jeopardize the lives of the other members of his working gang.

In these circumstances it does seem somewhat unusual that it should be the union officialdom which is giving the loudest assurances that, to quote the *Dispatcher*, "Actually, the only situation where men will work harder is where they haven't been working at all."

This may turn out to be true. But there are no guarantees of it embedded in the agreement. And if it is true, it will only be because the men themselves are vigilant and the union itself is militant in supporting their "beefs." The contract is, as I have indicated, terribly complex, and is susceptible of a variety of interpretations as to the applicability of smaller gang sizes or larger sling-load limits, on the part of both workers and employers. In addition to the traditional grounds of safety violation, in what is still one of the most hazardous occupations in the United States today, the workers are entitled to object to changes on grounds of "onerousness." No doubt even the 10 to 20 per cent of the San Francisco longshoremen who are functionally illiterate will soon be arguing the nuances of that word with at least as much fervor as their children in high school and college. Whether they will be able to do anything about it is another matter.

For the union has a psychological and a financial stake in the success of this agreement. This despite the fact that Max D. Kossoris, director of the Western Regional Office of the Bureau of Labor Statistics, argues that the shoe is on the other foot, since PMA will be pouring five million dollars a year into the union treasury, regardless of how well the members co-operate in living up to the terms of the new agreement. It is true that the agreement, as originally contemplated, called for the adoption of a system whereby, instead of the work rules being bought out, employers' gains would be measured and the employees would be paid only for the actual man-hours saved. (Mr. Kossoris himself was engaged for a year by PMA, with the consent of the ILWU, to devise such a system of measurement.) In the midst of negotiations, the measurement-of-gains concept – to which the union had agreed – was dropped, because, the employers claim, it was too cumbersome and technical, and the idea of an annual lump-sum payment was substituted. Nevertheless I think that this interpretation underestimates those pressures on the union leadership which I mentioned at the beginning of this paragraph.

Harry Bridges is in the anomalous position of being an internationally known labor leader (notorious or distinguished, depending on the angle of vision), with an actual membership of only a few thousand, and shrinking at that. With this new agreement he has re-entered the agreeable limelight, and, what is more, he has thrown down a challenge to those who threw him out of the official labor movement, the Meanys and the Reuthers, whom he continually excoriates for being more concerned with "respectability" than with "militancy," to come up with new agreements which will be as far-reaching and as "respectably" received as has been this agreement which he has maneuvered so shrewdly into existence. (This seems the most satisfactory explanation of why Bridges pressed for the new agreement in 1960 rather than waiting until the expiration of the old contract in 1962 to bargain off the work rules. The explanation of his opponents, that he sold out, is unsupported by evidence; his own explanation, that he was anticipating further restrictive legislation by the new administration, has its own flaw: while it is true that John F. Kennedy asserted last September in Salt Lake City that "An effective attorney general under present federal law could . . . depose Harry Bridges as head of the longshoremen," and that this is one campaign pledge that the Kennedy brothers may earnestly attempt to fulfill, it also seems apparent that PMA would hardly have been willing, and in fact eager, to part with twenty-nine million dollars to junk restrictive work rules if it were certain that Congress would go ahead and do the job for free.)

Furthermore, Bridges is discharging an obligation to those who built the union and fought the good fight. This is an old man's contract. The immediate beneficiaries will be the old-timers with twenty-five years of seniority, who will be able to retire with up to $7,920 cash money. Bridges's home base, Local 10, San Francisco (which voted up the contract five to one), has an average age of fifty-six. The center of his opposition, Local 13, San Pedro (which voted down the contract two to one), has an average age of thirty-six. In an aging union, I think it can be fairly said that the proposed immediate beneficiaries were all but unanimous in their decision to "go along with Harry," while the younger men were split in their reactions.

It is rather unlikely that Bridges will insist upon the union's grimly supporting "beefs" to the limit if they, no matter how justified, interfere with his generation's getting its due. He has already assured me that he is not going to stand for "phony militants" upsetting the smooth functioning of the new agreement; and his vice-president, Bob Robertson, struck an ominous note in the *Dispatcher* on January 13, 1961: "No fast operator, on either side, should start thinking of cutting a fat hog for himself, or making a name for himself, by disrupting the *orderly* process of change that will be necessary . . . if any sharpy on either side tries to create dissension, there will be plenty of sincere people to do some yelling. Are there people who don't want to see this plan succeed? I'm afraid so. Some of our own members don't want it to get off the ground." In such an atmosphere, it will be a hardy union member who will persist in pressing a grievance or in asserting that the new agreement works an "onerous" hardship.

Two additional safeguards in the new contract will serve to reinforce worker compliance with PMA-union leadership interpretations. For one thing, in clause after clause it is specified that changes will be agreed on not at the Local level, but at the coastwise level. Here again, Bridges was quite frank with me in granting that this can be, and probably will be, used to whittle down Local autonomy and concentrate more power in the hands of the international leadership; and the people with whom I spoke in San Pedro, from President George Kuvakas on down, are bitterly agreed with Bridges that the new contract will be a knife to gut their dissident Local, to render it powerless to protest, should the new agreement not only knock off an anticipated eight hundred jobs, by eliminating multiple handling, but also impose a harder working life on the membership. For another thing, the contract provides that "payments into the Fund shall be abated" up to the maximum employer obligation of $13,650 per day, "in the event of a work stoppage in any port or ports in violation of the provisions of this document." Here is a five-year built-in insurance that hotheads and militants, whether "phony" or not, will think twice before depriving their older union brothers, the men who built the organization, of the negotiated rights of their declining years.

But supposing that everything works out beautifully, that the longshoremen go along with the agreement in good faith, and that their employers exercise self-restraint in utilizing their new-bought domination of the work situation. The elderly men will retire, either voluntarily at sixty-five, or mandatorily at an earlier age, with a cash payment to speed them on their way, if lessening man-hour needs should require a shrinking of the labor force beyond the normal 4 per cent annual attrition. The younger men will be absolutely assured of a vested interest in their jobs and will be able to look forward to the same deal as the older men. If it works out this way, couldn't it be described as a millennial labor-management accord, one which frees management for the job of modernization and mechanization while it protects the old worker who has given his life to the industry and the young worker who is committing his life to the industry?

It could – but there is a fly in the ointment. This fly is the group of dock workers known as "B" men, about 1500 workers up and down the Coast, who are specifically excluded from the benefits of the new agreement. There is no question but that a substantial number of these men – no one knows how many, and it will vary from port to port – will be squeezed out of the bottom end of the industry, so to speak, even while the older men are being squeezed out of the top end into retirement. Therefore men *will* be losing their jobs under this new agreement, and it seems to me a piece of semantic legerdemain on the part of union and management publicists to insist that this is not so, simply because "B" men are not "fully registered" union longshoremen. The fact is that these are men who are committed to the shipping industry and are presently essential to it. (They now do most of the hold work in San Francisco, Stockton, and other ports.)

Who are they? This is insufficiently known, and represents one of the most fascinating and illuminating – if depressing – aspects of the whole West Coast waterfront story. Take the case of Bridges's Local 10, which for some years filled out the labor needs of management by supplying "permit" or "work card" men, in effect apprentices or postulant members, in addition to the "casuals" or "Social Security" men, like policemen or firemen or the unemployed, who came down to the waterfront to earn a day's pay. In the spring of 1958 the Local decided, in conjunction with PMA, to replace the members it was losing by attrition. It ran an ad in the local papers and received about fourteen thousand applications for membership – such was the attractive power of the union and of longshore work in the Bay area. The following spring some 570 of the applicants were accepted after interview, and shortly thereafter the figure rose to nearly 800.

PMA was anxious for a more stable and reliable work force than that available from the pool of casuals; it confined its investigation of applicants pretty much to questions of their responsibility and possible existence of a criminal record. The union was anxious for new members who would be loyal and union-conscious; the leadership hoped that the great number of Negro applicants would behave like many of their relatives and friends, who always went down the line for Harry; furthermore, in opening its books to members with union background or maritime experience, it welcomed a substantial number of DP's from other unions which had also been expelled from the CIO on charges of Communist domination, or from unions which had themselves ousted substantial numbers of alleged Communists.

Thus both management and labor stood to gain by this influx of new blood: the former, because it was obtaining the services of men eager to enter the industry, ready to turn to every day, and more than willing to work all the dirty cargoes that the fully registered men handled only reluctantly; the latter, because it was going to be able to replace the retiring and the dying with men who were, by and large, devoted to Harry Bridges and his kind of trade unionism.

But then negotiations got under way for what was eventually to emerge as the five-year mechanization and modernization agreement – and the "B" men, who had first been told frankly that they were being taken on to get extra work, and then promised at a series of special meetings that they would become full-fledged union members in six months to a year, found that, by mutual agreement, a freeze had been clamped on the industry. Save for a handful who had squeezed into full membership, some 615 "B" men in the Bay area now await the end of the freeze and, what seems most likely, their gradually being starved out of the waterfront. (Ironically, the "B" men of San Pedro may be in better shape, even though more work will be lost there, because the Port of Los Angeles, unlike San Francisco's waterfront, is growing so rapidly that in a few years it will become one of the great ports of the world; it is also ugly, with its omnipresent oil-pump levers pecking away like monstrous insects, in precise inverse ratio to the beauty and charm of San Francisco.)

There are optimists who believe that economies resulting from the new agreement may revive coastwise shipping, now virtually moribund because of highway trucking; there are even those who expect an impending revival of the China trade, once the mainstay of West Coast shipping. Either could absorb the cut in man-hours and even make necessary the permanent employment of the "B" men as members of an augmented labor force. But a hardheaded economist like Max Kossoris, in an article in *Monthly Labor Review* for January 1961, speaks not of "whether" but of "after": "After most of the Class B longshoremen and the casuals have been eliminated from the industry, how will the rest . . . of the cut in man-hours be absorbed?"

These men are not a statistic. As I have already indicated, it is the fact that they exist that should matter – not how many of them there are. When I asked an executive of PMA whether it wasn't really true that most of these men would be losing their livelihoods as a result of a contract publicized as a job-saving agreement, he replied, "The 'B' men are a matter for Harry Bridges's conscience."

So I asked Harry Bridges, and he replied, "Although the 'B' men are not considered a part of the industry, they're better off working here two or three days a week than they would be now in industry at large. In our opinion, they'll be all right for the next two or three years."

The "B" men themselves just don't know. Some are still inclined to trust Harry; most, however, are increasingly bitter and vengeful. A few, with no trade-union background, may become so vengeful that they will attempt to sue the union: this may be why the union is once again holding special meetings for them, meetings which had not been called since the beginning of the freeze. I am more concerned, however, with the dedicated militants than with the anti-union. These are men, many of them, who entered the working class voluntarily and who, after rough years in the NMU or the MCS or the UAW, fighting for the Communist Party line because that line happened to coincide with their own idealism and socialist principles, are now at the end of their rope, at the end of the line. Finally fed up with Stalinism in '52 or '56 or whenever, they turned to the ILWU because Harry Bridges seemed still to be leading a democratic working-class anticapitalist force. Many of them carried the ball for Bridges in other unions when he needed bail money, or legal aid in fighting jail and deportation; they were willing to do just about anything for him, and in fact some of them did do just about anything for him. Now they find that they are expendable. An injury to one, they discover very, very late, is no longer an injury to all.

The terrible disillusionment of these idealists finds its parallel among the scattered opposition to Bridges in the fully registered union members, including some of the older men. Again, I am not speaking primarily of the opposition on the right, which ranges from white-superiority workers frustrated by Bridges's automatic bloc vote from Negroes (some of whom have been getting theirs back by "Crow Jimming" the whites) to "professional Catholics" who wear the cross but have been known to wheel and deal with the Communists. I have in mind those dissidents who, because they are socialists or Trotskyites or ex-Wobblies or ex-Stalinists, persist in operating as though the principles of solidarity and brotherhood were antecedent to self-aggrandizement, the accumulation of power, or the captivating glare of publicity. I number these among the finest men I have ever had the privilege of getting to know, but I must in all conscience report that their prospects in the ILWU are dim indeed.

Not only do they have little, if any, contact with the "B" men, the ones who will be frozen out of the industry by the contract; from fear or distrust, they have almost nothing to do with each other. Being reasonable men, they are not always certain that Bridges is automatically wrong on every issue; and so, as each operates with his small band of followers, they gradually lose heart and turn their intelligence to the resolution of other problems, whether personal or social. "What are all the old lefties doing?" I asked one of these disillusioned men, and he replied with a weary smile, "They're sitting home nights."

Although it is entirely possible that he now has more in common, intellectually and temperamentally, with Paul St. Sure than he does with his own rank and file, Harry Bridges has in the past given great leadership to the workers of the West Coast. And although he has also done them some very questionable services indeed, it is a brave man who will rise to oppose him, knowing that he is opposing not only the leader's record, not only his practically unanimous support in the Negro ranks – which have always been accorded scrupulous equality and now form a majority of the membership of the San Francisco Local – but also his caustic tongue and his skill at both oratory and demagogy. When I asked him how he intended to educate his membership to the subtleties of the new agreement and to the necessity for self-discipline if it is to work, he replied readily, "We'll give it to them Castro-style, at our meetings." And at least a half-dozen longshoremen have reported to me, with shame or fury, the meeting at which Bridges rose with his cold grin to taunt the fully registered men for their qualms about dumping the "B" men: "You want to play politics with the 'B' men? Then bring them in and give them equal working rights. But you're not going to do that. You know it and I know it."

And they didn't. Whether they would have, if Bridges had appealed to their best instincts that afternoon instead of their worst, is doubtful. It is doubtful too whether he has guessed wrong about the temper of his people during the 1960's, that they (including the leaderless and aimless young redhots of San Pedro) will settle for what he has won for them in the new contract and will not yearn – or struggle – for that which he has yielded up in return.

A leading PMA official, recently traveling in the Soviet Union, was closely questioned at the Ministry of Marine, where he paid a courtesy call, about capitalist reaction to the new "mechanization and modernization" agreement. The official replied that most of the American press had received the agreement favorably, that many editorials had hailed it as an epoch-making solution to some of the human problems posed by automation and mechanization for industry at large, but that the *Wall Street Journal* had condemned it as "Communistic" because it paid hard cash for buying back prerogatives that should always have been management's. The Minister ruminated for a moment, and then murmured to his translator, "Tell the gentleman that I agree with the *Wall Street Journal.*"

This story may reveal more about the nature of the Soviet Union, or of its bureaucrats' conception of communism, than it does about this new contract. But it may serve to remind us too that a way of life is passing from the scene. Already men *are* working harder on the waterfront and are grumbling, but impotently, as they come to realize once again the meaning of the practices they voted out of existence. When the new contract expires in 1966, the men who have lived under it will be a lot less easily distinguishable from the rest of the American workers than they are today. Not only will the radical dissidents of whom I have been speaking be harder to find; so will the other oddballs, the men with brains who liked to work with their hands, the occasional novelist, painter, or philosopher whom one encountered on the waterfront because it was – as loyal union member Eric Hoffer put it to me – "a good place to talk and a good place to think, a mixture of physical and intellectual stimulation." By 1966 Eric Hoffer will have retired with his pension, and both the union and the waterfront will be far less hospitable havens for whatever Hoffers this nation may be fortunate enough to produce in the future.

Dissent, Autumn 1961

Labor's Cultural Degradation

Those of us who persist in clinging to certain archaic notions about the human degradation attendant upon capitalism, and who in consequence cannot shake off the suspicion that this might be a better world with the arrival of something we call socialism, are often taxed with the lack of foresight of Karl Marx. Not only is Marx held posthumously accountable for all the crimes committed in his name or in the name of socialism – from the Stalinist slave-labor camps to the Socialist management of imperialist pacification in Algeria – but he is also charged with having failed to foresee that capitalism would be able to provide not less and less, but more and more and more of the good things of life for its proletariat. It is true that in recent months these sardonic cries have become somewhat muted, as the unemployed are once again arrested for stealing food and display other signs of reluctance to proceed quietly from overemployment to home relief; but still the claim is made that the working class under capitalism (especially in Magic America), far from being increasingly exploited and degraded, is living at least as well as anyone else in the world, if not better.

Well, what about it? Are we to deny that the packinghouse worker and the auto worker can and do buy color television, three-taillight automobiles and Chris-Crafts to go with their fishing licenses? And if we admit it, shouldn't we also admit that capitalism is after all capable of satisfying all the wants of the underlying population, allowing for occasional recessions?

I for one do not think so. I for one think that the working class is not having its basic emotional wants and psychological needs satisfied. I for one think that the working class – regardless of whether it is envied by other proletarians who would like to drive cars instead of riding bicycles, or would like to ride bicycles instead of walking – is being cheated, swindled, and degraded as ferociously as ever its English counterparts were a century ago when Marx and Engels were anatomizing them. The fact that it may not be aware of its exploitation does not alter the reality of its situation. The fact that, even with an appreciable portion of it presently subsisting on unemployment insurance, its material status is still light-years ahead of its European (to say nothing of its Asian or African) counterparts is relevant only as it sheds a little light on the potential of plenty that would be available to all mankind if industrialization and the accumulation of capital were to take place at a rational pace on a world-wide basis.

Consider the condition, say, of the Chicago slaughterhouse worker at the turn of the century. Upton Sinclair railed magnificently, and with ultimately telling effect, not only at the economic subjugation of workers forced to toil sixty and seventy hours a week for a pittance, but also at the conditions under which they worked, at *what* they had to do for a living, and at *how* they were ruthlessly cleaned out in the saloons when the long day's work was done. It was his contention that the workers were being degraded and enslaved not only during their working hours, but afterward as well, when they turned to the consolation of booze to help them forget how they were spending their lives.

Let us grant at once that these workers are no longer forced to toil (not even the moonlighters) sixty and seventy hours a week. Let us grant at once that they are now paid much more for working much less than they did at the turn of the century, and that, thanks to their union, their conditions of employment have been immeasurably improved. *What* they do does not seem to have altered as appreciably. Since Chicago packing houses no longer offer public guided tours, let us note what was said not long ago by one of America's most distinguished women, who felt impelled, in her ninth decade, to address a letter to the *New York Times* (April 30, 1958):

> I have been horrified within the last few weeks by learning that the old cruel way of slaughtering animals for food is still being widely used, and that still, just as in my youth, there is no law to forbid it. This is to me absolutely incomprehensible because we are not a cruel people: we do not want to eat what comes to us through pain and suffering. And yet, as I know of my own knowledge, the facts about the slaughterhouses were investigated and publicized well on to sixty years ago. . . .

Miss Edith Hamilton does not dwell in her letter on the effects of this cruel work on those hired to perform it, nor need we linger here over the question, beyond observing that it is not one currently asked by those engaged in promulgating the myth of the happy worker.*

As for *how* workers are gulled and mulcted in the hangouts which Sinclair described as traps designed to stupefy the worker, and which we today might characterize as the liquid television of half a century ago, only those who live in the dream world of official mythology imagine that they no longer fulfill the evil function they did in the days of *The Jungle.*

> An armored truck [*A. H. Raskin tells us in the* New York Times Magazine *of May 4, 1958*] stood outside the unemploy-

* *Footnote, 1961:* The passage of the federal humane-slaughter law in 1960, to which I refer on page 3, resulted from the agitation of concerned people like Miss Hamilton; I have not visited a slaughterhouse since the mandatory change-over from the bone-crushing sledge hammer to gas or needle, but I should think it would mean a much less painful day for man as well as beast in the new packing house.

ment insurance office in a down-at-the-heels neighborhood five minutes ride from Detroit's glistening civic center. On the truck's side was a sign: "Charge for cashing checks. Up to $50 – 15 cents. Over $50 – 20 cents." Two-thirds of the workers streaming out of the office thrust their checks through the slot and paid tribute to the man in the truck. . . . Inside the office the manager frowned: "That armored truck is violating the law, but the cops don't bother the owner. And the wives like it, it keeps their men out of the beer gardens to cash their checks."

But new techniques for the inducement of oblivion have far outstripped the traditional saloon, with its check-cashing window and its soft-sell technique of simultaneously taking the worker's money and enabling him to forget that he has just spent his day hitting screaming animals on the head, tightening bolts on auto bodies, or seeking the opportunity to find such employment. Indeed, the new techniques of merchandizing both "leisure" and forgetfulness have now developed to the point where they can be said to play as large a part in the degradation of the worker as does his actual employment. The English writer Richard Hoggart puts the matter quite succinctly in his *The Uses of Literacy:*

> Inhibited now from ensuring the "degradation" of the masses economically, the logical processes of competitive commerce, favored from without by the whole climate of the time and from within assisted by the lack of direction, the doubts and uncertainty before their freedom of working people themselves (and maintained as much by ex-working class writers as by others), are ensuring that working people are culturally robbed. Since these processes can never rest, the holding down, the constant pressure not to work outwards and upwards, becomes a positive thing, becomes a new and stronger form of subjection; this subjection promises to be stronger than the old because the chains of cultural subordination are both easier to wear and harder to strike away than those of economic subordination. . . .

What is perhaps ugliest about the whole process, however, is that competitive commerce is now meshing the chains of cultural subordination with those of economic subordination. The worker is not simply lulled into forgetfulness of his daily idiot routine by the TV western: he is simultaneously pressured into permanently mortgaging himself by acquiring the objects manufactured by the sponsors of his daily ration of opiates. The peddlers of persuasion have now developed such techniques of sophistication and grown themselves into such large-scale enterprise that they engage the talents and the creative passions of a substantial segment of young college graduates in the fields of sociology, psychology, economics, and the English language itself. They regard the worker-consumer as a manipulatable object, rather than as a human being with individual needs and aspirations; they address him, in consequence, with a cynicism that can only be described as shameless, and they exploit him culturally as ruthlessly as he was exploited economically a generation ago. Thus Dr. Ernest Dichter, president of the Institute for Motivational Research, recently informed the Sales Executives Club of New York and the Advertising Federation of America:

> A year ago it was correct to advertise the purchase of air-conditioners under the slogan, "You deserve to sleep in comfort." Today, it may be psychologically more correct to shift to a moral approach, utilizing spartan, work-oriented appeals such as, "You can't afford to be tired all day," or "You work better and produce more after a refreshing night." Dr. Dichter termed this one approach for giving the consumer "moral permission" and "a rational justification" for buying products that represent the "good life." . . . Motivation research's view on price cuts, according to Dr. Dichter, is that they must be accompanied by advertisements that explain to the consumer the reasons for the change. Otherwise, "there is a grave danger that the consumer will become more than ever convinced that he was being cheated during a period of prosperity." Dr. Dichter also urged that salesmen become philosophers as well. To help dispel the sales lag, "he has to sell us not only a product but the desirability, the correctness of purchasing the product." (*New York Times,* March 19, 1958.)

Those who manage to accommodate themselves to a lunatic order of things have in general reacted to observations like those in the preceding paragraphs in one or a combination of the three following ways:

(1) They assert that the great virtue in our social order is that, in addition to providing the working class with the necessities and the amenities of a secure and civilized existence, it also provides the worker for the first time in history with an unparalleled variety of cultural possibilities, ranging from the great thinkers in inexpensive paperback books to the great composers on inexpensive LP's.

(2) They claim that the manufacturers of distraction are giving the public what it wants, and that if the proletarian turns in his off-hours not to Plato but to Spillane, not to Beethoven but to Alan Freed, this is no more than a reflection of the traditionally abominable taste of the masses, which preceded and will endure beyond the current American order.

(3) They point out that – if it is indeed true that we are the victims of an unremitting, concerted commercial assault on our nerves and our senses – this degrading and relentless battering affects not just the working class but all of us, and that it is therefore romantically inaccurate to single out the proletarian as the particularly exploited victim of the mass-media panderers.

All three defenses are interconnected; a response to all must start with an insistence upon the lately neglected fact that it is the man on the bottom of the heap, the man who does the dirty work, who has the fewest defenses against the unending barrage of sex and violence and the propaganda of commerce. He *is* the particularly exploited victim of the mass media; he is *not* given an honest possibility of developing an individual taste for individual works of the human imagination; he does *not* have the range of cultural choice available to college students, white-collar people, and middle-class citizens of the republic.

As Daniel Bell observes of the work situation itself, in his *Work and Its Discontents,* "a tension that is enervating or debilitating can only produce wildly aggressive play, or passive, unresponsive viewing. To have 'free time' one needs the zest of a challenging day, not the exhaustion of a blank one. If work is a daily turn round Ixion's wheel, can the intervening play be anything more than a restless moment before the next turn of the wheel?"

The man who leaves the packing house or the assembly line is neither physically nor psychically prepared to appreciate the quality paperback or the classical LP. Nor are they readily available to him in any case; the merchandisers of the mass entertainments reserve the right to restrict certain of their wares, or conversely to cram others down the gullets of their victims. It is no more accidental that the only civilized TV programs are presented on Sundays, when the average viewer is either sleeping it off or visiting relatives, than it is that the much-touted book racks are packed in the poorer neighborhoods not with Plato but with anonymously mass-produced borderline sado-pornography.

It is not only that the mass-media exploiters are capitalizing on the cultural backwardness of the great majority of the American people. Worse: they are actively engaged in the *creation* of new types of subliterature (see the paperback racks), submusic (radio and jukeboxes), and generally subhuman activities (television), which they dump on a defenseless public in saturation quantities. No demand can be said to exist for such products of greedy and distorted minds until they are first created and then reiterated to the point of nausea or numbed acceptance. In the process of production and reiteration, whatever remains of an independent, traditional working-class culture — as Mr. Hoggart spells it out painstakingly in *The Uses of Literacy* — is gradually eroded.

The middle classes and the intelligentsia can at least be said to have alternative choices for their leisure hours. Thanks to the numerical increase of the college-educated and to their steadily increasing purchasing power, the masters of mass consumption have made available to them the cultural treasures of the ages through the media of books, records, and even FM stations. But these have not been, nor will they be, addressed to the working class, to the vast inarticulate masses, who are deemed by their betters to have lower tastes than the primitive Africans and Asians to whom the State Department exports Marian Anderson and Louis Armstrong. What could be at once more patronizing and more bankrupt than the claim that the flood of swill daily pumped through our cultural pipelines fairly represents all that the ordinary man can ever be expected to appreciate? If it is true that this capitalist society has all but wiped out economic degradation and oppression, why can it produce only consumers assertedly hungry for cultural products as degraded as those of any previous epoch of human history? The fantastic technological and scientific advances of recent years — not the singular product, we see now all too clearly, of American capitalism — do not merely call for an accompanying cultural advance, up to now unobservable among us; they will be positively insupportable without such an advance, without a new definition of the meaning of culture and of the individual human potential.

Meanwhile, the fact of the apparent hunger for cultural rubbish combined with the salesman's pitch, and their apparent mass acceptance, should not blind us to the basic shabbiness of the degradation and the exploitation of those who, all too unaware of what is being done to them, may even be asking for more of the same. I must turn once again to Richard Hoggart, who speaks to the point on this matter:

> If the active minority continue to allow themselves too exclusively to think of immediate political and economic objectives, the pass will be sold, culturally, behind their backs. This is a harder problem in some ways than even that which confronted their predecessors. It is harder to realize imaginatively the dangers of spiritual deterioration. Those dangers are

harder to combat, like adversaries in the air, with no corporeal shapes to inspire courage and decision. These things are enjoyed by the very people whom one believes to be adversely affected by them. It is easier for a few to improve the material conditions of many than for a few to waken a great many from the hypnosis of immature emotional satisfactions. People in this situation have somehow to be taught to help themselves.

It should not be discouraging that there are few voices like Mr. Hoggart's on this side of the Atlantic. Surely it is better to speak late than not to speak at all, and by one's silence ensure the continuing and intensified exploitation of those least able to resist its seductive and ultimately corrupting effects. Every voice which says No is itself a demonstration of the existence of an alternative to the cultural degradation of the masses.

The American Socialist, July-August 1958

The Myth of the Powerful Worker

Winchester, Virginia

A small group of unhappy and bewildered Americans is gathered musingly about a little table in a trailer parked beside a gas station on the outskirts of this quiet, pleasant Shenandoah Valley town. The town, called the Apple Capital by its boosters, is the home place of Senator Harry F. Byrd, who owns something like 2 per cent of all the apple trees in the United States. The Americans, seated uncomfortably on a broken-springed couch and three kitchen chairs, beneath a couple of girlie calendars and a scrawled reminder of an impending meeting of their local union, munch on hamburgers and Southern-style beans (the trailer is mostly a cookhouse, with a refrigerator and a little rotisserie), and ponder the fact that a trial examiner for the National Labor Relations Board has just ruled that they are violating the Taft-Hartley Act. They have been on strike against the O'Sullivan Rubber Company for over two years, and after having been disenfranchised in a decertification election, they are now advised that they cannot continue picketing the plant down the road, and that their international union, the Rubber Workers, which has been giving them twenty-five dollars a week strike benefits so that they do not go hungry or lose their homes or possessions, must cease and desist from its nationwide boycott of O'Sullivan products.

While they stare at each other, lined-faced family men, toothless oldsters, motherly widows, and shy young women, wondering how it came about that all the power of the federal government seems to be invoked against them simply because of their desire for decent relations with their employer, a professor of economics from Harvard University is testifying in Washington before the subcommittee on labor of the Senate Committee on Labor and Public Welfare. The nation's capital is only two hours to the east, across a green and lovely Virginia countryside dotted with baronial estates devoted to the raising of fine horses and fine cattle; but those who sit in the high-ceilinged committee room just down the hall from Senator Byrd's office might be on another planet, a million light-years from the baffled strikers in Byrd's home town. Senators Kennedy, Goldwater, Ives and Morse are listening quietly and politely to a parade of academic and professionally interested witnesses from both sides of the fence expounding their ideas on new legislation affecting the NLRB and the Taft-Hartley Act.

The economist, Professor Edward H. Chamberlin, is telling them that "Organized labor is on the whole rather well up the income scale, yet the anachronism that labor is downtrodden and deserving of some special kind of public sympathy carries on. It derives, in part, from a cultural lag."

The professor may not have the sympathy of all his listeners in the committee room, but there are others besides the National Association of Manufacturers (which commends him to the readers of the NAM *News*) who hold to his position: indeed there are times when one might suspect that he speaks not only for the conservative Right, but also for the host of former friends of labor, and ex-radicals who smile wearily when they are informed that there are still embattled strikers in this golden land. And the casual visitor to Washington who pads from one marble palace of labor to another, through the acres of broadloom, from the incredible Teamsters Union Taj Mahal to the hardly more credible temple of the Union of Operating Engineers to the plushy International Association of Machinists building to the well-appointed Philip Murray building to the quietly luxurious AFL-CIO building, might be pardoned for thinking — unless he troubles to discover that there are still some dedicated and worried men working for their ideals amid all the opulence — that the professor is right and that "labor" — that great abstraction — has reached the Promised Land after all.

The O'Sullivan strikers of Local 511 do not think so, but even though they have a clothing depot set up to receive gifts from those who care, they are not pressing the point that they are "downtrodden and deserving of some special kind of public sympathy." They do a lot of hunting for deer and small game, a lot of fishing for everything from herring to trout, a lot of odd jobs around the town; they hold bake sales to raise money for things that the union can't afford to provide, like schoolbooks for the kids; and although it is hard to find steady work (always the ostensible reason is that they would be only temporary until the strike ended), nobody is going hungry. But people like Mrs. Martha Webster, a gentle, tired widow who went to work for O'Sullivan with her brother and her brother-in-law twenty-seven years ago, and who had never heard of unions until she joined the one that she now supports ardently, as an embattled striker; Mrs. Carrie Boyd, a jolly widow who is mostly Cherokee, seldom reads the papers but knows what she is fighting for after some fourteen years as an O'Sullivan worker; Arthur and Asa Smith, who helped build the plant back in the Twenties and put in about thirty years of their lives there before going on strike; Charles Rittenour, who when he went on strike was making $1.30 an hour after eleven years at O'Sullivan, and whose face is a little more lined now because his oldest boy (he has five children) has leukemia; and Bruce Muse, who started in at O'Sullivan twenty-five years ago at fifteen cents an hour, making $1.87 for a twelve-and-a-half-hour day, and going around to his friends' homes evenings to try to talk union after the twelve and a half hours were over — these people are the victims of a piece of legislation most of them had never heard of. After having voted 343 to 2 to affiliate with their union, and 355 to 2 to strike, they found themselves the targets not only of an intransigent company, but also of an apparently implacable and vindictive government as well. What is more, they are not merely the fluke victims of an accidental legal clause (which the new Kennedy bill would repeal)*: millions of American workers are now being victimized in one way or another by the Taft-Hartley Law, which is now being applied so rigorously by the Eisenhower-appointed NLRB that even back in 1954 *Business Week* was saying, "from a practical standpoint, it's obvious that T-H has changed in operation."

To understand why, it is necessary to recapitulate a bit of the Winchester experience, as well as that of workers in other places and other industries who are suffering as a result of legislation and administration which had hitherto engaged their attention less deeply than had the private life of the Prince of Monaco. It is difficult even for a more sophisticated individual than a Virginia worker-housewife to understand what Section 9(c)(3) is going to mean personally until the paychecks stop.

In April 1956, the NLRB certified the United Rubber Workers as exclusive bargaining agent for O'Sullivan workers, after the 343–2 election. Negotiations followed, but there was disagreement on the question of a general wage increase (the company average was forty cents to sixty cents an hour below similar organized shops), and the employees struck the plant on May 13 after the 355–2 secret strike vote. The company immediately began to re-

* *Footnote, 1961:* The Landrum-Griffin Law does now allow, at long last in 1961, that workers striking for economic reasons may vote alongside the strikebreakers who have replaced them, in proceedings such as attempted decertifications of previously recognized unions.

cruit strikebreakers from the West Virginia hills (it is a commentary on conditions in the area that people were willing to scab on their neighbors for $1.25 an hour), and to pepper the strikers with telegrams urging their immediate return on penalty of job forfeiture.

At this point the strikers – the vast majority of whom had never before belonged to a union, paid much attention to politics, or even voted – had their first collision with the majesty of the law. The State of Virginia, not ordinarily noted for its social pioneering, had been one of the first to pass a "right-to-work" law. Under its terms, the strikers were hardly allowed so much as a frown as they stood at the gates, surrounded by state police, and watched the sheltered newcomers going in to take over work that they had been doing for upwards of a quarter of a century.

"We never thought that it would last more than a day or two," says one of the lady strikers, "or that the company would be so glad to be rid of us after all those years we put in for them. Actually, we should have given the scabs the same reception that Nixon got down in South America – but then, there was the right-to-work law, and those state police."

From that point on the company was in the driver's seat. It prolonged negotiations, broke them off, rejected the assistance of the Federal Mediation and Conciliation Service, resumed negotiations, stalled again, meanwhile hiring about 200 new employees. In January 1957, the United Rubber Workers inaugurated a consumer boycott of O'Sullivan, the first such boycott ever undertaken by the union in all its history. The company, which had obviously been reading the fine print, filed a new election petition with the NLRB in April and a decertification petition in May.

Now, according to Section 9(c)(3) of Taft-Hartley, "No election shall be directed in any bargaining unit or any subdivision within which, in the preceding twelvemonth period, a valid election shall have been held. Employees on strike who are not entitled to reinstatement shall not be eligible to vote. . . ." Thereupon, the year having elapsed and the strikers having been replaced, the NLRB disfranchised the O'Sullivan strikers and, with majestic impartiality, proceeded to poll the strikebreakers, who voted 288 to 5 against the union.

This may seem a little unfair. Indeed, this peculiar provision in a law ostensibly designed for "encouraging the practice and procedure of collective bargaining and by protecting the exercise by workers of full freedom of association, self-organization, and designation of representatives of their own choosing," was so designated by President Eisenhower. He pledged an A. F. of L. convention in 1952 (six weeks before Election Day, to be sure): "I know the [Taft-Hartley] law might be used to break unions. That must be changed. America wants no law licensing union-busting. Neither do I."

Even if the President were to strain every nerve and sinew to keep this pledge, which is not exactly what he has done, it is an open question whether the Congresses which have followed his noble words would have contented themselves in their labor legislation with simply striking out the ineffable Section 9(c)(3), which had distressed even Senator Taft himself.

But this was only the beginning of the education of the O'Sullivan strikers. In October 1957, the O'Sullivan company returned to the NLRB to charge that the union, by conducting its picketing, and engaging in its consumer boycott of O'Sullivan products, was in violation of Section 8(b)(1)(A). This section reads: "It shall be an unfair labor practice for a labor organization or its agents to restrain or coerce employees in the exercise of the rights guaranteed in Section 7. . . ."

So, in February 1958, the NLRB issued a complaint and on May 15, the trial examiner, finding no merit in the union's claim that it was no longer seeking recognition, but was simply exercising its right of free speech by displaying such picket signs as

WARNING
PENALTY FOR STRIKEBREAKING
A LIFETIME OF SHAME AND
REGRET
URW ON STRIKE AFL-CIO
ON STRIKE MAY 1956 to ?
DON'T BUY O'SULLIVAN
PRODUCTS
HEELS MADE BY A COMPANY
WITHOUT A SOUL

recommended that the union cease and desist from "restraining and coercing employees of O'Sullivan Rubber Corporation in the exercise of rights guaranteed by Section 7 of the Act by picketing said Company for the purpose of obtaining recognition and a contract . . . ," cease and desist from "conducting a boycott campaign against the Company's products . . . ," post in conspicuous places a formal notice that they are so ceasing and desisting, mail such notices to the NLRB for posting on O'Sullivan bulletin boards as well, publish in the *United Rubber Worker* a notice that the boycott is over, and notify the Regional Director of the steps taken to comply.

In Winchester, the strikers drift in and out of their trailer on their way to go fishing or to look at the picket line down the road in front of the plant where they had put in so many years, and they wonder aloud why their noses are being rubbed in it.

"I never was one for politics," muses a gray-haired lady as she bends over the icebox to get out some food for the menfolks. "It's a little hard for me to understand why the whole government seems to be so determined to be against us. I know the company would do most anything, but the government . . ."

But by and large the strikers are more sophisticated now. They know that the trial examiner's recommendations must go to the NLRB in Washington, that their union will appeal, that the case will probably wind up in the courts, and that precedent is against them. They know that all they can do is grit their teeth and hang on; they are caught in a box, and thank God for the union. They also know that in a sense they have themselves to blame for never having bothered all their lives to pay their poll tax.

"What for?" demands Maurice Miller, president of the Local. "To vote for Byrd and his boys? We never had a choice, so we never bothered with the head tax. But now we've learned the hard way – I'd say we're close to a hundred per cent registered, and we're paying our COPE dollars so the unions can get into politics and see if we can scare up a couple pro-labor men to run in this neck of the woods."

Framed in the doorway of the trailer, a long-faced striker stares up at Miller and says, in the deliberate way of men in these parts, "I swear to you, I'd soona vote for the blackest nigga in the State of Virginia than for a Byrd man. Hope to die if that ain't true. They took us for granted because they could ignore us, and we took them for granted because we didn't know any betta."

With all due respect to the O'Sullivan strikers, they could win no more than a footnote in any balanced account of contemporary America if they represented only themselves. But in January 1956, the employees of Machinery Overhaul Corporation at Palmdale, California, voted 65–28 to be represented by the International Association of Machinists. After protracted negotiations the union struck, and after the required year's wait, the company, having in the meantime hired a shop full of strikebreakers, demanded decertification of the union: all too predictably, the strikebreakers voted 90–1 against the union. Again all too predictably, the NLRB found thereafter that the IAM, by continuing picketing, had committed unfair labor practices in violation of good old Section 8(b)(1)(A). In April 1958, the strikers were ordered by the NLRB to cease and desist from picketing the shop where they had formerly constituted two thirds of the employees. All of these strikebreaking decisions, it should be noted, stem from last year's startling *Curtis Brothers* decision, which reversed past precedent favorable to unions, and which dissenting NLRB member Murdock characterized in these words: "The majority's erroneous interpretation of Section 8(b)(1)(A) seems to be prompted in large part by its desire to censure the union's conduct and find some section which can be utilized to ban it."

It is plain fact that thousands of organized (and countless unorganized) workers all over the country are suffering from the Taft-Hartley law and its interpretation by the Republican-appointed NLRB.

Forty-five million unorganized workers in the United States can never better themselves through organization by such unions as the Textile Workers, Retail Clerks and the white-collar unions as long as Taft-Hartley remains as law and is interpreted as it is being interpreted by the NLRB. These workers are simply not organizable; and the lawyers and union staffers in the plush Washington offices, whose job is to thread their way through the mazes of NLRB decisions and administrative rulings, are by and large almost as frustrated and furious as the workers of Winchester, Virginia. Let us examine some of the reasons why.

First of all, there are the provisions of Taft-Hartley itself. We have already seen how some of these have changed the hitherto quiet lives of the people of Winchester and of Palmdale, California. In Toledo, Ohio, the Retail Clerks International Association had been bargaining with four stores together, which called themselves Retail Associates. In November 1957, the union struck one of the stores, Tiedtke's, which promptly withdrew from the employer group and settled with the union. Thereupon the union struck a second member store, LaSalle & Koch (an R. H.

Macy affiliate); this strike continues, but the store is open and, as in Winchester, grandmothers walk the picket line, cherishing their new-found militancy but wondering what goes on inside the store and inside the government.

For now the maneuvering had begun. Retail Associates, acting for its three remaining members, asked the NLRB to hold an election among the employees of LaSalle's, Lamson Brothers, and Lion Dry Goods, arguing that the bargaining unit had changed. The strategy was obvious: with the unionized employees of Tiedtke's excluded from the vote, with the 400 striking employees of LaSalle's excluded from the vote, and with the 350 strikebreakers of LaSalle's included in the vote, the Retail Clerks union couldn't possibly win. The union thereupon withheld its technically necessary non-Communist affidavits in an effort to keep itself off the ballot and thus forestall an election. It went before the NLRB and argued that it had the same right to withdraw from bargaining with the multi-store group that one of the store group did; and it asserted its right to bargain with the three stores individually.

With extraordinary rapidity, the NLRB ruled against the union, thus condemning it in advance to what the Rubber Workers had already been going through in Virginia. As Joseph A. Loftus narrated the story in the *New York Times* of April 11, 1958, the board "took the unusual step of notifying the parties by telegram of its decision less than forty-eight hours after it had heard oral argument." In so doing, the board overturned its own ten-year-old precedent, which forbade a union not technically in compliance with filing requirements from participating in an election; it opened the door to employers who would like to force their employees belonging to such powerful unions as the Mine Workers or the Typographers to submit willy-nilly to an NLRB election; and it drove the infuriated Retail Clerks to the courts, no less, to seek an injunction against the NLRB election. Sol Lippman, union counsel, bluntly called the decision "a naked effort to break a strike," and went before U. S. District Judge Edward M. Curran to demand injunctive relief.

The NLRB attorney actually pleaded that LaSalle's was losing money because of the strike – a strange argument for a government official in a quasi-judicial position. The Associated Press story of April 22 gave another interesting sidelight on the reasoning of the NLRB attorney:

> Mr. Come argued that it was not certain how the election would come out if held on schedule on a multiple-unit basis. He said some of the LaSalle employees who have replaced strikers might vote for the union.
>
> "You don't think they are going to vote themselves out of a job, do you?" the judge asked.

Thereupon the judge issued the preliminary injunction sought by the Clerks, and the case will now be fought through the courts, while the middle-aged ladies march the picket lines in downtown Toledo.

If it seems strange today that labor unions should go to the courts to demand the aid of what has been for generations one of the most dreaded weapons used against labor – the injunction – that can only be taken as a measure of the extent to which the labor movement has become alarmed, not just about Taft-Hartley itself, but about the erosive effect of recent NLRB rulings.

While some of the most deeply entrenched unions have been howling the loudest in outrage (the International Typographical Union, operating for generations under what have amounted to closed-shop conditions, says Taft-Hartley has already cost its members $30,000,000),* the truth of the matter would seem to be that it is the workers in the less powerful unions, and even more so the not-yet-organized workers, who are affected most directly by the

* *Footnote, 1961:* Finally, in 1961, the Supreme Court ruled against the NLRB and for the Typographical Union.

anti-labor bias of what one lawyer refers to as the National Labor Reversals Board. It costs from $3,000 to $10,000 to pursue a case through the circuit court, with the result that some unions simply cannot afford to contest what this lawyer calls "board law, not worth the paper it's printed on," in a court of law; indeed, he finds it currently so difficult to get a complaint issued by the board that he discourages his clients from filing charges with it at all. It should be noted parenthetically that corporations are legally entitled to list as business expenses the cost of fighting unfair-labor-practice court cases.

What is this "board law"? Here the layman finds his feet sinking into legal quicksand, and as he reaches out frantically for solid objects to cling to in the morass of opinions, precedents (some with names like the "Orkin the Rat Man" case), and administrative responses to changes in the political climate (i.e., the board's swing from a New Deal to an Eisenhower stance), he finds himself grasping at the straws of Latin phrases and at footnotes in which numbers outnumber words. Senator Wayne Morse of Oregon had a go at it on the floor of the Senate back in 1956, delivering himself of a ninety-page oration based in large part on a paper by Mozart G. Ratner, formerly Assistant General Counsel of the NLRB, entitled "Recent Changes in National Labor Relations Board Policies." Both of these documents are well worth reading, and one may surmise that the only reason for their not having a greater impact at the time was their lack of sex appeal as well as general public apathy toward labor problems at a time of full employment.

It would be tempting at this point to narrate some of the cases cited by Ratner and Morse, but a good deal has happened since then, and a good deal continues to happen. Let us mention only the case of the B.V.D. strikers, cited with good reason in both monographs. At Pascagoula, Mississippi, a group of women workers had organized themselves into a homemade union and then sought out the International Ladies' Garment Workers' Union for help. The NLRB denied reinstatement and back pay to thirty-seven strikers on the ground that they had continued to picket after acts of violence had been committed against the B.V.D. property by unidentified third parties. There was no attempt to prove that the women strikers instigated or even participated in the acts of violence; there was no evidence of conspiracy on the part of the strikers or of their having any control over the perpetrators. The board held that these ladies, some of whom were putting their children through school and were the main family breadwinners, were not entitled to get their jobs back because they should either have stopped picketing or dissociated themselves from the violence by "admonishment, denunciation or public pronouncement." This astonishing assault upon a group of innocent women, with all it implied not just for their right to their jobs but for their basic right to picket (and how can you conduct a strike without picketing?), forced the ILGWU to take the case to the courts. No wonder Professor Willard Wirtz, writing in the Northwestern University *Law Review*, commented that "the new NLRB . . . has proceeded to 'reinterpret' the [Taft-Hartley] Act in such a manner as to change its practical application substantially beyond anything seriously considered in recent Congresses."

We have to bear in mind, too, that the layman's notion that you can simply go to court (if you can afford it) and get everything straightened out that has been done to you administratively is more than a little simple. The courts are most reluctant to overrule the NLRB, and because of the "substantial evidence" rule, it is extremely difficult to get the board reversed in court on a question of fact. If you are not prepared to argue law rather than fact against the board, the chances are you will only waste your time and money in the courts. One Washington labor lawyer told me flatly: "If I were an employer lawyer, I could break any union just by using Taft-Hartley and the NLRB."*

In this connection, we might take note of a Washington story in the *New York Times* of May 27, 1958:

> The Supreme Court held today that an employee kept out of a plant by the threats of striking union members might sue the union for damages in the state courts instead of going to the National Labor Relations Board for relief.

Chief Justice Warren, joined in dissent by Justice Douglas, asserted:

> There is a very real prospect of staggering punitive damages accumulated through successive actions by parties injured by [*union*] members who have succumbed to the emotion that frequently accompanies concerted activities during labor unrest. . . . By reason of vicarious liability for its members' ill-advised conduct on the picket lines, the union [*the United Automobile Workers, already defending some twenty-nine other suits totaling $1,500,000 as a result of the Decatur, Alabama, strike*] is to be subjected to a series of judgments that may and probably will reduce it to bankruptcy.

This brings us to the tricky question which some Washington attorneys regard as the greatest drawback of the present NLRB: its narrow definition of its own jurisdiction. Without going into the complex details, we may say only that several years ago the board drew an arbitrary line and refused – presumably for reasons of budget and work load – to take jurisdiction in cases where the employer was basically "local" in character, as determined partly by the dollar value of business inflow or outflow. NLRB member Murdock promptly pointed out that there was neither a pressing shortage of funds, nor inability to handle case load (which was no higher than it had been

* *Footnote, 1961:* The unions had hoped for substantial changes for the better under the new Kennedy Administration; so far, however, improvement seems highly dubious in 1961.

five years earlier), nor any serious backlog of cases. He believed that the new jurisdictional standards would eliminate between a quarter and a third of the board's jurisdiction. It was his judgment, fortified by quotations from his more conservative colleagues, that the slash in jurisdiction was motivated by what you might dignify as philosophical considerations: the desire on the part of the board majority to cut back on "federal bureaucracy" and return to the states (most of which, if they have troubled to enact labor legislation at all, have adopted only "right-to-work" laws and similar employer aids) as much authority as possible on labor questions.

Labor lawyers like Arthur Goldberg and Elliott Bredhoff, counsel for the Steelworkers Union, claim that by thus taking itself out of the picture in such a substantial proportion of cases, the board has cut off the application of federal labor law from those working for hard-core employers and from marginal areas where workers are most in need of government protection. If you have been wondering where the individual human being re-enters the picture, think for a moment of the saleslady in a store or the chambermaid in a hotel, neither of whom can now turn to her government for protection if she wants to unionize — unless she happens to work for a "big" employer.

However, it must be noted that the Supreme Court has complicated matters by refusing to grant the states jurisdiction over some of these cases, thereby creating a "no man's land" for several million workers; that the Florida hotel cases are currently before the Supreme Court; that Congress is very likely going to have to do something about the no-man's-land area; and, indeed, that some labor lawyers in Washington are currently far more exercised about matters other than the board's refusal to take jurisdiction in many cases.*

* *Footnote, 1961:* The board is now required to take any cases it formerly took; in other words it can no longer disavow previous jurisdiction in 1961.

What are these other matters? Some of them are pretty ugly. Plato E. Papps, attorney for the International Association of Machinists, in a bitter article in the University of Detroit *Law Review*, entitled "The Aluminum Workers – Revisited," charges that:

> . . . It is hardly risky speculation to ferret out the true motives of the presently-constructed National Labor Relations Board. . . . It is patently obvious that NLRB changes in policy have invariably been in favor of management. The cumulative effect of the many small shifts has been considerable. Curtailment of the economic power of labor organizations is but one of a categorized array of anti-labor policies. And even where no explicit change in policy can be garnered from administrative rulings, the "Eisenhower Board" analyzes facts in such a way as to find fewer violations of the Act by employers in contrast to unions. It is necessary to explore only the dissenting opinions of Member Murdock to ascertain how "Republican political facts of life" form the keystone of board persuasion. The recent expiration of Member Murdock's term on the board brings to an end, incidentally, the irritable reminders that Congress did not intend the Taft-Hartley Act to be the manipulative bauble of the National Association of Manufacturers.

In support of these conclusions, Mr. Papps quotes the following comments from articles in the Utah *Law Review*, the *Labor Law Journal*, the Columbia *Law Review*, and the University of Chicago *Law Review*: ". . . Substantial changes have been made in the NLRB decisions since the advent of an Eisenhower majority. . . ." "The recent decisions of the board have tended . . . to favor the employer's interests over the union. . . ." "The recent major policy decisions reveal a total disregard for the fact . . . that Congress declared it to be the policy of the United States to encourage unionization for the purpose of restoring equality of bargaining power between employers and employees."

The most comprehensive and devastating summary of what these changes have actually involved is to be found in an article called "Labor Law Upside Down: The NLRB and Member Rodgers," written by Joseph E. Finley and published as a pamphlet by the Public Affairs Institute. Mr. Finley, a labor lawyer who makes no bones about his bias, traces the turnabout in labor law to the appointment to the board in 1953 of Philip Ray Rodgers, a Taft protégé. Most particularly since then, he claims, the NLRB has been curtailing union organization, resorting to injunctions, making inexcusable rulings against unions, suppressing union activities over broad areas, and making a feeble defense of its pro-management rulings.

For one thing, in the minds of the NLRB a *threat* has now become a *prediction*. If your boss tells you that he'll have to close down his plant if you vote for a union, or if he tells you that he won't bargain with the union, he's not threatening you – he's merely "predicting" what he may be forced to do, and therefore is not guilty of an unfair labor practice. The lawyers call this "prediction of a legal position."

Moreover, sophisticated employers, thanks to the new board, have now discovered that the realm of permissible campaign propaganda has been vastly enlarged. Finley cites the case of the Zeller Corporation, which, after bombarding its employees with mailings and anti-union publications, sent them a copy of a letter from one of its customers which inquired about the company's labor relations. Employees, the company pointed out to its own workers, "can readily see how we can retain customers and secure new business without the presence of a union." This, although it was a misrepresentation, was ruled by the board to be permissible propaganda.

Worse than either of these – at least in the opinion of this writer – is the extraordinary latitude given to employer "expressions of opinion" in the sacred name of "free speech." The cases that Finley cites are bad enough, in all conscience; but there are others he does not cite, particularly in the backward areas that the Textile Workers

Union has been trying almost fruitlessly to organize, that are so heartbreaking as to make anyone except the most case-hardened want to weep.

These are not the Thirties, we are reminded over and over. These are the Fifties, unions are strong (too strong, even some liberals are saying), workers are not deserving of any special sympathy. Yet today women who earn eighty-five cents an hour waiting on you in stores vote against having a union to defend their rights because they are frightened by their employer, or lied to by him, and have no government agency which will defend them against threats or lies made in the name of free speech. Today, throughout the South, thousands of men and women who work in textile mills at below-standard wages, in below-standard conditions, vote against unions because they are showered with racist propaganda of the lowest kind.

For some weeks now, John W. Edelman, Washington representative of the Textile Workers Union, has been fruitlessly appealing to Senator McClellan, chairman of the Select Committee – not on Labor Racketeering, as it has become known – but "to Investigate Improper Activities in Labor-Management Relations." He has asked for the opportunity to show that in Gaffney, South Carolina, in Alexander City, Alabama, in Tallapoosa, Georgia, in Stuart, Virginia, and in other towns throughout the South, there exists a pattern of anti-union violence and obstruction.

Back in 1950 a Senate subcommittee found that:

> The extent and effectiveness of the opposition in the Southern Textile industry is almost unbelievable.
>
> In stopping a union-organizing campaign, the employer will use some or all of the following methods: surveillance of organizers and union adherents; propaganda through rumors, letters, news stories, advertisements, speeches to the employees; denial of free speech and assembly to the union; organizing of the whole community for anti-union activity; labor espionage; discharges of union sympathizers; violence and gun

play; injunctions; the closing or moving of the mill; endless litigation before the NLRB and the Courts, etc. . . .

It is Edelman's claim that substantially the same conditions prevail today, in 1958, but so far Senator McClellan has shown no desire to divert the committee's attention from the more eye-catching exposures of venal union officials. We may legitimately ask what has happened to the national sense of proportion, and the fitness of things, when the misdeeds of a handful of loathsome slobs are deemed more worthy of our moral indignation than the deprivation of millions of Americans.

How do Taft-Hartley and the NLRB fit into this picture? Between 1943 and 1946, almost 50,000 Southern textile workers were brought under Textile Workers' labor agreements; since Taft-Hartley, this union's organizing drives have been for the most part dishearteningly unsuccessful. Take the case of the Burlington chain. Burlington is the largest single textile company in the United States, employing about 50,000 workers in about a hundred plants in this country alone. This is no backwoods outfit. It is also not above being involved in the distribution of anti-Semitic and anti-Negro propaganda, in having its supervisors tell employees that the union is 100 per cent for racial integration, in having its plant managers tell employees that the union has given large sums to the NAACP, in informing its employees that white workers would have Negro shop stewards if the union got in. Why not? The NLRB has already ruled that employers have the right to "free speech," and that if employer-subsidized Chambers of Commerce and clergymen peddle anti-union race hate during organizing drives, there is no "proof" that the employers are using them as anti-labor "agents" to commit unfair labor practices.

But free speech seems to be a one-way street. In the T.W.U.'s futile effort to organize the workers of the Chatham Manufacturing Company in Elkin, North Carolina, all meeting places within an area of thirty miles were denied to Chatham workers: the Elkin YMCA, the local movie theaters, the Elkin school, the Benham school, the Boonville school, the Boonville movie house, the Surrey County Court House. Meanwhile, the workers were being bombarded not only by the local clergy and the local press, but by a hate sheet called *Militant Truth.* The Elkin *Tribune* was not above reprinting such paragraphs as the following from this hate sheet:

> The boys who head the CIO and would control the policy go under such names as Rieve, Baldanzi, Belanger, Shupka, Jueter . . . Rosenberg, Rubenstein . . . Stetin, Tullar, etc. Where do you think these men come from? Are their backgrounds, their beliefs, their faith anything like yours and ours?

The union lost the election. The union is still losing elections. Let me repeat that there are forty-five million unorganized workers in the United States. As Joseph Finley points out in his pamphlet, there are by now "numerous cases where unions have gone into election campaigns with far more than a majority of the employees signed to membership cards, then have received the brunt of an employer's 'predictions,' 'opinions' and 'permissible propaganda,' and have come out losing by margins of three and four to one."

I only wish it were possible for me to elaborate on some of the other points made by Finley — his charges that the NLRB has been suppressing union activities over a broad area, including secondary boycotts, on-the-job union rights, seniority rules, union security, collective-bargaining rights and protection against discriminatory discharges. But space permits mention only of his final pages on the record of NLRB member Philip Ray Rodgers, who voted against unions in every single case cited by Finley, including those labeled by federal judges as "farfetched," "irrational" and "unjust and intolerable." Finley has compiled a little chart of the voting record of Mr. Rodgers which reveals that, in

1955, he cast sixty-six votes for management and two for labor; in 1956, forty-nine for management and one for labor; in 1957, forty-five votes for management and none for labor: "When a man votes for management 98 per cent of the time over a three-year period in critical cases, the conclusion is inescapable. He is no longer a judge, but a partisan adversary."

Well, the conclusion would seem inescapable, too, that if we are going to have investigations of union skulduggery, we ought to have an investigation of whether honest unions are getting a fair shake at the tribunal of the National Labor Relations Board.* The NAM is deeply impressed by the fact that complaints to the NLRB of workers against their *unions* have zoomed upward recently, spurred no doubt by the recession and the anger of laid-off workers at all officialdom; the rest of us ought to be deeply concerned whether the rights of unorganized workers to form unions and bargain collectively are being adequately protected by a board which has been so zealously protecting employers' rights of "free speech," "permissible propaganda," and "predictions" of catastrophes in the event of union victory.

Meanwhile, the observer who compares the lean and quizzical faces of the O'Sullivan strikers with the somewhat better-fed faces in the sleek halls of labor in the nation's capital, may be pardoned for wondering just how much American workers, and the American people in general, have gained from the labor leaders' ostentatious effort to keep up with the Joneses in Washington, only to find themselves a minor vote-trading power bloc in a city of really big power blocs. Perhaps the leaders really belong

* *Footnote, 1961:* Representative Pucinski (D., Ill.) now heads a House Subcommittee investigating charges that the NLRB has deliberately discriminated against unions.

back with the led – from which independent base they might begin to understand for the first time what the potentialities of power *really* mean.

The Nation, June 28-July 5, 1958

Less Work—Less Leisure

> I regard the five-day week as an unworthy ideal . . . More work and better work is a more inspiring and worthier motto than less work and more pay . . . It is better not to trifle or tamper with God's laws.
> —*John E. Edgerton, President of the National Association of Manufacturers* (*1926*)

Akron, Ohio

Times have changed since the gentleman quoted above invoked the Deity in opposition to Henry Ford's revolutionary five-day week. Not that hard-pressed executives ceased thereafter to cite divine guidance as the source of their labor relations. A decade after Mr. Edgerton pointed to the Lord, sit-down strikers at the largest rubber plant in the world, Akron's Goodyear plant, provided one of the first tests of the new CIO, and in a nineteen-below-zero St. Valentine's Day blizzard, the scraggly crowd of determined workers marched up Market Street into the teeth of the gale. Little more than a year later, in March 1937, the 10,000 workers of the Akron Firestone plant struck after four years of futile effort to get the company to recognize their union. Harvey Firestone was at his estate in Miami Beach. The teletype from Akron to Harbel Villa kept Mr. Firestone informed, but, we are assured by the authorized Firestone biographer, it "did not alleviate his feeling of distress at this cleavage. 'When the strike broke out in Akron it jarred me for a day or two. Then I concluded there must be some reason for it and that we could not help it, but the thing we should do was not to fight it but to stand on what we thought was right and then let matters stand, as it was God's will we were to have a strike and there was a good reason for it, and it would be righted in the right time. . . .' "

In the Akron of today, it is hard indeed to realize that it was only twenty years ago that Harvey Firestone sent that philosophical message to his son, that it was only twenty years ago that the Firestone strikers threw up shacks of canvas, wood, and tin as picket shelters at the freezing factory gates. Now this industrial city is clean, prosperous and not slum-ridden, and to the casual visitor the workers themselves are transformed, too; they are no longer the grimly huddled proletarians of those terrible and dramatic days. At a glance, they seem to epitomize the publicity ideal of the smiling middle-class American. And the union that helped to lead them out of the pit of the depression, the United Rubber Workers, is today not merely a well-housed and comfortably situated fraternal organization; it is a democratically operated, decently administered labor union, properly and profoundly concerned with the naggingly complex problems of its membership, and still so proud of its militant origins that it disputes with its big brother union, the Auto Workers, the claim to originating the weapon of the sit-down strike.

Just as it is hard to realize that the affable, self-assured workers cruising Akron's streets in late-model cars are often the same men who pounded up those streets as defiant strikers two decades ago, so it is hard to believe that much of the present leadership of their union, from President L. H. Buckmaster on down, consists of the very same men who founded the union and endured beatings and imprisonment in the course of their early struggles. Yet you will bump into them as you travel around town — George Bass in the International Office, Joe Childs at a restaurant, Jack Little at a meeting of his local; men whose names are already lengendary, but who give the impression — along with the union's rank-and-file activists and "politicians" — of being more worried about the immediate future than proud of their accomplishments in what is already the remote past. Indeed, one might almost be tempted to characterize this mood, particularly among the rank and file, as one of uncertainty, of tentativeness of direction, of lack of confidence in whatever the ultimate goals may be. It is a mood strikingly different from the explosive *élan* of those who went out and built the CIO because they were convinced beyond question that they were going to convert the rotten life of the American worker into the good life.

Ever since those dismal depression days, a portion of Akron's rubber workers have worked a six-hour day and a six-day week. The six-hour day was first instituted by the companies as a work-sharing (or poverty-sharing) device, but soon became so popular with the workers that they wrote it into their union constitution (one of their constitutionally enshrined objectives is "To establish the six-hour day and the thirty-hour work-week with wage increases to compensate for the shorter time so that there will be no reduction in weekly earnings from such action"), and into their contracts with the Big Four of the rubber industry. Today it is an emotionally charged article of belief, and even the most cursory inquirer in Akron soon becomes convinced that the delegate from Local 101 to the union's 1956 Los Angeles convention was hardly exaggerating when he cried from the floor: "We in the six-hour plant regard it as almost a religion."

It is this unique long-time experience with the shorter work-day that has lately made Akron a focus of interest as a possible forecast of what all America will be like in the era of the less-than-forty-hour week, an era that presently seems inevitable even if the Deity should once again be invoked by those who oppose its arrival. Already the town has been researched and written up by *Fortune* and the *Wall Street Journal*, and it is increasingly referred to by those who write about and ponder the problems that will attend the shorter work-week: Will people use the increased leisure wisely? Will workers tend to hunt up second jobs? What will the social effects eventually be?

Unquestionably, the outlines of the social pattern of the

future are here to be seen. But the first thing the visitor learns is the complexity of that pattern, and certainly before we are so brash as to generalize from this unique industrial instance we should at least note some of the special factors that must be taken into consideration in any speculation about the uses of leisure.

First, although about 30,000 rubber workers do work a six-hour day, six days a week, with the plants operating four shifts a day, they represent only about 15 per cent of the employees of the rubber industry. Most rubber workers, by special contractual agreements, are now on a straight eight-hour day with premium pay if they work the sixth day.

Second, even in some of the six-hour shops there are departments or divisions (mostly the crafts) which work eight-hour shifts.

Third, in only two cities outside Akron do Rubber Workers' locals have six-hour contracts.

(These first three points acquire a special significance when you realize that the hourly rate for the eight-hour man is contractually lower, even for the same work, than that of the man in the six-hour plant – but that he may take home somewhat more money if his plant regularly works a sixth or overtime day. To put it mildly, the union membership is not united on the question of which working day is better.)

Fourth, Akron cannot be regarded as a typical American industrial city, if only because its population is virtually homogeneous with a relatively small percentage of immigrants. They call Akron "the capital of West Virginia." It would seem obvious that people who have come up by the thousands out of the hill country to make steady money building tires are going to use their leisure somewhat differently from those who came over from Europe to make ladies' garments or pig iron, but also to escape oppression and to build a future for their children.

Fifth, the city is relatively characterless – partly because the Southerners are still so deeply rooted in their home country that they return at every opportunity, and partly because the rubber barons have not seen fit to dispense largesse in any considerable amount in the community which produces their wealth.

Sixth, it seems most unlikely that any general shortening of working hours across the country will follow the unique Akron pattern. More probably we are going to see unions pressing for work-weeks like the Garment Workers' seven-hour, five-day week, or the Auto Workers' momentarily abandoned but very much alive proposed eight-hour, four-day week. The difference in effect of each system is almost incalculable. For example, who is going to be more willing and able to work at a second job: the man who works a six-hour, six-day week, or the one who will work an eight-hour, four-day week?

Seventh, there has been no large-scale, careful study of the ways in which Akron rubber workers make use of their leisure. With the exception of a cursory union survey, there has not been an attempt to find out exactly how many of them hold down a second job. Therefore, given the complexity of the six-hour-eight-hour pattern, no one can say with confidence that the man who works shorter hours does in fact lead a measurably different life – in terms of what he does with his off-hours – than his fellow on the more traditional eight-hour day. In all honesty we must be limited at this point to impressionistic hunches and conjectures, which in the present instance are based on observation and on conversation with workers.

What can we learn from the experience of these Americans who have been living with the short work-day for a generation? Quite a lot. First of all, some 60 per cent of the Akron working women are married. Thirty thousand housewives in this area are not only housewives but wage-earners too, and not on an emergency wartime basis but as steady industrial workers, accumulating seniority, looking for paid vacations and working toward retirement pensions alongside their men.

Not exactly alongside, however. The wife in Chicago or New York who works will probably leave home with her husband in the morning and meet him at home for supper. Not so in Akron, where the four six-hour rubber-plant shifts make it easier for the wife to work a shift which will still enable her to keep house, and for the husband to work one which will enable him to baby-sit while his wife works. If, in addition, he has a *second* job, which as we will see is often the case, he is going to be able to spend only a few hours a week alone with his wife. Their children, often looked after by Grandma or by baby-sitters, are causing heads to shake anxiously over increasing juvenile delinquency. Togetherness is never going to penetrate very far into the household where the adults are holding down multiple jobs; for every three marriage licenses issued here last year, there was one suit filed for divorce. And we have to bear in mind that this looks more and more like a permanent phenomenon, as working wives strive not just for that extra pay check (the federal government takes a healthy bite out of it every year), but for security, for hospitalization, medical care, vacations, pensions.

We might note parenthetically at this point that a Gallup poll taken last year indicated that, on a national basis, women were opposed to the idea of a four-day week by a three-to-one margin. No reasons were given, but it seems only logical that a housewife who normally puts in a twelve-hour day and must continue to do so (like the farmers, who were predictably opposed to the four-day week by a four-to-one margin) would resent such a lightening of the burden of others. Besides, there is the fear that the husband who is off for three days may become less responsible, drink more, run around more. Nevertheless, I should be very much surprised if a poll were to show anything like this feeling among the women of Akron, who have learned from experience that the shorter day gives them more of what they want — even if it is only the opportunity to go out and become wage-earners themselves.

What else have the Akron rubber workers been doing with those extra hours? The stroller down South Main Street on a Monday evening, when the stores are open late, will get one or two ideas, provided he isn't run over (per capita auto registration here last year was second only to that in Los Angeles). Husbands and wives are clustered in the brilliantly lit do-it-yourself supermarkets, picking over wall coverings for the bathroom and floor coverings for the rumpus room. Home ownership is high – seven out of ten Akron families live in their own homes – and men who work only six hours a day can put in a good deal of time fixing and repairing, building a garage, paving a driveway, adding an extra room.

The bowling alleys are jammed, the poolrooms do well, the neighboring waters are stocked with power boats, and last year Summit County sold the fantastic number of 67,400 hunting and fishing licenses to local residents (there are a little over 300,000 people in Akron).

The churches can't complain, either. The people up from West Virginia, Kentucky, and Tennessee take their religion seriously, many of them tithe as a matter of course and of conscience, and they go in heavily for revivalism and fundamentalism. The Temple of Healing Stripes has free bus service to its Divine Healing Services; evangelists hold Old Fashioned Brush-Arbor Revivals and show Signs! Wonders! Miracles! every night in the summertime; and Rex Humbard is supervising construction of the Cathedral of Tomorrow, Calvary Temple, The Largest Church Auditorium Built In This Generation.

Other cultural manifestations are somewhat more muted. Living theater is practically nonexistent, there is no professional symphony, and although the Public Library is good, one can search the city in vain for a bookshop devoted to selling new books. (There are, to be sure, several which specialize in ecclesiastical tracts of various denominations, and a shop in the very shadow of a rubber plant which, despite the protestations of its owner that he caters to a steady clientele of "bookworms," seems to attract primarily young workers looking for what the proprietor calls "strictly legal" sex and girlie books.)

At this level, then, Akron rubber workers do not seem to spend their extra off-hours very differently from their brothers across America. What the others are doing, *they* are doing — and then some. We can even say this of the one big question not touched on thus far, the second job. A Federal Census Bureau survey published in the summer of 1957 found some 3,700,000 persons to be multiple job-holders. This figure is about double what it had been six years before, and it works out to about 5.5 per cent of the country's total employed.

Now there cannot be a single person in Akron who would claim — although everyone is guessing — that the percentage of rubber workers holding down two jobs is that low. Best guesses seem to agree that anywhere from one in seven up to one in five rubber workers holds a second full-time job, with a small fraction even managing two jobs on different shifts at different rubber plants. In addition, something like 40 per cent engage in some sort of part-time outside work. With such a discrepancy between the Akron picture and the national picture, the inference would seem obvious, although there are many rubber workers who heatedly deny it: the shorter day, even with a higher pay scale, increases the number of men who obtain second jobs as garage attendants, taxi drivers, bellhops, grocers, butchers, clerks, insurance salesmen, realtors, brokers, barbers, repairmen, bakers — yes, and engineers too.

I am afraid that what I have said thus far will leave the reader feeling cold and clammy; but the general picture must be clear before we can attempt to understand its meaning in the lives of the individual actors — the workers themselves. It is to be expected that *Time*, surveying the "moonlighting" (two-job) situation, should point out that there are those who "hail moonlighters as heirs to the spirit of the nation's founders and insist that hard work never hurt anybody." But when Arthur Schlesinger, Jr., asserted last fall that "The most dangerous threat hanging over American society is the threat of leisure . . . and those who have the least preparation for leisure will have the most of it," one wonders whether he realized that it was the *enforced* leisure of the layoff that was soon to threaten American workers, and that all too often it was the memory of previous enforced leisure that was driving them into moonlighting, into destroying their leisure by racing from one job to the other while the jobs were still there to be had?

It is unlikely that Mr. Schlesinger was thinking in these terms. One can agree with his warning only if one takes a long-term view; it can hardly be immediately comforting to those workers who have not accumulated sufficient seniority to avoid being laid off in the current slump, like the two ladies with fourteen years' seniority who sat biting their lips, jobless, in an Akron coffee shop. Or (to cite a perhaps less suspect source) like Kenneth Marxmiller of the Caterpillar plant in Peoria. "It affects my wife more than me," said Mr. Marxmiller to a *Life* reporter (January 27, 1958). "She just sits and cries. . . ."

Nor is it likely that Mr. Schlesinger could foresee how rapidly his analysis would be vulgarized into the grossest sort of caricature. The *Saturday Evening Post* of January 11, 1958, has a short story entitled "Holiday for Howie" and subtitled: *At first glance it seemed terrific, a four-day work week! But then he found there was a catch in it.* . . . The catch, it turns out, is that Howie rapidly gets bored with all that leisure. He takes to sleeping late on those long weekends, and when his wife declines to go gallivanting around the country with him (her responsibility to house and children continues on his days off), he looks up an old school friend, now a rich bachelor leading an idle, dissolute life. They drink together, which is what Howie had been looking forward to, but the friend reveals that he is not really happy or free; he is drinking himself to death from boredom and loneliness. Shocked, Howie goes to the beach to Think Things Out:

> He hadn't learned to handle time. All he could do was try to kill it. . . . And all the while, crazily, more time being made. Household gadgets to save time for the housewife, for what? So that she can spend the afternoon playing cards? And all the freeways built to save time, for what? So that people traveling at breakneck speed can get home ten minutes earlier to have an extra cocktail before dinner? And science adding years to a man's life, for what? So that at eighty he can learn to dance? . . . Speed, and time to be filled, is that all our civilization has contributed? He felt like crying and he didn't know why.

Lying there, Howie discovers the secret — Time opens out for him into Eternity. He hurries home to explain this to his wife — a large order — and to tell her that he has decided to take a second job, one which will fill two of his three free days, because:

> ". . . Time is not for me. Some people can handle it. I can't. . . ."
>
> "Oh, Howie." There was love and admiration in her muffled voice. And vague regret.
>
> "Cheer up, Doll. Think what we can do with the extra money — lots of things. Think what we can get — a new car, with all the gadgets! Color TV! Air conditioning! We'll really be living! Smile, Doll!"
>
> THE END

It is characteristic of the corrupt subliterature of the mass media, as it used to be of Fascist propaganda, that it is thoroughly capable of seizing on some of the most agonizing and centrally important human problems and distorting them into grotesque and semicomic horror stories, which relate only weirdly to the way people really think and feel.

Then what do the workers believe? Every Akron worker with any consciousness of his position in society starts with one unalterable and clearly understood premise: he is a member of a declining labor force. On November 1, 1951, the Goodrich plant in Akron had 11,475 employees on its rolls; on May 4, 1956, it had 8500 employees. It is true that the company moved some of its operations to more modern and hence more competitive plants elsewhere, as well as to plants working eight-hour shifts (with lower hourly rates); but this only serves to sharpen the worker's realization that automation, rationalization, and continually developing industrial technology are, before his very eyes, cutting down on the number of human beings needed to manufacture goods.

He sees himself in a situation not unlike that of the farmer. With productivity steadily increasing at the rate of about 3 per cent a year, he will be able to protect himself and his family only by moving from the manufacture of goods to the delivery of services, as the farmers have gradually moved to the cities, or by spending fewer hours per week producing goods. The two-job situation can be partially interpreted as the beginning of such a shift—very often the second job is a service job, whether it be cutting hair or selling real estate. I was not too surprised to hear several workers say that they believed eventually the government would have to subsidize labor as it has subsidized the farmer. "You can call this socialism if you want," one added aggressively. "The point is the problem is bigger than we are and it has to be solved in a big way."

Here again is something the Akron worker has come to see: the problem of the shorter work-week, of increased leisure versus a second job, is bigger than he is, it is bigger even than his 220,000-member union. It has implications that may make it too big even for his senior partner, the million-member Auto Workers Union, whose lead he has traditionally followed (although the development of the plastics industry and of such products as foam rubber and pliofilm are making Akron somewhat less directly dependent on Detroit's prosperity). And he is badly split.

He is split not only when an eight-hour local opposes a six-hour local (the international union, which has been seriously trying to achieve work-week uniformity so that it can bargain across the country for pay-rate uniformity, presented its program clumsily to the last convention and was voted down by the six-hour men and the abstainers). He is split in discussions within his own local. And most serious and pregnant of all, he is sorely split in his own mind.

Every rubber worker with whom I spoke was agreed that the rising unemployment in Akron would vanish at once if all men working second jobs were to leave them. Were they therefore agreed that all two-jobbers should be compelled to give up the second job? No.

Again, no one knows for sure, but there seems to be a consensus that the men who are out moonlighting are mostly in the thirty-five-to-fifty age bracket. Men older than that often have their homes paid off; their wants are more modest; they are looking forward to retirement and pension. They are over the hump. The youngsters in the six-hour shops have never worked any longer hours; this seems plenty long enough to spend in a filthy, noisy place where the acrid stench of hot rubber is never absent. And some of them can and do go to Akron University while they are working. It is the men who remember the depression who apparently comprise the bulk of the two-jobbers – they and the young men with wives and children who have concurrent payments to meet (sometimes of staggering amounts) on house, car, TV, furniture, and appliances. And, as the very men who oppose the two-job frenzy demand: "Can you blame them?"

What is wrong, then, with a man going out and getting a second job? In reply the workers themselves will tell you horror stories far more shocking than any dreamed up by a slick fictioneer. They will tell you of a Negro worker found to have twelve years of seniority at one rubber plant and thirteen at another, and finally forced to choose between them, when the fact that he had been working seventy-two hours a week not for a few months, but for a dozen years, was brought to light. They will tell you of workers taking second jobs at small independent eight-hour rubber shops and being told frankly by their new boss that he had secured contracts on the basis of their working for him for less than the union scale in the Big Four. They will tell you of two men splitting an eight-hour shift at a gas station in their "leisure" time, and thus depriving one job-hunter of full-time work. They will tell you of their brother union members driving cabs for scab wages, cutting hair for scab wages, painting houses for scab wages. They will tell you of their terrible shame when a member of their union's policy committee was found working a second job as a salesman in a department store even while the store was being picketed by the Retail Clerks' union for not paying a decent minimum wage. They will insist that the rubber companies themselves look the other way when a worker takes a second job (unless his efficiency is drastically lowered), because they know that the man with two jobs will be less likely to attend union meetings, that he will more easily accede to downgrading, that in general he will be far less militant than the man who relies solely on the income from his job in the rubber plant.

And then, almost in the same breath, they will say that this is a free country; that you can't stop a man from trying to get ahead; that if a man wants to drive himself to death for the privilege of sleeping in a $30,000 house it is his privilege; and that it is only reasonable for a man still as basically insecure as an industrial worker to make it while he can, to catch up while times are still good, to acquire some of the luxuries while they are still within his grasp.

Is this a preview of America's (and indeed the industrialized world's) future? As the work-week shrinks, will we be treated to the spectacle not of thousands, but of millions of workers scrambling to undercut one another, protected in the primary job by their union and bidding their labor for secondary employment at ruinously low rates? Will leisure become a term of mockery covering *longer* hours spent in working to obtain, and then to replace, household objects carefully engineered for rapid obsolescence? On this point, at any rate, some of the workers mix faith and optimism. They tend to agree, although they put it differently, with the magazine *Factory Management and Maintenance* (November 1956), that the "Crux of the matter, on either a four- or five-day week, is whether general economic conditions and the worker's pay scale would put pressure on him to carry a second job for the added income, or allow him to enjoy the added leisure of a four-day week with a single job."

But the road toward that happy day is going to be, and is now, hard, rocky, and painful. "Certainly it should not be expected that there should be eight hours of pay for six hours of work," Goodyear's Board Chairman P. W. Litchfield and President E. J. Thomas told their employees in 1953. Despite the fact that they did not invoke the Deity, they were not fooling. Employers generally are going to resist the better-pay-fewer-hours onslaught with everything they've got; unions will be forced by the logic of the situation to carry that onslaught forward with everything they've got.

When the dust has settled – and a good many human beings have suffered in the struggle to achieve it – we will probably find ourselves in the era of the shorter work-week. *Then* Mr. Schlesinger's warning of a populace trained to work but not to live will be seen in all its force – and in all likelihood it may be too late to do anything about it in a missile-maddened, consumption-crazy society premised on lunacy and built on hypocrisy. It is not to be expected that the unions, deeply absorbed as they are in daily grievance wrangles and protracted contractual fights, are going to devote themselves to thoroughgoing studies and forecasts of the leisure hours of their membership. Besides, as one tough but weary old militant put it to me ruefully: "We've been so worried these past years about subversives that we haven't hired or inspired any of the young hotheads. The banks and the law firms aren't afraid of the independent-minded kids – they snap them up – but we've been scared of radicals here in the union and as a result we're not attracting the kind of minds who could help us plan for a different future, the way we used to attract them when we were first organizing."

The problem of what two hundred million of us will do with our increasing leisure time – and just as we have been watching Akron, so two billion will be watching the two hundred million – is so awesome in its magnitude as to be terrifying. Isn't that all the more reason for it to capture the imagination of our younger generation of social scientists, as the conquest of other worlds is supposed to be capturing the imagination of the physical scientists?

We must persist in the confidence that the best of the new intellectuals will break free of the internal isolationism, the exclusive concern with career and family, which has preoccupied them in common with most Americans for the past decade and more, and will undertake audaciously the task of outlining a social order in which both work and leisure will be rationally based. What is needed is a social order in which, most important of all, the masses of man will be protected against the swelling flood of "entertainment" opiates in order that they may be energized to search freely for new patterns of spontaneous living for themselves and their children.

The Nation, February 22, 1958

The Myth of the Happy Worker

> "From where we sit in the company," says one of the best personnel men in the country, "we have to look at only the aspects of work that cut across all sorts of jobs – administration and human relations. Now these are aspects of work, abstractions, but it's easy for personnel people to get so hipped on their importance that they look on the specific tasks of making things and selling them as secondary . . ."
> – *William H. Whyte, Jr., The Organization Man*

The personnel man who made this remark to Mr. Whyte differed from his brothers only in that he had a moment of insight. Actually, "the specific tasks of making things" are now not only regarded by his white-collar fellows as "secondary," but as irrelevant to the vaguer but more "challenging" tasks of the man at the desk. This is true not just of the personnel man, who places workers, replaces them, displaces them – in brief, manipulates them. The union leader also, who represents workers and sometimes manipulates them, seems increasingly to regard what his workers do as merely subsidiary to the job he himself is doing in the larger community. This job may be building the Red Cross or the Community Chest, or it may sometimes be – as the Senate hearings suggest – participating in such communal endeavors as gambling, prostitution, and improving the breed. In any case, the impression is left that the problems of the workers in the background (or underground) have been stabilized, if not permanently solved.

With the personnel man and the union leader, both of whom presumably see the worker from day to day, growing so far away from him, it is hardly to be wondered at that the middle class in general, and articulate middle-class intellectuals in particular, see the worker vaguely, as through a cloud. One gets the impression that when they do consider him, they operate from one of two unspoken assumptions: (1) The worker has died out like the passenger pigeon, or is dying out, or becoming accultured, like the Navajo. (2) If he *is* still around, he is just like the rest of us — fat, satisfied, smug, a little restless, but hardly distinguishable from his fellow TV-viewers of the middle class.

Lest it be thought that (1) is somewhat exaggerated, I hasten to quote from a recently published article apparently dedicated to the laudable task of urging slothful middle-class intellectuals to wake up and live: "The old-style sweatshop crippled mainly the working people. Now there are no workers left in America; we are almost all middle-class as to income and expectations." I do not believe the writer meant to state — although he comes perilously close to it — that nobody works any more. If I understand him correctly, he is referring to the fact that the worker's rise in real income over the last decade, plus the diffusion of middle-class tastes and values throughout a large part of the underlying population, have made it increasingly difficult to tell blue-collar from white-collar worker without a program. In short, if the worker earns like the middle class, votes like the middle class, dresses like the middle class, dreams like the middle class, then he ceases to exist as a worker.

But there is one thing that the worker doesn't do like the middle class: he works like a worker. The steel-mill puddler does not yet sort memos, the coal miner does not yet sit in conferences, the cotton mill-hand does not yet sip martinis from his lunchbox. The worker's attitude toward his work is generally compounded of hatred, shame, and resignation.

Before I spell out what I think this means, I should like first to examine some of the implications of the widely held belief that "we are almost all middle-class as to income and expectations." I am neither economist, sociologist, nor politician, and I hold in my hand no doctored statistics to be haggled over. I have had occasion to work in factories at various times during the Thirties, Forties, and Fifties. The following observations are simply impressions based on my last period of factory servitude, in 1956.

The average automobile worker gets a little better than two dollars an hour. As such he is one of the best-paid factory workers in the country. After twenty years of militant struggle led by the union that I believe to be one of the finest and most democratic labor organizations in the United States, he is earning less than the starting salaries offered to inexperienced and often semiliterate college graduates without dependents. After compulsory deductions for taxes, social security, old-age insurance and union dues, and optional deductions for hospitalization and assorted charities, his pay check for forty hours of work is going to be closer to seventy than to eighty dollars a week. Does this make him middle-class as to income? Does it rate with the weekly take of a dentist, an accountant, a salesman, a draftsman, a journalist? Surely it would be more to the point to ask how a family man can get by in the Fifties on that kind of income. I know how he does it, and I should think the answers would be a little disconcerting to those who wax glib on the satisfactory status of the "formerly" underprivileged.

For one thing, he works a lot longer than forty hours a week — when he can. Since no automobile company is as yet in a position to guarantee its workers anything like fifty weeks of steady forty-hour pay checks, the auto worker knows he has to make it while he can. During peak production periods he therefore puts in nine, ten, eleven, and often twelve hours a day on the assembly line for weeks on end. And that's not all. If he has dependents, as like as not he also holds down a "spare-time" job. I have worked on the line with men who doubled as mechanics, repairmen, salesmen, contractors, builders, farmers, cabdrivers, lumberyard workers, countermen. I would guess that there are many more of these than show up in the official statistics: often a man will work for less if he can be paid under the counter with tax-free dollars.

Nor is that all. The factory worker with dependents cannot carry the debt load he now shoulders — the middle-class debt load, if you like, of nagging payments on car, washer, dryer, TV, clothing, house itself — without family help. Even if he puts in fifty, sixty, or seventy hours a week at one or two jobs, he has to count on his wife's pay check, or his son's, his daughter's, his brother-in-law's; or on his mother's social security, or his father's veteran's pension. The working-class family today is not typically held together by the male wage-earner, but by multiple wage-earners often of several generations who club together to get the things they want and need — or are pressured into believing they must have. It is at best a precarious arrangement; as for its toll on the physical organism and the psyche, that is a question perhaps worthy of further investigation by those who currently pronounce themselves bored with Utopia Unlimited in the Fat Fifties.

But what of the worker's middle-class expectations? I had been under the impression that this was the rock on which socialist agitation had foundered for generations: it proved useless to tell the proletarian that he had a world to win when he was reasonably certain that with a few breaks he could have his own gas station. If these expectations have changed at all in recent years, they would seem to have narrowed rather than expanded, leaving a psychological increment of resignation rather than of unbounded optimism (except among the very young — and even among them the optimism focuses more often on better-paying opportunities elsewhere in the labor market than on illusory hopes of swift status advancement). The worker's expectations are for better pay, more humane working conditions, more job security. As long as he feels that he is going to achieve them through an extension of existing conditions, for that long he is going to continue to be a middle-class conservative in temper. But only for that long.

I suspect that what middle-class writers mean by the worker's middle-class expectations are his cravings for commodities — his determination to have not only fin-tailed cars and single-unit washer-dryers, but butterfly chairs in the rumpus room, African masks on the wall, and power boats in the garage. Before the middle-class intellectuals condemn these expectations too harshly, let them consider, first, who has been utilizing every known technique of suasion and propaganda to convert luxuries into necessities, and second, at what cost these new necessities are acquired by the American working-class family.

Now I should like to return to the second image of the American worker: satisfied, doped by TV, essentially middle-class in outlook. This is an image bred not of communication with workers (except as mediated by hired interviewers sent "into the field" like anthropologists or entomologists), but of contempt for people, based perhaps on self-contempt and on a feeling among intellectuals that the worker has let them down. In order to see this clearly, we have to place it against the intellectual's changing attitudes toward the worker since the Thirties.

At the time of the organization of the CIO, the middle-class intellectual saw the proletarian as society's figure of virtue — heroic, magnanimous, bearing in his loins the seeds of a better future; he would have found ludicrous the suggestion that a sit-down striker might harbor anti-Semitic feelings. After Pearl Harbor, the glamorization of the worker was taken over as a function of government. Then, however, he was no longer the builder of the future good society; instead he was second only to the fighting man as the vital winner of the war. Many intellectuals, as government employees, found themselves helping to create this new portrait of the worker as patriot.

But in the decade following the war intellectuals have discovered that workers are no longer either building socialism or forging the tools of victory. All they are doing is making the things that other people buy. That, and participating in the great commodity scramble. The disillusionment, it would seem, is almost too terrible to bear. Word has gotten around among the highbrows that the worker is not heroic or idealistic; public-opinion polls prove that he wants barbecue pits more than foreign aid and air-conditioning more than desegregation, that he doesn't particularly want to go on strike, that he is reluctant to form a Labor Party, that he votes for Stevenson and often even for Eisenhower and Nixon – that he is, in short, animated by the same aspirations as drive the middle-class onward and upward in suburbia.

There is of course a certain admixture of self-delusion in the middle-class attitude that workers are now the same as everybody else. For me it was expressed most precisely last year in the dismay and sympathy with which middle-class friends greeted the news that I had gone back to work in a factory. If workers are now full-fledged members of the middle class, why the dismay? What difference whether one sits in an office or stands in a shop? The answer is so obvious that one feels shame at laboring the point. But I have news for my friends among the intellectuals. The answer is obvious to workers, too.

They know that there is a difference between working with your back and working with your behind (I do not make the distinction between handwork and brainwork, since we are all learning that white-collar work is becoming less and less brainwork). They know that they work harder than the middle class for less money. Nor is it simply a question of status, that magic word so dear to the hearts of the sociologues, the new anatomizers of the American corpus. It is not simply status-hunger that makes a man hate work which pays *less* than other work he knows about, if *more* than any other work he has been trained for (the only reason my fellow workers stayed on the assembly line, they told me again and again). It is not simply status-hunger that makes a man hate work that is mindless, endless, stupefying, sweaty, filthy, noisy, exhausting, insecure in its prospects, and practically without hope of advancement.

The plain truth is that factory work is degrading. It is degrading to any man who ever dreams of doing something worth while with his life; and it is about time we faced the fact. The more a man is exposed to middle-class values, the more sophisticated he becomes and the more production-line work is degrading to him. The immigrant who slaved in the poorly lighted, foul, vermin-ridden sweatshop found his work less degrading than the native-born high school graduate who reads "Judge Parker," "Rex Morgan, M.D.," and "Judd Saxon, Business Executive," in the funnies, and works in a fluorescent factory with ticker-tape production-control machines. For the immigrant laborer, even the one who did not dream of socialism, his long hours were going to buy him freedom. For the factory worker of the Fifties, his long hours are going to buy him commodities . . . and maybe reduce a few of his debts.

Almost without exception, the men with whom I worked on the assembly line last year felt like trapped animals. Depending on their age and personal circumstances, they were either resigned to their fate, furiously angry at *themselves* for what they were doing, or desperately hunting other work that would pay as well and in addition offer some variety, some prospect of change and betterment. They were sick of being pushed around by harried foremen (themselves more pitied than hated), sick of working like blinkered donkeys, sick of being dependent for their livelihood on a maniacal production-merchandising setup, sick of working in a place where there was no spot to relax during the twelve-minute rest period. (Someday – let us hope – we will marvel that production was still so worshiped in the Fifties that new factories could be built with every splendid facility for the storage and movement of essential parts, but with no place for a resting worker to sit down for a moment but on a fireplug, the edge of a packing case, or the sputum- and oil-stained stairway of a toilet.)

The older men stay put and wait for their vacations. But since the assembly line demands young blood (you will have a hard time getting hired if you are over thirty-five), the factory in which I worked was aswarm with new faces every day; labor turnover was so fantastic and absenteeism so rampant, with the young men knocking off a day or two every week to hunt up other jobs, that the company was forced to overhire in order to have sufficient workers on hand at the starting siren.

To those who will object – fortified by their readings in C. Wright Mills and A. C. Spectorsky – that the white-collar commuter, too, dislikes his work, accepts it only because it buys his family commodities, and is constantly on the prowl for other work, I can only reply that for me at any rate this is proof not of the disappearance of the working class but of the proletarianization of the middle class. Perhaps it is not taking place quite in the way that Marx envisaged it, but the alienation of the white-collar man (like that of the laborer) from both his tools and whatever he produces, the slavery that chains the exurbanite to the commuting timetable (as the worker is still chained to the time clock), the anxiety that sends the white-collar man home with his briefcase for an evening's work (as it degrades the workingman into pleading for long hours of overtime), the displacement of the white-collar slum from the wrong side of the tracks to the suburbs (just as the working-class slum is moved from old-law tenements to skyscraper barracks) – all these mean to me that the white-collar man is entering (though his arms may be loaded with commodities) the gray world of the working man.

Three quotations from men with whom I worked may help to bring my view into focus:

Before starting work: "Come on, suckers, they say the Foundation wants to give away *more* than half a billion this year. Let's do and die for the old Foundation."

During rest period: "Ever stop to think how we crawl here bumper to bumper, and crawl home bumper to bumper, and we've got to turn out more every minute to keep our jobs, when there isn't even any room for them on the highways?"

At quitting time (this from older foremen, whose job is not only to keep things moving, but by extension to serve as company spokesmen): "You're smart to get out of here. . . . I curse the day I ever started, now I'm stuck: any man with brains that stays here ought to have his head examined. This is no place for an intelligent human being."

Such is the attitude toward the work. And toward the product? On the one hand it is admired and desired as a symbol of freedom, almost a substitute for freedom, not because the worker participated in making it, but because our whole culture is dedicated to the proposition that the automobile is both necessary and beautiful. On the other hand it is hated and despised – so much that if your new car smells bad it may be due to a banana peel crammed down its gullet and sealed up thereafter, so much so that if your dealer can't locate the rattle in your new car you might ask him to open the welds on one of those tail fins and vacuum out the nuts and bolts thrown in by workers sabotaging their own product.

Sooner or later, if we want a decent society – by which I do not mean a society glutted with commodities or one maintained in precarious equilibrium by overbuying and forced premature obsolescence – we are going to have to come face to face with the problem of work. Apparently the Russians have committed themselves to the replenishment of their labor force through automatic recruitment of those intellectually incapable of keeping up with severe scholastic requirements in the public educational system. Apparently we, too, are heading in the same direction: although our economy is not directed, and although college education is as yet far from free, we seem to be operating in this capitalist economy on the totalitarian assumption that we can funnel the underprivileged, undereducated, or just plain underequipped, into the factory, where we can proceed to forget about them once we have posted the minimum fair labor standards on the factory wall.

If this is what we want, let's be honest enough to say so. If we conclude that there is nothing noble about repetitive work, but that it is nevertheless good enough for the lower orders, let's say that, too, so we will at least know where we stand. But if we cling to the belief that other men are our brothers, not just Egyptians, or Israelis, or Hungarians, but *all* men, including millions of Americans who grind their lives away on an insane treadmill, then we will have to start thinking about how their work and their lives can be made meaningful. That is what I assume the Hungarians, both workers and intellectuals, have been thinking about. Since no one has been ordering us what to think, since no one has been forbidding our intellectuals to fraternize with our workers, shouldn't it be a little easier for us to admit, first, that our problems exist, then to state them, and then to see if we can resolve them?

The Nation, August 17, 1957

Work as a Public Issue

> . . . you'll be old and you never lived, and you kind of feel silly to lie down and die and to never have lived, to have been a job chaser and never have lived.
> — *Gertrude Stein, "Brewsie and Willie"*

We have come by insensible stages to the point of denying that serious problems still exist in this nation. With the single exception of juvenile delinquency (all too often considered not as a problem demanding solution but as a convenient theme for comic books, cheap novels, worse movies, and self-satisfied head-shaking), we have resolutely determined — influenced perhaps more than we realize by the ceaseless cajoling of an advertising culture — to look only on the sunny side of things, to believe indeed that if there is a dark side it exists only in the shadow cast by the Iron Curtain, or in the pathetically underdeveloped lands. The surface statements are so much easier to live with. Thus, in regard to daily labor: Workingmen are now protected by powerful industrial unions; in any case, their employers have become more sophisticated and less ruthless; they are covered in sickness by Blue Cross, in unemployment by insurance, in old age by Social Security; they earn enough to purchase an array of commodities never before available even to Oriental potentates. How then can they be wretched or ashamed of what they do? How much more pleasant to believe that those who testify to the contrary are as extreme and out of touch as those who plead for recognition and consideration of such problems as the menace of mutual annihilation, the international degradation of popular taste, or the despoliation of the landscape by "developers," at the rate of three thousand acres every twenty-four hours.

Yet there is something more to this middle-class reluctance to face certain unpleasant realities, or to permit their legitimization as public issues. In the case of work, if we grant the possibility that millions of American workers may in truth be terribly discontented with their jobs, doesn't this arouse a consequent suspicion: that the growing white-collar classes are reluctant to admit this likelihood not only because it would disturb the comfortable mass-media concept of America as a land of blissful togetherness, but even more importantly because it would do violence to their own self-esteem by calling into question the basic worth and individuality of what they themselves are doing to earn a living? No one likes to be reminded that he is not in some way important as a contributing member of society. A restless young architect may very well tend to reject any picture which portrays the American mass-production worker as profoundly dissatisfied with his lot. While this architect may be regarded by his family and neighbors as a "professional man," he himself is all too sharply aware that he is doing nothing more than the most dull and deadening draftsman's work in a vault ranked with his similars, who know him to be nothing more than they are – all-but-anonymous units in the firm's labor force. In short, it is painful for him to be confronted with the evidence that the difference between him and the factory worker may be only one of degree. It is a pun that can hurt.

Nor is the young architect unique. Surely we must now realize that the young attorney, clerking in a huge law factory, or the young business administration graduate, disappearing into the paternal embrace of the giant corporation, can rarely get from his daily work the satisfaction – to say nothing of the thrill – that his father did. The fact that Americans are spending billions annually on "hobbies" does not mean to me that they are living richer lives, but rather that they are seeking elsewhere the satisfactions of personal fulfillment that formerly came from the job of work itself.

The hidden bonds of boredom and frustration that link the lives – if they only knew it – of the professional man and the workingman are close to the surface in the working pattern of the burgeoning millions of clericals and technicians, which is so similar to that of the numerically declining working class. The typist in the clattering cavern of a typical insurance office, indistinguishable from her sisters who tap the machines at their serried desks, the file clerk punching her Hollerith cards under the fluorescents in any of a dozen labyrinthine bureaucracies, the stock clerk running off labels in the automated shipping department of a rationalized department store – all these may have their half-attentive ears filled all day with Strauss waltzes piped in by solicitous employers, their mouths filled with coffee piped in twice a day at the insistence of their union or their personnel supervisors. But what are their minds filled with? Year by year, day by day, what they do becomes increasingly routinized in the interest of production and efficiency, just as does the labor of the assembly-line worker.

I think we can confidently expect that more will be said of this problem in the years ahead, particularly as it becomes more apparent that the labor of the white-collar girl, or the technical man, is growing increasingly routinized and difficult to distinguish from assembly-line labor, both in its lack of relation to the finished product and in its ultimate effect as alienated labor on the self-respect and the mental responsiveness of those performing it.

At this point, however, it might be wise to attempt to distinguish the principal tendencies among those who have been so seriously concerned with work as to consider it a basic problem.

It has been grappled with on the one hand by technicians and on the other by social theorists. The technicians have not only conducted a considerable number of important experiments designed to measure such things as the relation of fatigue to boredom and the introduction of various incentives in a humanized work situation; they have also exercised considerable influence on the managerial classes. The reason for this influence is obvious enough: if you can show a plant manager that productivity will increase if he refines his techniques of handling his employees, you are going to have his ear. By the same token, I do not wish to act as a promoter in these pages for schemes based on the manipulation of working people with the end of maximizing profits. No doubt the technicians and the business administrators would fervently deny that their aim is to manipulate people; but to me such a conclusion is the inescapable end product of an approach which begins not with human beings and their aspirations but with productivity and techniques for increasing it.

As for the social theorists, here too I think we can discern two main tendencies. The first, perhaps best articulated by David Riesman, concludes that it is impossible to build a modern industrial society, with an indefinitely rising standard of living, without the concurrent phenomenon of more and more people working at more and more standardized tasks. Nevertheless it perceives several rays of light: one, automation, which at least will reduce brute labor and repetitive work to a minimum, and at best will bring forth factories and offices in which workers will find their tasks more complex and hence more challenging; another, a vast increase in leisure with an inevitable four-day week and a consequent shifting of primary human interest from the job to the leisure-time activity.*

* *Footnote, 1961:* Thanks to the generous invitation of Dr. Fred B. Wood, I was enabled not long ago to observe the research and systems development divisions of the International Business Machines complex at San Jose, California. I may not have made the grand tour quite as had Nikita Khrushchev, but I did

The second theoretical tendency, led by men like Erich Fromm, Erich Kahler, and Daniel Bell, is unwilling to grant the inevitability of a social order in which sensibility is blunted and individual creativity stifled by forcing men and women to spend all their adult lives at tasks beneath their human dignity, tasks made palatable not by their so-

---

lunch with some very keen and cultivated people indeed, and I was suitably impressed by the blank but many-eyed outsides and the staggeringly intricate insides of RAMAC, surely the most elegantly complex automatic device ever designed by man to free himself from laborious drudgery for the solving of complex problems: the machine rents for two thousand dollars an hour, a reasonable price when you consider that in one hour it will do computations that would keep a Ph.D. in mathematics busy eight hours a day for five years. But it was when I came to the assembly line itself that I was really amused, impressed, and flabbergasted. There sat long rows of women threading and weaving bits of wire together, and performing other handwork tasks essential to the construction of IBM's RAMAC. These nonunion ladies, surrounded by Muzak, muted sunlight, and the THINK signs of the great paternalist and individualist Thomas Watson *père,* are apparently still as essential to the mathematician who wants RAMAC to do his dirty work for him as they used to be to those of our grandmothers who could afford egrets on their hats or lace on their undergarments. Until someone figures out a way to make the marvelous machines without the skilled and busy fingers of the women workers, the machines will continue to rent for two thousand dollars an hour — and it will be a bit premature to insist upon the worker's having disappeared with the egret.

cial utility or their relation to any existing human desire, but solely by their wage. It searches for a way out by posing certain questions. Can people who work in factories be educated to participate in decision-making affecting their own working lives? Can productive facilities be decentralized to the point where their management can be at least partially controlled by the workers themselves? Can the experiences of small, utopian communities and small nations be profitably assimilated by highly industrialized countries?

Clearly there are soft spots in both theoretical positions. In the case of the "realists," can they expect us to embrace automation as a panacea simply because in certain specific industrial instances it introduces the necessity of a more highly trained work force? Is the supermarket clerk who from his hiding place stocks the gravity-fed shelves of canned goods going to be any happier than his father, who at least used to look his customers in the eye, and even on occasion talk to them? Will the operator who turns a dial at the prompting of a flickering oscilloscope feel any more warmth toward his work than the assembler who pounds an endless stream of truck doors into place with his mallet? And can we really believe that workers who increasingly hate what they do will make intelligent use of their increasing leisure time? Is it not more likely that, half numb on the job, they will settle off the job for those mass opiates which render them wholly numb?

And as far as the idealists are concerned, who seriously claims that the efforts of the Yugoslavs or the Israelis can be translated into the American industrial experience? Who has demonstrated that the time clock — its very existence an insult to anyone who presumably looks forward to his work — can be eliminated from assembly-line factories? Who is convinced that production can be democratically scheduled in a steel mill as in a communal jewelry-designing workshop? Who is sure that we are really so rich as to be able to afford a decline in productivity, if that should be a demonstrable result of putting people before productivity?

But to ask these questions, let us realize, is not to scoff at those who conscientiously address themselves to matters urgently important in the lives of millions of us. It is, rather, to indicate the terrible breadth of the chasm that separates those who *think* from those who *do*, those who *ponder* problems of power from those who *wield* power.

Inevitably, the existence of this chasm gives rise to improbable, often ludicrous situations. Paradox piles upon paradox in the land of opportunity, where millionaire candidates can vie for the favor of immigrant workers, and where the leader of Soviet communism, denied the ear of organized labor, can appear before capitalist politicians and businessmen, an honored guest gotten up in an Italian suit and handmade shoes, and assert, "As a former worker I extend particular greetings to the toilers who create the wealth of society."

Surely not the least of the paradoxes is the fact that while we know perfectly well what is wrong with the rest of the world, we are hard put to it to arrive at a consensus on the American way, which is supposedly synonymous with the right way. We are perhaps more democratic than any other nation, we have certainly been more productive; does this mean we are any happier? At the moment there is no way of knowing, for while we pride ourselves on our ability to determine to the decimal how our neighbors will vote, or how many of them can be mesmerized into buying a dentifrice that looks like a candy stick or an auto that looks like a beached whale, we simply don't know – yet another paradox – whether they are happy, whether they truly enjoy doing the things they have had to do to make this the most productive land on earth.

This observer suspects that they do not, that by and large they are more likely to lead lives of quiet desperation than of quiet satisfaction with work, family, and acquisitions. Let me concede at once that among those who argue the matter this is a minority view (which for some reason often provokes anguished outrage) and that it is based on a mixture of observation and hunch; but no more can be said, can it, in support of the common contention that Americans are a people who take pride and pleasure in what they do?

It is only in recent years that this subject has begun to be discussed. Before that, for something more than a decade, the national mood had been one of self-congratulation. Ordinary people seemed to be devoting their lives more or less pleasurably to the accumulation of an endless stream of commodities; even the intellectuals were commencing to confess in their house organs that America was more beautiful than they had previously conceded. But then the Russians sent up Sputnik, and the economic bubble burst at home. And it began to be legitimate to ask not only what had happened to American technology, and whether American education was capable of turning out more than mediocrities and juvenile delinquents, but who was responsible for recessions, why we permitted our magnificent landscape to be irremediably defaced with jerry-built, split-level slums, and how it had come to pass that although our foreign policy was not only invariably right, but heaven-inspired, we were increasingly mistrusted and feared by our former admirers. And, finally, there were those who posed the question as to whether our working lives actually yielded sufficient satisfactions to compensate for the eroding sacrifices demanded by the work. In short, a few of us have at last begun, haltingly and often not without embarrassment, to state publicly that this nation, far from having solved anything beyond certain comparatively simple production-distribution problems (which are currently being solved at least as thoroughly by other nations too), now confronts problems awesome in their magnitude and demanding not merely an easy patriotism but a steadfast humility and a willingness to go to the heart of the matter. The question I am considering here is whether one of those problems – the meaning of work – can be brought forth from the philosopher's study and placed where it belongs – in the political arena – as a public issue in the widest sense of that term.

So now we can return to the implications in the title of these remarks. Surely the questions I have just raised must indicate that in this country today the problem of satisfying work is indissolubly linked with that of fruitful leisure. The problem of leisure is interlocked with that of the content and control of the mass media; which problem in turn cuts to the heart of a commercially oriented culture. In short, the probing of what at first consideration may seem a comparatively limited problem is actually nothing less than a revolutionary act, calling into question our very social structure.

It need hardly be added that there are no present indications of public readiness for revolutionary acts of this order, any more than for placing on the agenda as public issues some of the other social problems referred to earlier. Nonetheless, those of us who believe that American democracy derives its continuing vitality from people rather than from things, and from the people's response to the conditions of their lives, must remain confident that the inexhaustible reserves of rebelliousness of the willful human spirit will one day assert themselves against the stultifying vegetativeness of the modern American work routine.

Saturday Review, December 12, 1959

2.

Robinson Crusoe — the Man Alone

Gladly he gives this tale to all mankind
To tread the hills and shores with countless feet.
Henceforth the globe itself swims in his mind,
The last unknown and insular retreat.
— *from Crusoe, by Karl Shapiro*

Tough-minded journalist that he was, Daniel Defoe would have blanched if he had known that future generations would classify him snugly as the Father of the Novel. Indeed it was precisely in his greatest works of fiction that he was at pains — because the temper of his time demanded it — to claim that he was only setting down the unvarnished facts, and that he had no intention of concocting romances or other questionable works of the imagination. But if this is a historical oddity it is hardly the most remarkable paradox psychologically of this complicated man: one must be particularly struck by the disparity between the materials he sought out so methodically and the literary uses to which he put them. This disparity is most intriguing in the case of *Robinson Crusoe;* an examination of it may perhaps reveal to us a little more, not just about the personality of Defoe, but about the vaster problem of human loneliness, which spreads like a stain as more and more of us are pressed closer and closer together.

In the spring of 1944 I was cycling along the North Sea coast with several companions, equipped with neither map nor guidebooks, only with a turkey and other picnic necessities borrowed from the merchant ship on which we were employed. One of the most pleasant occurrences of that delightful day in peaceful County Fife was our sudden discovery of a statue about the size of a cigar-store

Indian standing forthrightly on the front lawn of a modest row house in the town of Largo. There was barely room for the statue, and when we saw that it had been erected in memory of Alexander Selkirk, we nodded wisely, exchanged some comments about *Robinson Crusoe,* and continued on our way.

But that statue remained in a corner of my mind, obstinately, as such things will. The world is full of statues of all sorts, and I have stared at my share: statues of authors and statues of their creations, statues of Montaigne and Balzac in Paris and of Tom Sawyer and Huck Finn in Hannibal. But I am not aware of many statues erected to the memory of those who have inspired the authors of great works, or who have served as the models for their characters. Is there a statue of Gogarty in Dublin, of Mrs. Wolfe in Asheville, of Thalberg in Hollywood, or of that little piece of madeleine in Paris?

I knew rather vaguely, I suppose, that Alexander Selkirk had been a seafaring man, that he had been shipwrecked for a time, and that Defoe had somehow made use of his adventure, but it was not until, browsing through Walter Wilson's rambling three-volume *Life and Times of Defoe* (1830), I came upon a hair-raising footnote that I began to sense what kind of fellow Selkirk had been. After he was rescued from his desert island, he returned in 1712 to Largo. There, says Wilson casually, "His parents, who were still living, received him with joy; but his recluse habits induced him to shun the haunts of men, and he constructed a cave in their garden, where he sought repose in solitude. . . ."

The fact is that, far from having been shipwrecked, he had had himself put ashore on a desolate island at his own request – and there he remained alone for four and a half years before being taken off and returned to happy little Largo, his parents' garden, and the cave which he hastened to dig. This voluntary commitment has been amply commented on (although I don't think it has been interpreted quite as I interpret it), but I am unaware that any modern writer has so much as mentioned the cave in the garden, with the exception of Walter de la Mare, in his wonderfully engaging *Desert Islands*.

Thomas Wright, in his Bicentennial Edition of *The Life of Daniel Defoe*, does have a fairly thorough account, sans cave, of this peculiar man. Alexander Selkirk had been born Selcraig (just as Robinson Crusoe had been born Kreutznaer, and Daniel Defoe, for that matter, had been born Foe), the seventh son of a cobbler, like Hans Andersen, as Walter de la Mare points out, and so many folktale heroes. "Wild and restless," he ran off to sea for six years after creating a disturbance in church at the age of nineteen. He returned only to beat up his brother for giving him salt water (it was a mistake), and to beat up another brother, and his father, and finally even his mother, for trying to stop him. On Sunday morning, the 30th of November, 1701, he was obliged to stand up in church in front of the pulpit and acknowledge sin, be rebuked in the face of the congregation for it, and promise amendment in the strength of the Lord.

Understandably, this passionate young man went to sea again the following spring, with Dampier, the celebrated buccaneer, who had two ships to plunder French and Spanish vessels. Thomas Stradling, "a man of ferocious and quarrelsome temper," was master of Selkirk's ship, the *Cinque Ports*, and Dampier himself commanded the *St. George*. Arrived at the Juan Fernandez Islands off the coast of Chile early in 1704, the two men quarreled and separated; but Selkirk too became embroiled with Stradling and had himself and his effects rowed ashore to Más a Tierra, an island roughly twelve by three miles.

When, however, he saw the boat returning, the horrors of his situation vividly presented themselves; and, rushing into the surf up to the middle, he stretched out his hands towards his comrades, and implored them to come back and take him on board again. The only answer was a jeer. The boat reached the ship, the ship spread her sails, and Selkirk was alone on his island.

Unable to abandon the hope that Stradling would relent and come back for him, the unhappy Selkirk found himself chained to the beach; and, even when gnawed with hunger, rather than go in search of fruits and other products of the woods, he contented himself with shell-fish and seal's flesh, and whatever else he could obtain without removing inland. He hated even to close his eyes. Often he cursed the folly that had brought him to this terrible solitude, and sometimes, starting up in agony, he would resolve on suicide. Voices spoke to him both in the howlings of the sea in front and in the murmur of the woods behind. The shore was creatured with phantoms. Then – cooling his fevered brain – came sweet visions of his childhood, the home at Largo, his mother, the fields he had rambled in, the words he had heard in the old kirk, thoughts of God.

After eight long months of melancholy and horror, in which he was "scarce able to refrain from doing himself violence," he vanquished his blues, as De la Mare puts it, and set to work. He burned all-spice wood, fed on fish, turnips, and goats' meat, and came gradually to cope creatively with life on Más a Tierra. He had a couple of narrow escapes, once from a fall of a hundred feet, another time from marauding Spaniards, and when his ammunition ran out he raced barefoot after the island's goats and their kids, capturing and killing no less than five hundred of them.

On the 31st of January, 1709, he was picked up, scarcely articulate but otherwise healthy, by two more marauding ships, the *Duke* and the *Duchess*, on one of which was no other than Dampier. Selkirk was made mate of the *Duke*, and subsequently master of one which the marauders captured, and returned home with about eight hundred pounds of prize money, or plunder. As De la Mare notes, this "prince and prototype of all castaways" was "not so happy, he said, as when he hadn't a farthing." Selkirk enjoyed considerable notoriety after his return to England in October of 1711. He was interviewed by Richard Steele, was made the subject of a paper in *The Englishman*, and had several narratives of his life written, as well as four published accounts of his adventures. In De la Mare's words, Steele, who saw Selkirk quite often,

> believed that even if he had been ignorant of Selkirk's story, he would still have detected the ravages of solitude in his "aspect and gesture." He "showed a certain disregard to the ordinary things about him, as if he had been sunk in thought."
>
> After a few months' absence Steele met him again "in the street, and though he spoke to me I could not recall that I had seen him. Familiar discourse . . . had taken off the loneliness of his aspect, and quite altered the air of his face."

It was after this that Selkirk made his way home and constructed the cave which De la Mare oddly glides over (I say oddly because it was one of the charms of the late poet that he could seize on an item like this and expatiate on it at great and pleasant length). The cave could not contain Selkirk either, however. This "unsociable" man emerged to fish and to wander around: it was thus that he met a girl named Sophia Bruce, whom he found tending a cow. They eloped to London, but when it was all over, Sophia was left alone and Selkirk continued on his lonely way. He drifted back to Largo, got into another scrape there which sent him packing, and after knocking around Bristol and Liverpool, he went to sea once again. All too fittingly, he died at sea in 1723. "He is said," De la Mare adds, "to have bequeathed his effects to 'sundry loving females' — including two who claimed to be his widows. But of this episode Defoe made no practical use." In 1885 his brooding statue went up on his front lawn. Had I known about the cave when I stared at the statue of Mr. Selkirk, I would certainly have gone around back and tried to discover if any vestiges of it remained, these hundreds of years later.

Now what strikes one immediately is that this man, who had himself put ashore on a desolate island in a moment of anger, who hid in a cave in another moment of anger, who estranged himself from his family and was kicked out of town in another moment of anger, was if not psychotic certainly what we would nowadays term a seriously disturbed personality. Tempting as it may be to analyze the components of the disturbance, I must resolutely disclaim either the skill or the desire to undertake such an analysis. I am content to point out that the disturbance existed, and would rather have you return with me to the period of Selkirk's fame, when journalists chased him for his story much as journalists of the 1950's chased the skipper of the *Flying Enterprise*, Captain Carlsen, who refused to abandon ship after it cracked in a hurricane, but remained aboard alone in a vain effort to save it. One of those journalists was an aging Cockney hack named Daniel Defoe.

Scholars are apparently still arguing as to whether Selkirk and Defoe actually met. Thomas Wright says categorically that Defoe "made a journey from London to Bristol apparently for the express purpose of seeing" Selkirk at the house of a Mrs. Damaris Daniel, and that Selkirk "placed in Defoe's hands all his papers." On the other hand, back in 1916 William P. Trent was arguing in his *Daniel Defoe* (an intelligent and enlightening book, but so steeped in the dying genteel tradition that its author could not bring himself to reproduce the full subtitle of *Moll Flanders*, much less to quote from it or to recommend it to general readers) that "the makers of myths have not hesitated to affirm that Defoe made use of the papers of the returned sailor — who has not been shown to have had any — and cheated him into the bargain. A meeting with Selkirk has also been affirmed by some, and the house where the supposed conference took place has been pointed out in Bristol."

Well, whatever the truth as to the possible encounter, we do know that Defoe was thoroughly up on the adventures of the Scottish sailor, that he was a careful researcher, and that in many, many of its details *Robinson Crusoe* does parallel Selkirk's story. I would prefer to think that they met, if only because I enjoy imagining the confrontation, in the comfortable home of the lady with the elegant name, of the dour adventurer and the dapper, elderly word-slinger; but I must admit that it really doesn't matter. What counts is that this profile-writer, who was in journalism for money as he had been in half a dozen other enterprises to support his wife and six children, from hosiery to jobbing to spying to editing, worked up yet another in his incredible series of true-life romances, with no other purpose than to pick up some quick cash, and that from his re-imagined version of the travail of the neurotic castaway came one of the great pure classical tales of all time.

We might pause for just a moment here to glance at Defoe's own life in order to sharpen our perspective on the man who became a great novelist almost in spite of himself, and who won immortality by transforming an abnormal episode into a saga of man's conquest of nature. I think the use he made of Selkirk's adventure, or rather his transformation of it, will be somewhat clearer if we locate Defoe and see him as he was when he emerged into the great creative outburst of his sixties.

Defoe's Presbyterian parents trained him for the ministry, and although as a young man he decided that he was not fitted for it, he received a comparatively good education. Apparently he got a good grounding in science too, and he says of his Colonel Jack at the age of fourteen: "I loved to talk with seamen and soldiers. . . . I never forgot anything they told me . . . young as I was, I was a kind of an historian; and though I had read no books, and never had any books to read, yet I could give a tolerable account of what had been done, and of what was then a-doing in the world. . . ."

He became a commission merchant, lived in Spain for a time, married (not happily, it is important to note), wrote poor poetry on the side, and by 1692 had failed in business to the extent of about a quarter of a million dollars. Thereafter he was never really out of financial trouble. He got off by making a deal with his creditors; he went into the brick and tile business, became a prolific journalist and pamphleteer, and started to mix in politics. He found—

and so did his readers — that he had the ability to write about current issues in a style that was direct, simple, and clear. But with the death of his patron, King William, and the accession of Queen Anne in 1702, Defoe, although an enormously popular Dissenter, became a hunted man. In 1703 he was arrested, thrown in jail, tried, and sentenced to pay a fine, to stand three times in the pillory, to be indefinitely imprisoned, and thereafter to be paroled. The extraordinary thing about this ugly episode, aside from the public humiliation of a man who had already earned certain claims to distinction, was that Defoe himself managed to turn it to good account: the mob treated him as a hero; instead of being mocked and jeered in the pillory, he was cheered and feted in the midst of his exposure, and his *Hymn to the Pillory* was very well received indeed.

Thereafter Defoe devoted himself more and more to political journalism. The politest word that can be found for much of his life and work in these middle years is that both were unsavory. He sold his skills to the highest bidder, spied for those in favor and sneered at those out of favor, and year after year churned out economic essays, unsuccessful poetry, humorous tidbits and political correspondence, feverishly accumulating dowries for his marriageable daughters. The act of writing, apparently of writing *anything* as long as there was money in it, became as ingrained and habitual with him as it has ever been with any hack. Not infrequently he wrote semifictional biographical puffs for quacks or odd birds, and he seemed to delight in working up quasi-factual accounts of the lives of unusual characters.

Such was the man who, at the age of sixty, sat down to knock out a lively account of the adventures of a castaway, and who, in the incredible five years that followed, unburdened himself of the three parts of *Robinson Crusoe, Duncan Campbell, Memoirs of a Cavalier, Captain Singleton, Moll Flanders, A Journal of the Plague Year, Colonel Jack, Roxanna,* and *A New Voyage Round the World.* No wonder that Trent comments, "It becomes still more astonishing when we are reminded that during these years Defoe's bibliography must be credited with at least six other volumes . . . that his journalistic labors . . . remained considerable . . . that he wrote at least a score of pamphlets . . . and finally that it seems highly probable that he spent several of his summers taking horseback journeys in order to secure materials for his interesting and valuable *Tour Thro' the Whole Island of Great Britain. . . .*"

If we think of Daniel Defoe as a typical Englishman, a typical Londoner, perhaps a typical Cockney (he was even born within hearing of Bow Bells), and of his tale of a man on an island as a typical English novel, with its emphasis on factuality, fortitude, and optimistic common sense, we find that we are cheered on by English critics of all persuasions, from Sam Johnson to Virginia Woolf to V. S. Pritchett (let us except Macaulay, who said coldly of Defoe: "Altogether I don't like him"). Indeed, it is precisely those writers who one might think would harbor reservations about Defoe's genius who are most fervent in their adulation, who support most fervidly Daudet's estimation of Defoe as England's national author and Robinson Crusoe as "the typical Englishman par excellence, with his adventuresomeness, his taste for travel, his love of the sea, his piety, his commercial and practical instincts," and so on and so on. Thus Virginia Woolf writes of Defoe: "He belongs, indeed, to the school of the great plain writers, whose work is founded upon a knowledge of what is most persistent, though not most seductive, in human nature. . . ."

But it is Walter de la Mare who phrases most precisely this English pride in Defoe's normality, his rationality, his lack of neurotic undertones. Speaking of *Robinson Crusoe,* he says shrewdly,

It is not so much in spite of its limitations as to a large extent because of them that it remains one of the most famous books in the world. It taxes no ordinary intelligence. There is nothing delicate, abstruse, subtle to master. It can be opened and read with ease and delight at any moment, and anywhere. Its thought is little but an emanation of Crusoe's seven senses and of his five wits. Its sentiments are universal.

I have no intention of calling these verdicts into question. There is no point in forcing a reading of *Robinson Crusoe* which would see it as something other. But I keep harking back to that odd Scotch sailor who hid himself in a cave, and I cannot but suspect that one of the greatest of Defoe's achievements is one which has hardly been touched on by all his admirers in the last few centuries. It is De la Mare, once again, who comes closest to it, and so I must quote him once again:

. . . if Defoe had really faced, as he might have tried to face, the problem set in *Crusoe* his solution could not have been in that book's precise terms. All praise and thanks that it is what it is, a triumph in its kind; and yet one may pine for what, given a more creative imagination and a different Crusoe, the book might have been if the attempt had been made to reveal what a prolonged unbroken solitude, an absolute exile from his fellow-creatures, and an incessant commerce with silence and the unknown, would mean at last to the spirit of man. A steadily debasing brutish stupidity? Hallucinations, extravagances, insanities, enravishment, strange guests?

Selkirk after but four years' silence was scarcely articulate. Crusoe after his eight and twenty years, addresses the three strangers who he finds trussed-up on the beach with the urbanity of a prince, the courtesy of an Oriental, and in faultless Spanish. . . .

Well, this touches more closely on what seems to me at any rate one of the most intriguing facets of both *Robinson Crusoe* and its author: his ability to *normalize* the *abnormal,* to write of extreme experience in terms of sensible human reaction to it, to describe the lives of extraordinary people in ordinary language and in readily comprehensible but not patronizing terminology. Parenthetically, those who are curious as De la Mare was curious as to how a different Crusoe might have reacted might consult an eighteenth-century narrative in the form of a journal kept by a sailor who had been put on the Island of Ascension in May 1725 by the commodore and captains of the Dutch fleet "for a most enormous crime." The castaway, who lasted apparently until mid-September, left his incomplete journal lying beside his skeleton, where both were found later by Captain Mawson of the *Compton.* He describes in most affecting and horrible detail his inability to catch the island goats, which both Selkirk and Crusoe had captured and killed, and his being forced to drink turtle blood mixed with his own urine. It is to be found in Charles Neider's anthology *Man Against Nature,* and is worth examining as one instance of the sufferings of a man on an island who was not blessed with the good fortune, skill, and ingenuity of Crusoe.

To return to our theme. What strikes me as extraordinary is Defoe's instinctive ability to take the gruesome self-immolation of an antisocial drifter and convert it into the intriguing and *uplifting* tale of a healthy-minded, practical fellow. Indeed, the very opening chapters inform us of Defoe's intention: instead of demanding to be put ashore on the desolate isle in a fit of rage, as had Selkirk, Crusoe is shipwrecked – and thus at the outset absolved of any direct responsibility for his plight. Isn't this almost the exact opposite of the working method of many modern poets and novelists, who start with the seemingly normal, the deceptively ordinary, and proceed to reveal to our horrified but fascinated gaze (and to the disgust, let it be added, of those trained to appreciate an older, more "positive" kind of writing) that what lies behind the smiling façade is a cesspool, a jungle, or a desert strewn with bleached bones? When we give our children *Robinson Crusoe* for their birthdays we are tacitly concurring with Defoe's estimate of himself as a moralizer and purveyor of unexceptionable sentiments, based on splendidly factual narratives – which we now see have been culled from sources as neurotic as the moralities and sentiments of any modern novel.

"The reappearance of Selkirk into the civilized world,"

De la Mare comments, "was certainly for Defoe a stroke of luck, but then, Selkirk, for full seven years before Defoe made use of him, had been 'a common prey to the birds of literature.' It was sheer ability that not only recognized the literary value of this nugget, but prevented Defoe from being too clever in his tale – though clever in all conscience he could be."

This is so, but it remains to point out that Defoe's seizing upon Selkirk's tale was hardly unique in his literary life, either in the character of the tale itself, or in the use he made of it. Defoe seems to have long been fascinated with those who were cut off from the world either through force of circumstance, by a quirk of nature, or from their own willfulness. In the midst of one of his most prolific journalistic periods, he was, it is important to bear in mind (the description is Trent's),

> a shunned bankrupt and turncoat, living in chambers in London or with his wife and children in a large house in Newington, seeing little or nothing of the gay society of the epoch, not even acquainted with the fellow men of letters who with himself give the age its chief luster, but, none the less, in no sense a recluse, rather the keenest observer of his day, the most intelligent, alert, and well paid of the prime minister's secret agents and the most accomplished journalist England had produced – perhaps the most remarkable the world has ever seen.

This is the man who in 1719 published a pamphlet entitled *Dumb Philosopher; or, Great-Britain's Wonder*, subtitled "Surprizing Account how Dickory Cronke, a Tinner's Son in the County of Cornwal, was born Dumb, and continued so for 58 years; and how some Days before he died, he came to his Speech."

This is the man who, maintaining his special interest in the plight of those cut off because they were deaf and dumb, became rather dismally embroiled with his beloved daughter Sophia's suitor Henry Baker, a specialist in the training of those so afflicted; and who, in April 1720, brought out *The History of the Life and Surprising Adventures of Mr. Duncan Campbell*, subtitled, "A Gentleman, who though born Deaf and Dumb, writes down any Stranger's Name at First Sight; and their Future Contingencies of Fortune. . . ."

This is the man who in 1726 brought out *Mere Nature Delineated,* about a boy who had been found running wild in a German forest and had been brought to London for medical examination. It is interesting to observe how Defoe describes this Peter the Wild Boy:

> . . . they tell us, he was found wild, naked, dumb; known to, and knowing nobody. That he lived a vegetative life, fed on grass, moss, leaves of trees, and the like; that he acted below brutal life, hardly a sensitive, and not at all a rational.
>
> They hardly allow, that he walked or stepped erect, but rather creeping on hands and knees, climbing trees like a cat, sitting on the boughs like a monkey, and the like; tho' in that part we must not carry our fancy beyond the fact, because we see him at present standing upright, as the soul-informed part of mankind do. . . .

This is the man, then, who wrote *Robinson Crusoe.* It is true that my listing of and quotation from his works has been highly selective. But for one thing, others of his works can be interpreted as paralleling, so to speak, those remarked above; for example, it is hardly stretching the story line of a masterpiece like *Moll Flanders* to see it as Mark Schorer does: "Like *Robinson Crusoe,* this is a desperate story of survival, a story that tries to demonstrate the possibility of success through unremitting native wit." For another, I have wished not to analyze Daniel Defoe exhaustively, but only to indicate that certain personalities and themes fascinated him if not obsessively, at least recurrently, and that this may have been because these people and these notions echoed certain tormenting problems in his own personal life – the problems of the man alone. It is true that Defoe was a busybody, a progressive-minded money-maker, and in many ways a representative man of his time; but it is also true that he was unhappily married, that he was deprived of many of the stimulations he sorely needed, and that he died wretchedly, an old man hiding out from his creditors and abandoned by his ungrateful children.

The theme of *Robinson Crusoe* parallels, in its duality, the life of its author (which is why, I feel, Defoe seized with such sure instinct on the handy facts of the Selkirk experience). Crusoe on the one hand in the classic posture of human extremity: loneliness; on the other, an unsentimental, hardheaded chap learning to make do with what he salvages from the wreck of the ship and manages to acquire on the island. So Defoe was, as we have seen, at times ostracized and cut off from the best society of his time; and yet, as the judicious biographer James Sutherland observes, he "enjoyed the mere variety of human life, the bustle of active people, the shopkeeper scratching his head with his pen, the fine lady cheapening a piece of silk, the beggar limping by on his crutches, the stir and commotion of market-day in a small town, the forest of shipping on the river at Gravesend." It is no wonder that his readers were "the small shopkeepers and artisans, the publicans, the footmen and servant wenches, the soldiers and sailors, those who could read but who had neither the time nor the inclination to read very much."

The most recent biographer of Defoe, Brian Fitzgerald, writing from what is apparently a Marxist orientation, puts it this way:

> He could compensate himself for all the failures of his life – for his bankruptcy, for the degradation of his imprisonment, and the claustrophobic fear of confinement that haunted him ever afterwards – by becoming the captain of his soul and the master of his fate on an imaginary uninhabited island in the North Atlantic. He could compensate himself for the humiliations he had suffered in public life by doing the actions of government he had never been able to perform in reality, by showing his capacity for ruling and directing and colonizing. No longer need he concern himself with the remote and more abstract problems of human society; he could, through the power of his imagination, become the monarch of all he surveyed. . . .

Whatever our reservations about the manner of Mr. Fitzgerald's expression, we must grant that this does make sense, as does his description of *Robinson Crusoe* as "the great allegory of the capitalist system. Crusoe," he says,

> who was Defoe projected, was the supreme affirmation of the individual. Like the lively, enterprising merchants and tradesmen, the middle class, the bourgeoisie, then in the full flush of revolutionary triumph, Robinson Crusoe renounces the past and prepares to make his own history. . . . Crusoe triumphed — as did the bourgeois capitalist — by his faith in himself, his naive optimism, which enabled him to overcome both his own folly in risking his fortune and the cruelty and the savage hostility of his fellow-men, and to found his ideal colony beyond the seas. He was the empire-builder, the man who challenged nature and won; his reward was calculated down to the last threepence, and it was well earned. But *Robinson Crusoe* is not only a paean in praise of capitalism. It, too, has revolutionary implications. Crusoe (as Professor Kettle has reminded us) sets off on his life of adventure and uncertainty *against* the advice of his middle-class father; and if in one sense his story is one in praise of the bourgeois virtues of individualism and private enterprise, in another — and more important — sense it celebrates the necessity of social living and the struggle of mankind through work to master nature. . . .

This fits in rather comfortably with Sutherland's assertion that "if Defoe's public was drawn chiefly from the middle and lower classes, that public had got an epic entirely after its own heart, with a hero it could understand and admire because he was taken from its own ranks. Crusoe may be all Mankind in difficulties, but he is first of all an Englishman of the lower middle classes making the best of things." His story is told in "the prose of democracy, a prose which in modern England with its inhibitions and its class consciousness has almost been parsed out of existence."

It may be objected that all this accounts, if it does that, for Crusoe's popularity in his own day, but not necessarily thereafter — the easiest kind of post-factum analysis. It may be objected that it borders on the obvious to assert that Daniel Defoe, like so many other creative minds throughout the ages, was piqued (if not tormented) by the problems of loneliness and isolation, but that he turned them to account for the cash customers of his day by presenting them as healthy problems, as susceptible of solution as the problems of trade or empire. The real question, it may be argued, is why *Robinson Crusoe* has persisted in its popularity in the several hundred years since its first printing, down through a time when interest would seem more likely to center not on what this ingenious islander does with his goats and his salvaged tools, but rather on his dreams and nightmares, on what he substitutes for female companionship for more than twenty-eight years, and on the symbolic richness of his punishment and redemption.

I have no answers to this question beyond those which have already been given by time and by scholars and critics whose equipment I, as a common reader, obviously lack. Before the beginning of the twentieth century, we know, there had already appeared at least seven hundred editions, translations, and imitations of the story. In our time their number has multiplied, perhaps beyond counting. In the eighteenth century, Sheridan wrote a popular pantomime, with David Garrick playing Crusoe; in the nineteenth, Offenbach composed the music for an opera based on the adventures of our hero; in the twentieth, Luis Bunuel, the gifted Spanish surrealist movie-maker, was intrigued enough with *Robinson Crusoe* – despite the fact that he claims not to have liked the book – to make from it a thoroughly absorbing movie, one which has moments of incandescence, with Daniel O'Herlihy as a perfectly right Crusoe. In the eighteenth century *Crusoe* was used as the basis for lectures in classical political economy; in the twentieth, as we have seen, as ideal fuel for Marxian analysis.

But now, in our own day, something does seem to be happening. The book which Maxim Gorky characterized apothegmatically as "The Bible of the Unconquerable" is being turned over to the kiddies. It is not being shared with them, like *Alice in Wonderland* or even *Huckleberry Finn;* in an age in which hillbillies gape at the Sadlers Wells Ballet on their barroom screens and intellectuals leaf desperately through their expensive paperbacks in search of entertainment which will not be entertaining, *Robinson Crusoe* does not seem to be often read by those past the age of confirmation (even Bunuel's intriguing and sensitive film is recommended for the impressionable young alone).

The reader who has been patient this long may now begin to suspect, with reason, that what I have been attempting to do is to push *Robinson Crusoe* for the adult trade. (Children have as yet no need to be so instructed – although even *that* audience is becoming so violently sophisticated that one may tremble for its future capacity to be enthralled by the doings of a single man, neither bubble-headed nor space-gunned, who teaches a parrot to talk and learns by trial and error how to bake bread and fire pottery.) To be sure, there are many ways of awakening, or re-awakening, reader interest in a classic work. We may rhapsodize over the plot, or story development, but only, it seems to me, if we can be reasonably certain – as in the case of a Portuguese or Tibetan classic – that it has remained generally unknown. We may linger admiringly over the author's periods and cherish the subtleties of his rhythmic ebbs and flows, but not, it seems to me, when the author wields the serviceable but uninspiring "prose of democracy." We may fall in with the current fad of playing locksmith, fumbling among the unwieldy bunch of keys that constitute our critical armory for the one that will magically unlock the work and reveal the symbolism presumably hidden within – but Thomas Wright, who maintained stoutly for years (basing himself on an offhand remark of Defoe's) that *Robinson Crusoe* was a deliberate allegory, a direct reflection of Defoe's own life, and that Defoe for nearly twenty-nine years had led a life of silence, was at length forced to admit that he had been the victim of his own theorizing; and I have no desire to lay the foundations for such a future admission.

We may finally – which is what I have attempted – look to see if, how, in what way, the passions and problems of the author have paralleled ours so many years later. If we then find Defoe to be contemporary – not in manner necessarily, nor even in outlook, but in *preoccupation* – then surely he merits pride of place alongside those in our time who have been preoccupied too with loneliness and isolation but who, much more torn than he with the agony of doubt, have hesitated to address themselves to the Unconquerable and so have become the tribunes of the Unsure.

Here, however, we enter other realms. I would not contest the obvious truth that *Robinson Crusoe* has been read over the years not primarily because of what it says, or omits, about loneliness, but because it appeals to the busy child in us all, because it is a practical and entertaining manual in the domestication of nature, and because it is a painless and unfrightening guide to the exotic. To the extent that it continues to be read, it can be seen as still providing the same kind of refreshment to the same kind of people. But I have been addressing myself in these lines I suppose to the Unsure, to those who increasingly attempt to distinguish themselves from the masses (among other ways) by ignoring escapist literature, even classical escapist literature, in favor of those books which do grapple with the problems of loneliness.

In the emerging mass society, the *angst* of the solitary intellectual is now being experienced, if confusedly, by ever-lengthening lines of bumper-to-bumper megalopolitans trained to dread nothing more fiercely than loneliness. Will *Robinson Crusoe*, with its cheery accent on the positive, still find acceptance among either the hyper-sophisticated or the great ordinary anonymous mass who have been its cherishers, as they have been the cherishers – at least until the coming of the mass society – of most great writings throughout the ages? One can only guess. It is entirely possible, for example, that it may be on the verge of yet a new wave of popularity for just these reasons, that now it will be read not as an epic of man's indomitability, but as a nostalgic reverie of those old days when it was possible to conceive of the vanquishing of loneliness and the disappearance of doubts, when it was possible to conceive that by conquering nature you had conquered all.

"He who wants to escape the world translates it," said Michaux. If by his translation he conquers, if only for an hour, "the last unknown and insular retreat," has he not earned all over again the honor of our rapt attention, as well as that of our invincible offspring?

The Antioch Review, Spring 1958

Footnote, 1961: The ancient terror of loneliness seems to be getting more and more confused in the popular mind with a dread of ever being alone. I wonder whether this latter may not have more to do with the much noised-about population explosion than is generally allowed. If people are not inculcated with an understanding of the necessity to arrange for the preservation of human privacy on our planet, to say nothing of opportunities for solitude and contemplation of an undefiled natural order, or for the maintenance of wilderness areas and respect for the balance of nature, they are apparently going to continue to ignore appeals – no matter how frantic or how well-reasoned – that they limit the number of their offspring. Of course this is hardly the only reason for the phenomenon, but the fact that millions of "liberty-loving" Americans and Europeans (whose populations are exploding too) seem to take positive pleasure in jamming themselves into crowded housing developments, beaches, parks, and highways ought to be taken into consideration by the demographers and the planners.

(Similarly, we are bombarded with baloney about our "peace-loving" nation and our "peace-loving" people, when there is no substantial evidence that the American people would react with any emotion other than horror if peace were to break out. Not only does a forty-seven-billion-dollar annual arms budget barely suffice to stabilize our unemployed at five million in a land that has never known devastation, but we are psychologically goaded to hate, to fear, and to need the presence of an external menace. Some psychologists describe the violent American – and, it must be added, Western European – "comic" books, "mystery" books, movies, and television as an "escape valve," meaning that passive exposure to a broad spectrum of consistently sadistic and brutal behavior may inhibit, rather than incite, antisocial activity, by relieving the consumer of his aggressions. Even if this is so, the waxing horrors of the mass media must be characterized as an "immoral equivalent" for war, and we are still left with the problem of finding William James's "moral equivalent" if we expect the desire for peace to well up in the bosoms of mankind. I believe with James that a socialist reconstruction of our value system is essential.)

Thanks to the fantastic increase in mobility made possible by the automobile and the airplane, even those who pride themselves on getting away from it all are enabled to find solitude – and in the process to despoil hitherto untrammeled areas. In Wyoming, I was assured by a ranger that "sportsmen" boldly chewing jeep roads up the steep sides of previously inaccessible fastnesses have gullied out thousands of acres of wilderness land. It is neither melodramatic nor cynical to observe that we are moving toward the erasure of privacy even in areas formerly considered sacrosanct, and that this tendency is strengthened by powerful forces in modern society. If formerly the church was regarded as providing refuge from worldliness and sanctuary for contemplativeness, today it becomes yet another monument to Togetherness, a headquarters for Bingo and basketball. In the San Antonio *Express* of July 2, 1959, I read of the Reverend John E. Weir's new church in Louisville, Kentucky:

> It will include a swimming pool, tennis court, snack bar, an unloading ramp for motorists, and the largest outdoor church bulletin board in the city . . .
>
> Churchgoers traveling by car will be able to unload on the second-floor level just outside the chapel. The parking lot becomes a playground with a touch of a button.
>
> Concrete slabs open to reveal a 40 by 60 foot swimming pool. Swings and a slide come out of their underground hiding places along with tennis net posts and basketball goal posts. The snack bar will be attached to the social hall . . . The bulletin board will be 16 feet long, 8 feet high, and 4 feet deep. It will include a miniature of the Holy Land, with a mirror on the back of the board reflecting the scene for passing motorists . . .

Marriage too, whether in or out of the church, becomes not a union of two human beings, but an occasion and an excuse for herding together in absolute contradiction of all that marriage has presumably implied throughout the bourgeois era. From the San Francisco *Chronicle* of April 3, 1961, I learned of the situation at the popular British honeymoon resort of St. Helier, Jersey, one of the Channel Islands:

A thousand brides bounced down to breakfast today with not a blush on their faces.

"The modern bride," explained hotelman Alex Aston, "does not blush. She's far too busy running a quizzical eye over the rest of the girls."

This phenomenon is part of a growing British development—the honeymoon en masse. As hotelman Aston explained: "The last thing a bride wants these days is to be left alone."

The thousand brides, equipped with a thousand bridegrooms, came to Jersey in the annual marriage rush set off by a British institution known as the tax man's wedding . . .

A pretty young bride who asked to be nameless confessed:

"My main honeymoon worry was being lonely. I mean you could easily get bored with no one but your fiancé (she meant husband) to look at all day. But we have already chummed up with some very friendly couples."

One hardly knows whether to laugh or to weep for the pretty young bride, who has anticipated her similars in *1984* by several decades. Is it beyond the bounds of probability to consider that it may become not merely socially acceptable, but *de rigueur*, for her to be delivered of her offspring in public just as now she enjoys her honeymoon en masse? Then there will remain only the ultimate experiences of coitus and death, and if population growth continues at its present rate, it may become an unacceptable luxury for either of these events to take place without the presence of other human beings similarly engaged.

Certain Jewish Writers

The original version of this essay was written in collaboration with Irving A. Sanes, who is responsible for most of its insights but not for the revisions I have made, and to whom I am most grateful for permission to reproduce here.

Of late there has been an extraordinary increase in the number of arguments advanced to demonstrate the human superiority of the Jew. They are based on the Jew's supposed "alienation" from general society. The very terminology of those who accept pat formulations of "Jewish alienation" is open to question. "Rootlessness" and "alienation" may readily be seen as romantic terms if one substitutes the more realistically descriptive terms *insecurity* and *rejection*. And although it may seem invidious to assert that material reasons compel the Jew to engage himself, to compete in the world of art, there is reason to believe that for the Jew the production of works of art is one means of gaining recognition, love, and a sense of community with other craftsmen. Surely it is important to note that during the Thirties, when it was practically possible for many Jewish intellectuals to identify with the militant working class (regardless of the ultimate effects on them of this alliance), there was little talk of "alienation." There was no need for the concept itself; and if there was self-pity, it was of a different order; for the intellectual could think of success, recognition, and integration as being bound up with the struggle to supersede the class and the system that denied him those rewards.

If today the artist no longer bases his hope on a *class* in society, he by no means has given up hope of being accepted by *society*. Although his high seriousness and faithfulness to the demands of his art make it appear that his means are irrational and contradictory, it is true only in the sense that all attempts to deal with emotional situations are so. The desire is a sensible and worthy one. As it concerns the Jewish artist the answer is more complicated only in that he has greater hopes for the saving process of art because he is more effectively rejected by society; he is most concerned with love and respect because he feels himself most excluded from it.

The reader who does not approach these Jewish writers with romantic preconceptions finds himself continuously stumbling over their ill-concealed self-hatred, despair, and masochism. It does not follow at all that Jewish writers ought to adopt "healthier" attitudes; but surely one can expect of their critics that they recognize masochism and evaluate it honestly. By romanticizing the Jew as the figure at the center of art they have only created one more stereotype: the Jew as Alienated Artist.

II

The natural tendency of minority groups to defend themselves from the sneers of the conforming majority by parodying their own differences has provided material for several generations of sociologists and folklorists. Although it may seem a far cry from the malapropish Greek restaurateur to the *avant-garde* Jewish poet, once either one is abstracted from the society that has formed him and is considered as a hothouse type, he becomes a cliché; and we can expect no increase in our understanding of Greeks or Jews. This is true no matter with what degree of sophistication the cliché-specimen is examined. In the context of our discussion the end product is all too often an over-sharp evaluation of the centrality of the Jew in the domain of the intellect.

Consider the gross but striking correspondence between the Jew as Artist and the Jew as Entertainer. Certainly, with such metropolitan comedians as Milton Berle, Morey Amsterdam, and Myron Cohen, a form of Jewish particularism is joined to a striving to stand somewhere above the audience and criticize the culture that has formed it and that pays its way. Every popular subject is immersed in the "destructive element"; what is most highly valued is the verbal gift. Very little use is made of the traditional comic techniques because the single device is cruelty to one's audience, based on the obvious superiority of the comedian's mind, with an occasional admixture of self-cruelty.

These comedians are furthermore the highbrows of popular culture, speaking a special language to a special audience.[1] One feels in watching them that they consider their minds to be weapons, developed in the struggle against an inferior society which scorned them. And again one feels that their superiority is based, not on what the intellect can accomplish, but on what it can *see:* corruption, self-interest, the material drive behind ideals. The scorn that passes for comedy is aimed at everyone who is so naïve as to think in other terms.*

[1] It might also be asserted of this audience, by those interested in creating yet another stereotype, that because of its background of exclusion, it seeks to relieve its intense malaise in the bitter intramural anti-Semitism of the nightclub comedians. But accent and intonation aside, is this audience not part and parcel of the large and anxious American bourgeoisie, whose pursuit of fun is only one more indication of life alienated from value and meaning? If, to some, the Jewish nightclubber seems more intense in his pleasure habits, we are justified in pointing out that hatred, mockery, and fear limit him to a smaller playground, from which his concentrated and typically American cries ring loudly in our ears.

* *Footnote, 1961:* It would be instructive to interpret the new generation of metropolitan comedians, so many of them Jewish – Mike Nichols and Elaine May, Mort Sahl, Shelley Berman, Lennie Bruce, Milt Kamen – against the background of these remarks.

The comedian too has become a kind of pathic observer. But what he observes has lost its value of perspective; he laughs at himself as much as he does at others; all the world follows the main drift, and he who would attempt to counter it is a "schmo." Yet, at the same time that he insults his audience, he sees himself as victim of the audience – making himself the butt of laughter, telling a story in a Yiddish accent, describing his family life as both a center of sentiment (Mama's cooking) and a grasping unit (the innumerable sponging relatives), and presenting a portrait of himself as somehow a misfit in a world whose normality, dull as it may be, is yet above him.

Life in America has done much to produce this kind of Jew. But the emphasis must be placed on the *American* half of the proposition. Of alienation there is plenty; there is even a kind of complex vision; certainly the comedian, like the intellectual, has developed the habit of living on his wits and his art. But what has formed this Jew has little or nothing to do with the Jewish ethical tradition. If the extent of his severance from society is more severe, it stems from the degree of hatred that is turned against him. Acting as though one were the pet victim of the world does not lead to a better understanding of the world; it can only lead to a false evaluation of the importance of one's suffering, and the creation of one more false stereotype. Hence, the danger of identifying all Jews with the immigrant Jew who settled in the New York or Chicago ghettos, or with his child, whose struggle to realize his independence led him to the hope of mastery by the control of art – almost, by a need to monopolize art.

III

The alienated man as subject and object of literature, and as the image through which one experiences the outer world, can be followed in the central figure of Delmore

Schwartz's family chronicle.[2] The Jewish family becomes the symbol of the historical forces that moved westward to America. The Jews are the chosen people in the sense that they are foreordained, "Chosen for wandering and alienation/in every kind of life, in every nation . . ." From the flight to America, from the impact of industrial civilization and the crassest expression of modern existence upon the "people chosen for pain" emerges the new cultural hero. The long history of suffering has torn illusion from his eyes; he is born with a cry of agony, almost immediately aware of the contradictory forces of Europe, America, capitalism, and Israel, all of which are embodied in his name.[3] It is invariably a name that sums up the tensions which he must resolve in loneliness and pain, one which has in itself, and from the beginning, "the basis of the art of poetry/the hard identity felt in the bone."

Born alienated, there is no progression for the protagonist from innocence to wisdom; we encounter him in Mr. Schwartz's later short stories as the lonely man, whose exile is the source of his strength, who turns inward because of his heritage of suspicion and rejection, a prey to "innumerable anxiety feelings which had their source in events which had occurred some twenty-five years before."

The strength of evocation of the symbolic Jew lies in the implication that, separated from Gentile society, he is still adequate to deal with it so long as his disillusion and craft are kept intact; its inadequacy is projected in the names that Mr. Schwartz gives to his protagonist. The ridiculous conjunction of a "Christian" Christian name with a Jewish family name warns the hero of the impossibility of ever crossing over to Gentile society. At the same time it sums up the imbalance of the alienated man

[2] Mr. Schwartz has not written a chronological narrative. The story of the hero and of his ancestors is to be found in *In Dreams Begin Responsibilities* (1938), *Shenandoah* (1941), *Genesis* (1943), and most recently in *The World Is a Wedding* (1948).

[3] The naming of the hero-child (Shenandoah Fish, Belmont Weiss, Hershey Green, etc.) recurs throughout Mr. Schwartz's work.

generating within himself a hatred for the Jewish name (himself), and the Christian name (society).

Nevertheless, and necessarily, society must be entered. The means adopted by the Jewish intellectual are reminiscent of the procedure Henry James thought necessary for becoming an English citizen: one is introduced into society and vouched for, as it were, by one's intellectual ancestors, the cultural heroes of the ages. But here the question of entering society, with even the best credentials, takes on an added difficulty. It can be summed up in these words of T. S. Eliot: "For the expression of imaginative reality, for truths of poetry and of religion, a man is best equipped when he uses the language of his ancestors, shaped by a particular racial sensibility and capable of conveying the messages of the inherited imagination."

If the Jewish artist subscribes to such a point of view he can only turn his creative energies to Hebrew forms of expression. That the American Jew recognizes the falsity of Eliot's statement is evident in his insistence on working in the idiom of his country and drawing upon the international experience. But his efforts are weakened by his refusal to believe that the Jewish problem is a social one. The tension of his work is apparent in the double image he constructs for himself, as both the victim and the heir of the ages. The difficulty lies in the inability of the artist to reconcile the advantages of being an alien with the necessity of being a member of society. His statement of malaise is a romantic and stereotyped one not because he does not utilize the elements of his difficulty in his work, but because he attempts to armor himself morally against the reality of his situation by abstracting the virtues of alienation on the one hand, and tradition on the other, and uniting them in his own person.

The effort of the complex personality to escape the stereotype mold into which he is cast is evident in both the prose and the poetic styles of Mr. Schwartz, who has spoken of his versification as having a "deliberate flatness," a heavy and slow quality "to declare the miraculous character of daily life and ordinary speech." But has he really succeeded with this device in regaining "the width of reference of prose without losing what the Symbolists discovered"? In *Genesis,* when the intensity of the declaimer's suffering (always in the passages of poetry) reaches a point that cannot be controlled within the "morbid pedestrianism" of his prose and bursts into an indulgent lament, the reader suffers, between prose and poetry, the same kind of embarrassment that the juxtaposition of Jewish and American names ("Shenandoah Fish") caused the protagonist. When an equilibrium is finally regained one returns to the modest language of daily statement with the feeling that it is a false exterior, a disguise whose aim is not to increase our awareness by enlarging our experience, but to shelter the poet, to save him from exposing his private emotions to a world that might not understand.

The relationships of tenderness and mutual sexual satisfaction, rare enough anywhere, it is true, are nowhere mentioned in Mr. Schwartz's extended autobiography. What *is* mentioned is their opposite: the discovery of betrayal and guilt in marriage, the implication that those possessing beauty and energy are certain to betray, that their potency is coupled with insensitiveness, while those who are sensitive are apt to suffer from a kind of "psychic impotence." Here again there is the example of T. S. Eliot, whose hollow men are incapable of making love because "there is a shadow which falls between the desire and the spasm." But with Mr. Schwartz the statement turns inward, the emphasis turns on the protagonist instead of on the poem, and we are again reminded of the artificial use that is made of disguising poetic form: if the personal and poetic idiom has been evacuated of high-flown language, it is only to hide the highly charged nature of the poet's feelings.

The Jewish artist's ambiguous social aspirations, his unconscious reluctance to interpret his self-hatred as a reflection of the discrimination that keeps him outside of general society, create a tension within the body of his work that is cramping in its ultimate effect. The literature itself becomes dull; philosophic generalities are substituted for social density, for an acting out of manners and morals that are peculiar to the time in which we live.

IV

In Isaac Rosenfeld's novel *Passage From Home* (1946),[4] we encounter once again the rootless Jewish intellectual, this time in embryo, in the process of discovering that his future lies outside the home. Once again we meet the self-conscious protagonist, his attention centered upon himself as the seer who carries Europe, his ancestors, and industrial America within himself. His hope for escape from Irving Howe's "tragedy of the family relationship" is accompanied by a gradual disillusionment with the means of escape, a sharpening of his vision that leads him to expect betrayal and misunderstanding as a condition of life. True, the communal forms of love still exist, we see them in Mr. Rosenfeld's Passover scene; but they are fleeting and anachronistic, just as are the ethical and scholastic precepts of Jewish life, even while they carry with them a sense of dignity (as in the Talmudic disputes of the aged rabbi and his friends). There emerge only the forms of tradition, implying dignity in adversity. Here too dignity is seen as another side of the coin of alienation, maintained with the most absolute – and critical – intellectual integrity.

As Daniel Bell has pointed out, the novel ends with an assumption of alienation. The young protagonist, Bernard, unable to confess to his father, confesses to himself; but "Now it was too late. Now there would only be life as it came and the excuses one made to himself for accepting it."

[4] Reprinted (Meridian Books) in 1961.

There must have been, for Mr. Rosenfeld himself, a stopping-off place somewhere between the discoveries of the adolescent Bernard and the attitudes of the adult protagonist of his later Kafkaesque stories which have been appearing in *Partisan Review* and *Kenyon Review* both before and after the publication of *Passage From Home*. But no trace of the leftist political adherence of Mr. Rosenfeld and his contemporaries during the Thirties can be found in their creative works. We may surmise that it was only a minor disturbance in the lifelong process of discovering their own loss of love – a loss which is incarnated in Mr. Rosenfeld's short stories – and of rooting out every pose, attitude, rationalization that might tempt the spirit to hope.

In Mr. Rosenfeld's (and also in Saul Bellow's) prose itself there is a desperate flight from tricks, from any stylization, from a signature that might differentiate their language from another writer's. In this anonymity exists the lonely man, the self-denigrating hero who, like the "private eye," does not like this world but accepts it as necessary and livable if he can take his beatings and reject his bribes, living his life as though his own peculiar form of integrity were the only valuable thing in the world; it is an integrity implying a complete knowledge of the corruption that can be fought only by craft, cunning, self-knowledge, and a limitless ability to "take it."

But like the "private eye" – the modern indefinite symbol of everyman's loneliness and dignity – the "lonely man" too becomes stylized. He lives in a world that many intellectuals have already charted with an ambivalent dread. Thus the short stories of Isaac Rosenfeld compose a kind of political parable pointing to the extreme developments of authoritarian states; and, as in the earlier poetry of Auden, the location of the battlefronts and the customs of the people have grown so confusing that one cannot discover which side the hero is on. He has rejected not only self-pity but self-value. It can no longer be, as Daniel Bell claims, that such a writer "still retains a deep critical sense regarding the inequalities, injustice, oppressive nature of an exploitative society." Any such reaction has become too unsophisticated: young Bernard himself passed that point in his "true *Bar Mitzvah*."

Like the "private eye," our new hero (on a higher plane, to be sure) takes corruption for granted; he is interested in different matters: understanding his own reactions and maintaining a quiet dignity, carving by his craft and his art some quiet corner in which he can examine his own guilt. But, of course, the analogy cannot be carried too far. The artist is too complex to be compared to the detective, for he is a deeper adventurer, with a harder mind, and neither the wish nor the hope to clear up the case. To eliminate the danger of coming to a conclusion he has constructed a world in which there are no conclusions. It is a world from which moral choice has been eliminated: only the facts of color, stature, language, and religious affiliation are known. The only proper attitude left is that of alienation: the suffering has become too deep to share.

V

In *Dangling Man* (1944),[5] the first novel of Saul Bellow, we find a prose style similar to that of Mr. Rosenfeld and a good deal of the same self-mockery.[6] Mr. Bellow's book

[5] Reprinted (Meridian Books) in 1960.

[6] Interested readers may want to compare the striking stylistic similarities between two early first-person stories, Mr. Rosenfeld's "The Hand That Fed Me," and Mr. Bellow's "Two Morning Monologues" (both included in the *Partisan Reader,* 1947). In the latter story, the narrator, whose name is Mandelbaum, speaks in the bitter accents of Delmore Schwartz's young Jew: "I didn't want my name in the paper. I've always avoided parading it. I can't stand that. I can't remember a time in my life when I didn't swallow before saying it." (The "poor New York Jew," by the way, now appears in the pages of the literary magazines with a regularity which is becoming monotonous. See, for example, Wallace Markfield's story, "Ph.D.," in the September-October 1947 *Partisan Review:* "Auerbach, little Jew of C.C.N.Y. . . ." his "thesis to be HISTORY AND ALPHABET OF AGONY.")

details, in the form of a diary, the anxiety of a young intellectual who has been placed in 1A but is never drafted. There is a cafeteria scene in which Joseph, who is keeping the diary, recognizes a Communist with whom he had been friendly in his own party days. When the Communist (a crackpot who sticks pins in maps, each pin a possible barricade) insults Joseph by refusing to acknowledge his greeting – and why did he try to force recognition if not to be victimized again? – Joseph creates a scene. As a result, he succeeds in embarrassing his companion, who was going to get a job for him.

The effects of Joseph's explosion of temper cause us to wonder if Joseph is not as much an "addict" as the Stalinist. And does he too not see himself in those terms, profoundly self-aware as he is? The question then arises: does Joseph demand to be recognized by the Stalinist as a human being, or is the scene more subtly contrived to show that he does not take himself with any greater seriousness than he does the Stalinist? Do we not have here, in short, a man who has looked deeply into himself and come up with mocking laughter; does not this inward irony, indeed, comprise the sum of the dignity of the hero in a world that leads from depression to war?

Joseph, Mr. Bellow's lonely protagonist, sharing with the characters of Delmore Schwartz and Isaac Rosenfeld the same hero-attitudes of introspection, disillusion, and rootlessness that are so recognizable and attractive to the modern reader, reflects on the war and says, ". . . I would rather be a victim than a beneficiary." It is this choice which finally identifies the Jewish stereotype.

VI

Art begins at the irrational, that subterranean area where the most important parts of our lives are rooted. The artist who plunges in brings forth to our consciousness some of the richness, ordered and illuminated, of his own experience. He who dares to make the perilous descent is usually tortured by the disparity between his separate vision and the naked world. In that sense the artist has always been alienated from his society; his art has been his life, open to those who similarly dare, closed and dangerous to the rest of mankind.

For the most part, the struggle that has led the artist to the depths has been engendered by the search for good in the labyrinths of evil. Since the decline of the Roman Church, this search has been conducted largely by creative and speculative protestant minds. Even today, when categories of good and evil, sin and salvation, despair and loneliness, have lost their original frame of reference, they still retain their power of evocation and are interpreted in terms of guilt, anxiety, rootlessness, and alienation.

From one point of view, the writers we are discussing are the descendants of the religious artists, whose psychology reflected the inner struggle over such conceptions. This struggle, intensified by the collapse of a monolithic intellectual structure, has deepened the contemporary thinker's skepticism and sapped his confidence in the reflective process to the point where he doubts even *his own* thought. His understanding of history as science is overwhelmed by his sensitiveness to the imponderable and fortuitous.

The "wandering Jew," at home nowhere, rejected everywhere, has become the deep symbol of rootlessness and chance. It is not strange that his lonely search for a community of love, his hard and necessary wiseness (almost, like art, a weapon for self-preservation) should occupy a central position in the creative work of contemporary Jewish writers.

But here we encounter a difficulty, an examination of which may disclose a measure of the inadequacy of these writers. The work of the religious artist was directed from its beginnings toward a religious goal; that work took on richness of meaning because art and goal had the same concrete content. Viewed with this unity of content in mind, the history of suffering and loneliness could be seen as both personal and impersonal — a part of the larger scheme that was compelling enough to reconcile man to his insignificance.

The authors whom we are considering, however, have scrapped the religious goal of the religious writers and have maintained only their tradition of alienation.

There is no Church for these Jewish writers. (Can they even dream of substituting the ethic of the Talmud?) They have come too far; the wisdom of disillusion has been too profound. Having accepted, in the Thirties, the consolation of socialism and the less imaginatively satisfying solace of materialism, they cannot now turn to an acceptance of Eliot's ethos. And so, with the hope of socialism dead in their minds, they have seized upon alienation as a positive value, thereby asserting that they are the heirs of all the great alienated writers of the last century. The argument can be reduced to this: alienation is a virtue; its reward is complexity of vision: the Jew is peculiarly alienated; therefore his complexity of vision is peculiarly great. If one but proclaims his alienation insistently enough, the proclamation itself will in time be accepted as artistic creation.

In a review of *Dangling Man*, Delmore Schwartz wrote: "Here for the first time I think the experience of a new generation has been seized and recorded." The experience is that Joseph, the narrator, has been forced "stage by stage, to even greater depths of disillusion . . . he is gradually stripped of the few pretenses and protections left him." That, generally, is the experience and the importance of all the work of the writers under discussion.

VII

Here in America a handful of artists, thrown together by the unending Diaspora, have recorded in diaries and stories, reviews and poems, their naked vision. They are the members of the "colony of the spirit" who shape their art so fiercely that talk of hope and beauty is gratuitous; art itself is all-encompassing.

But they are also the heirs of another, later tradition, whose methodology was designed to remove man from the realm of the peripheral and subjective, where the meaningful life was considered to have its inception within the subject, to an objective contemplation of the world. This new discipline insisted that the world could be changed by including as much material as was possible in the realm of the rational and bringing it under administrative control.

The conditions that made it possible for American Jewish writers to share in this new, materialistic tradition (the effects of which are still evident in the realism of their style) were most favorable in the Thirties. These were the years when they were shaping their thought and art, when hopes were high for an experimental and revolutionary solution of the problems of mankind. There was a real demand for the "relatively classless stratum" of intellectuals (as Max Weber has defined them) to develop an experimental outlook for the working class. This alignment was possible because, as Karl Mannheim has pointed out, the unattached stratum of intellectuals could adapt themselves to any point of view, "and because they alone were in the position to choose affiliations."

Open to them were the techniques of Marx and Freud with which they were able, on the one hand, to probe the conservative ideology of their society and, on the other, to embrace the vision of its opposite. Problems of good and evil lost some of their personal depth and were replaced by the esthetically less interesting concepts of class history, scientific method, and psychological realism. The danger was that they would no longer construct meaningful interpretations of human experience but would, rather, merely demonstrate in their writings the validity of those categories that were being forced into the intellectual foreground by thinkers like Freud and Trotsky.

The materialist-scientific tradition, on the whole, led

to the rejection of religion as reactionary and anachronistic. But once again the Jewish intellectual assumed for himself a symbolically central position in the scheme. Mr. Schwartz's protagonist is seen, buffeted through history, suffering the fate of the subjective hero; at the same time he views questions of nationalism, imperialist war, capitalist competition, and the sources of psychic impotence with the eyes of Marx and Freud. The question was: Who else but the agonized Jew has such vital need to change society?

Art is the form which the intellectual has chosen to resolve the tensions of these two contradictory currents of thought. And indeed, the literary tradition can be viewed as a third current that integrates the other two into a consistent and almost adequate resolution. In an important sense, the style has become the artist. But, as we have seen, beneath the style the necessary inconsistencies remain. These writers have created a bastard and transitional form that has loosened the restriction of both the novel and the poem. For, if the subjective view remains, the religious goal to which it was formerly linked has disappeared; if new techniques of rational investigation make it impossible, as Philip Rahv has pointed out, ". . . to return to pre-political modes of expression," these same techniques (always a danger to the artist who must make his solitary dive into the irrational)[7] are not adequate to ground the artist, with no role in social production and therefore no pervasive ideology, in a disintegrating society.

It is beside the point, of course, to speak of a solution to this problem. The artist's role is determined by his social position between the classes, by his intellectual heritage, by the state of the society in which he lives. He has usually been able to understand the nature and the interest of the classes between which he functions; paradoxi-

[7] Arthur Koestler is the best example of the writer who falls into the trap of using knowledge as a substitute for art.

cally he has been unable to understand his own role. Living on the brink he has only been able to view the disaster. It is small wonder that alienation has become, for him, the perspective of art.

But yet, since hope does not die easily, we continue to search for some other road, for some new artist who possesses the seriousness and craft of the group we have discussed and who, at the same time, touches on the relationships that exist *between* men; someone who will be capable of the act of creation implicit in Malraux's statement: "The greatest mystery is not that we should have been thrown up by chance between the profusion of matter and the profusion of stars, but that, in that prison, we should produce from ourselves images sufficiently powerful to deny our insignificance."

VIII

In his second novel, *The Victim* (1947)[8], Saul Bellow has made a solid beginning in the direction of bringing light to his "colony of the spirit": but only by means of leaving the colony.

At first glance one is struck by the closeness with which Mr. Bellow follows the narrative of Dostoevsky's *The Eternal Husband*, and impressed with the artistry with which he makes it his own. Indeed, a comparison of the characters in the two novels would show how Mr. Bellow reinterprets and intensifies the questions of guilt and responsibility, earlier posed by Dostoevsky, that lie at the heart of his novel.

Following Dostoevsky, Mr. Bellow creates, on the most obvious level, the stereotyped images of victim and victimizer. There is Asa Leventhal, the Jew, cranky and suspicious, whose efforts to establish himself in a hostile world are intensified by his fear that security — even mental stability — rests in precarious balance, liable to be

[8] Reprinted (Viking Compass) in 1956.

toppled by chance misfortune. Opposed to him is the Gentile, Allbee, his personal fury. Because of Allbee's New England background, his early easy success, his loyal friends, and his beautiful wife, we think of him as the counter-stereotype, the irrational, taunting figure of society, symbolized as the enemy.

But soon the relationships between the two men undergo a change. We notice with surprise that even on the surface level of the novel, the roles of victim and victimizer are reversed. We discover a Jew who is employed, respected, married, and in love – even taking for granted the fact that he is capable of being loved! – and a figure of importance in his family, for which he feels a sense of responsibility and affection. Allbee, on the other hand, is the dispossessed: a drunkard who has lost his wife, jobless, friendless. He even assumes some of the traits of the literary Jew: beyond shame and pity, he is not afraid to strip himself of every pretense and illusion. I am what I have become, he says, due to evil circumstances, due to forces beyond my control; if I tell you all this it is because I have nothing to lose; and yet, in the end, I don't blame you for my misfortune, I just want you to see what you have done to me and give you the chance to undo it; I might still be capable of living like a man.

But there, deeper yet, in the heat and crush of New York, in the narrow streets, the stifling rooms, the jammed subways, the inhuman restaurants, Asa Leventhal, the man too busy to read or think, feels that he is, after all, only a part of mankind, and his haunting misery reaches out to embrace others. On a trip to Staten Island he sees a tanker and thinks, ". . . it was terrible on a day like this . . . the men nearly naked in the shaft alley as the huge thing rolled in a sweat of oil, the engines laboring. Each turn must be like a repeated strain on the hearts and ribs of the wipers, there, near the keel, beneath the water." And immediately after, looking up to the buildings on shore, seeing the light over them, wild and savage, he reflects that a speck of such inhuman light exists in all men responding to "the heat and glare . . . or even to freezing salty things, harsh things, all things difficult to stand." Joined with sympathy is an understanding of evil, deep in all men, and for which all men are responsible.

What gives the book depth is not that Asa Leventhal is a Jew but the author's insistence that we are all responsible for the community and must reside in it, aware of chance and the yellow light, but also of the men toiling in the tanker beneath the waters. We are no longer faced with the image of the unique Jew. And from the words of Allbee, uttered at the close of this novel, we can perhaps sense a new spirit, wider than the colony from which the artist seems to have emerged: "When you turn against yourself, nobody else means anything to you either."

The Menorah Journal, Spring 1949

Footnote, 1961: Since these lines were written, the American Jewish writer has taken extraordinary strides forward. If Isaac Rosenfeld died tragically young, Delmore Schwartz became the youngest poet ever to be awarded the Bollingen Prize, and Saul Bellow went on after *The Victim* to make a deliberate break with his earlier style, manner, and preoccupation, and soon won a new kind of recognition with *The Adventures of Augie March.* And a whole new generation of Jewish writers – Norman Mailer, Bernard Malamud, Herbert Gold, Mark Harris, Ernst Pawel, Alfred Grossman, Philip Roth, Grace Paley, and others – of varying gifts but a common vivacity and appeal for the intelligent common reader of no matter what background have attracted international attention as serious American writers.

Writing in *Western Review* in 1958 on Mr. Malamud's *The Assistant,* I said:

While Jews have had an honorable place on the American literary scene since the 19th Century, that place has for the most part been marginal. It would hardly be unfair to say that while their brothers were busily engaged in Americanizing themselves and making the giant stride from sweatshop and tenement to office and suburb, American Jewish writers achieved prominence primarily as either bestseller sentimentalists or genre painters of ghetto and immigrant life. They were never able, not even after World War I, to conquer the ramparts of high art in the world of fiction; there were no Jewish writers to rank with Dos Passos, Fitzgerald, Faulkner, Hemingway. Really it is only since World War II that the American Jew has battered his way (as all writers must batter their way in this country) into the front rank of serious American fiction.

But if this development has been belated, it has been extraordinarily rapid too. Already it is impossible to call the roll of outstanding imaginative novelists and short story writers in this country without including the younger Jewish talents who have come to the fore in the last decade. This unusual development (I omit mention of the parallel and more predictable success of Jewish commercial writers in the movies and television) can be seen as analogous to the sudden emergence of Jewish painters concurrently with the great sweep of School of Paris painting of the last seventy-five years. From Pissarro to Pascin, Soutine, Modigliani and Chagall, it is impossible to imagine what that great creative upsurge would have been like without the participation and indeed the imaginative leadership of the Jewish graphic artists newly freed from centuries of proscription of brush and palette.

So too I venture to suggest that one day it will be impossible to conceive of what course American literature would have taken in the Fifties and Sixties without the active leadership of those American Jewish creative figures who turned from their fathers' conquest of business America to the conquest of the demon of Art.

As I see it now, this conquest has paralleled the very recent shift of the Jew as American from a marginal position to one of centrality – a phenomenon I noted in my Introduction. In such a location there is little room for self-pity on the one hand or pride in uniqueness on the other. We might measure the distance that has been traveled by contrasting Hemingway's Jewish athlete of the Twenties, Robert Cohn, the boxer, forever attempting with fists or flattery to join the club, the expatriate Americans who exclude him, to Philip Roth's Jewish athlete of the Fifties, Ronald Patimkin, who hangs his jockstrap from the shower faucet while he sings the latest pop tunes, and is so completely the self-satisfied muscle-bound numskull that notions of Jewish alienation are entirely "foreign" to him.

The writer who has covered the territory most completely in his own work (and is, perhaps in consequence, the most consistently forward-thrusting and imaginative) is Saul Bellow. I find it fascinating to observe how some of his "Jewish" characters, like Augie March and Tommy Wilhelm, are in many aspects as un-Jewish as their names, while some of his non-Jewish heroes, like Henderson, sometimes lapse into what can be regarded as Jewish speech mannerisms and reflective modes too. And I do not think it has been remarked elsewhere how the notion of the crank, the obsessive man, runs throughout his fiction, starting with the Communist crackpot topographer of *Dangling Man*. He uses the crackpot-invention idea not just as an indication of screwiness but as a common denominator of the old human urge to break the mold, an urge which is wacky and comic but also helps to differentiate us from the other members of the animal kingdom.

It will be remembered that the ship's carpenter with whom Augie March is cast adrift after they have been torpedoed is a logical nut obsessed with the idea of the ideal colony he is going to set up when they are flung ashore in a remote place.

In the title story of Mr. Bellow's collection of stories, "Seize the Day," the glorious swindler Dr. Tamkin also has more to him than can be measured by his gambling other people's money in futures and his fake psychologizing.

"An electrical device for truck drivers to wear in their caps," said Dr. Adler, describing one of Tamkin's proposed inventions. "To wake them with a shock when they begin to be drowsy at the wheel. It's triggered by the change in blood-pressure when they start to doze." . . . Mr. Perls said, "To me he described an underwater suit so a man could walk on the bed of the Hudson in case of an atomic attack. He said he could walk to Albany in it."

To which the hero of the story replies defensively: ". . . I get funny ideas myself. Everybody wants to make something. Any American does."

In the next story of the collection, "A Father-to-be," the hero is daydreaming in the subway: ". . . as a chemist, he asked himself what kind of compound the new Danish drug might be, and started thinking about various inventions of his own, synthetic albumen, a cigarette that lit itself, a cheaper motor fuel."

Nor is that all. The hero of "Looking for Mr. Green" "sat and listened while the old man unfolded his scheme. This was to create one Negro millionaire a month by subscription. One clever, good-hearted young fellow elected every month would sign a contract to use the money to start a business employing Negroes. This would be advertised by chain letters and word of mouth, and every Negro wage-earner would contribute a dollar a month. Within five years there would be sixty millionaires. 'That'll fetch respect,' he said . . ."

Even in the final story, "The Gonzaga Manuscripts," the little Spanish banker who supposedly holds a great poet's last papers is more interested in the title to a pitchblende mine in Morocco than in the poems: ". . . Pitchblende has uranium in it. Uranium is used in atom bombs."

It might almost be said that the daydreamed scheme, the cockeyed money-making device, replaces the nocturnal dream as a technique of rounding and deepening his people. Later on, Henderson, of course, is the "Rain King," the most grandiose schemer of all, the millionaire with screwball ideas on extracting frogs from an African well; and Herzog, tenderly ruminative hero of Mr. Bellow's novel in progress, composes mental letters of solace and stimulation to Dr. Carl Jung, Sir Winston Churchill, President Eisenhower . . .

All these can be interpreted in a way as typical of the familiar Jewish *luftmensch,* in quite another way as typical of the familiar American schemer. But what really raises them to a different level is that, because they are susceptible of being interpreted both ways, they are revelatory and refreshing to readers who may in fact know little of *either* tradition. Here is where art emerges from self-absorption, and here I suppose is the point of these remarks.

Italian Cinema, American Audience

Despite the misshapen form of the globe of the 1960's, there have been a significant number of positive achievements in the Western world since the degrading and hideous years of the 1940's. Any American observer would have to include among these achievements such parallel, if apparently unrelated, phenomena as the European industrial-technological resurgence (particularly in Germany and Russia) and, on the cultural scene, the explosions of American abstract art and of Italian neo-realist films.

It cannot be pure accident that it was in the United States perhaps even more than in their homeland that the striking accomplishments of Roberto Rossellini, Vittorio de Sica, Cesare Zavattini, and Federico Fellini have been swiftly appraised at their true worth. We are proud of the American contribution to the short story over the last century, as are the Italians of seven centuries of imperishable masterworks of painting; and if the cinema be taken at its best as a happy fusion of the arts of the storyteller and the painter, it is only natural that America – the home not only of Hollywood (where technique and commerce had combined to overwhelm creativity) but also of the modern short story and of the absolutely free modern painting – should have taken these movies to its heart. It was only natural that we should have been quick to grasp not merely what was moving and what was pictorial about Italian moving pictures, but also what was *new* about neo-realism.

The cannonading and the tortures of World War II had scarcely stopped when we were bowled over by the artistry and intensity of *Open City*, which came like a hammer blow, forcibly recalling us to an agonizing awareness of what we were already eagerly preparing to forget. And as soon as we call up the titles of the great movies which followed *Open City* — *Paisan, Shoe Shine, The Bicycle Thief, Miracle in Milan, Umberto D, La Strada, Nights of Cabiria, I Vitelloni* — it becomes apparent that the wholehearted appreciation of our response has been aroused by more than merely an intellectual appreciation of esthetic problems well met.

For what we found, and continue to find, in these movies, is a quality of compassion ominously lacking in the scramble of the other Europeans to rebuild and catch up, and shamefully absent from our own postwar existence, which seemed dedicated to obliterating from the national consciousness what we had done to Hiroshima and Nagasaki and the fact that our land had not been devastated. Even in painting, the one area of the arts in which it is all but universally acknowledged now that postwar America gained pre-eminence, we evacuated first the human form and then any reference at all to the natural world. The rest of us, perhaps as deeply affected as the painters by the course of events, or perhaps merely numbed by fear, selfishness, and ambition, gladly turned from our generous impulses of the Thirties to an exclusive preoccupation with personal advancement. By insensible degrees we arrived at a point of practically denying that there was any social warrant for, much less artistic potential in, concern for the poor, the suffering, and the helpless.

Others made the effort sporadically, but only the Italian movie makers of the postwar decade consistently continued and persisted in recalling us to our inseparable connection with the underlying peoples who comprise still the great bulk of mankind. Only their films, unreeled to us throughout the years of international concentration on political rigidity and personal aggrandizement, shamed us out of our selfishness – not (with the exception of a number of inevitable failures) through the manipulation of cheap sentimentality or the platitudes of the pulpiteer or the propagandist – but with a remarkably consistent artistry which in retrospect is as humbling and impressive as any other accomplishment in the arts in the modern era.

If any one figure can be taken as representative of the spirit with which the neo-realist movies have been infused, surely it is the orphan-hero of *Miracle in Milan.* This young man, so idiotically and purely innocent as to believe (and to live out his belief) that we must all love one another, becomes the natural leader of his shantytown because he limps when he encounters the cripple, shrinks to a hunch when he encounters the dwarf, and speaks from the side of his mouth when he chats with the man with the deformed jaw. In hurling himself so spontaneously into a sharing of the agonies and even the deformities of his friends and neighbors, this Prince Myshkin of the slums acts for us all, he *acts out* what we feel that we ourselves ought to do in actuality, or at least perform symbolically.

For in these movies, not one of which has been in color or on a wide screen, we enter the black, white, and gray landscapes and lives of the poor – and they in turn enter our emotional landscapes, our inner lives. As I have had occasion to mention elsewhere, the neo-realist cinema is essentially a cinema of poverty; we can suppose that the prefix has been added because a considerable gap in time separates these movies from Chaplin's earlier comic masterpieces about the poor, *The Gold Rush, City Lights,* and *Modern Times.* During that period, even though it was an era of wars and convulsions, the cinematic norm was – and still is – one of pompous inflation, the costume drama, the war epic, the Western saga.

But the fact, grasped by the Italians from bitter first-hand knowledge, is that the anonymous figures who populate their rubble-strewn landscape are universal as poverty is universal and glamour is not. Most people in the world do not live on an infinitude of endlessly mounting sequined MGM staircases, nor do they gaze each evening at a Technicolored sunset, filtered through nodding palm trees. We may on occasion be charmed by the dancers on the sequined staircases, or transported by the lovers fading into the tropical sunset, but these can never make the hair rise on the back of our necks as can the sight of the poor simpleton girl in *La Strada* trudging through the dirty melting snow, past the lonely Esso sign, or of the little boy in *The Bicycle Thief* waiting in the biting rain for his father before another such sign: for this is the landscape not of the tourist but of the poor.

It can be argued that the very best motion pictures of all time have been in the main not those seduced by the sweep of the camera's eye into grandiosity, but rather those which have focused – like Chaplin's and the Italians' – on the lives of the poor and the anonymous. However, it does not at all follow from this that there has been a narrow concentration in Italy on filming wretchedness and misery, or a view of life bounded by the canons of a strict, soulless, humorless realism. Quite the contrary. Even among the films already enumerated, without even a passing glance at the Italian movies (some of them very good and very amusing) that have given us close-up views of such buxom charmers as Gina, Sophia, and Silvana, we encounter a variousness of method, of approach, of styles of seeing life, as broad and many-faceted as that of many other artistic developments of the era which were not so handily labeled.

Indeed even within the framework of one movie we can observe how ironic contrast is gained by permitting the same landscape to be variously interpreted, in accordance with the gradations of sophistication of the viewers. In the case of *La Strada,* for example, we the audience see the world of carnival shows and strange towns, tied together by the bare highways and bleak roads of Italy, as sleazy and poverty-stricken. To the artless peasant girl, who is being initiated into this world, it is wondrously glamorous as well as terrifyingly new. This simultaneous revelation of the pathetic poverty of the scene and of its exotic glamour to the simple girl is in fact one of the uniquely cinematic achievements of this film.

Nor is the neo-realist film – or the comedy of poverty, as I should prefer to think of it – confined to a "realistic" interpretation of theme or character. The films of which we speak have ranged from tragic fable (*La Strada*) to comic fantasy (*Miracle in Milan*). More, they have not focused blindly on the plight of the urban proletariat or the rural peasantry: they have presented to us the tribulations of small boys (in *Shoe Shine* and in *The Bicycle Thief*), of old men (*Umberto D*), of prostitutes (*Nights of Cabiria*), of young men without prospects (*I Vitelloni*).

The bond that unites these films is neither theoretical nor narrowly ideological. To take the case of the last-named movie, it is not the fact (in itself questionable) that *I Vitelloni* could be categorized as neo-realist that makes it singularly affecting. It is rather that the film's artistic statement about the misery of being young and aspiring, but not needed or utilizable in a provincial society, is one which could, one suspects, be as terribly understandable to the educated but unemployable young Indian as to the Italians who are portrayed.

In short, we return to the matter of universality. The love of a lonely man for his dog, of a boy for his hard-pressed father; the need for a woman to be personally wanted, for a man to be socially needed; the absolute necessity for compassion if we are not all to founder in the seas of swinish self-absorption – these have been the simple stuff of artistic accomplishment in the storytellers of all ages, whether in printed words or in moving pictures. They are not and can never be confined within national boundaries or political categories. At our own best, we as Americans have represented these qualities to the rest of the world; in one art form, the cinema, the Swedes and the French and the Japanese (most especially in the neo-realist masterpiece *Ikiru*) have in recent years succeeded in translating them to the screen in a number of notable productions. But it is above all the Italian movie makers who have rediscovered for us the beauty and the pity and the terror in the hearts not of the eccentric or the great or the highly placed, but of the ordinary man; and in so doing they have revivified the perennial artistic paradox that once the ordinary man is so anatomized he becomes no longer ordinary, but Everyman. It is for this, finally, despite shortcomings, failures, and painfully abortive careers so painfully akin to those of our own American artists, that we must pay them honor as dedicated and gifted carriers of the Italian – and the Western – cultural tradition.

Chrysalis Review, Autumn 1961

Footnote: American movie makers attempt sporadically to distill film drama from the unspectacular lives of ordinary people. Most of these movies have been failures of heart, just as (oddly enough) the deaths of most of the great screen lovers have come from failure not of the liver or lights but of the heart – John Garfield, Errol Flynn, Tyrone Power, Clark Gable, Gerard Philippe, Henri Duval . . . The most recent of these attempts, which might be labeled as an American version of neo-realism, is the independently-made *The Savage Eye,* a recounting of the sexual and spiritual starvation of a newly divorced young woman. The theme is surely valid, and could be taken as an American equivalent of the sufferings of Gelsomina in *La Strada;* the setting, Los Angeles, misery capital of the Western world, is as apt for the theme as are the Italian roads for the tale of Gelsomina; and the fact that the movie was made as an "art" film, on weekends, without stars, economic pressures, or big budgets, must have ensured its freedom from the deformations imposed by the profit-takers. Yet the picture is not an honorable failure of a group of aspiring artists who overreached themselves. It is actively vulgar, and for that reason it is ultimately depressing, despite the fact that in the end the heroine presumably learns to "live with herself." The City and its Citizens are seen by the savage eye of the camera as one undifferentiated, unadulterated horror; and while it is carefully explained that this is the view of the disturbed and shocked heroine, we are given no refraction through the gaze of a compassionate heart. In consequence the viewer comes to feel that this lingering on distorted faces and gross bodies, on piteous, hideous ludicrousness, grotesquerie, and horror, must reflect a prior attitude of contempt on the part of the manipulators of the all-seeing eye. What is disturbing about this above all – and the pseudo-poetry of the sound-track commentator, far from eliminating it, only serves to reinforce it – is the implication that the manipulators (and by extension the ticket-buying patrons) are superior to the damned souls who are seen gambling, whoring, gourmandizing, reducing, faith-healing, and writhing in the flames of the American Inferno. But this is a superiority which has not been earned. Therefore at bottom it has nothing in common with the art of men like De Sica, Rossellini, Fellini, Zavattini, who, while they may see people as horrible, weep at them, laugh at them – but never smirk over them.

Three-Penny Opera— Three-Dollar Seats

A visitor to the Theatre de Lys in Greenwich Village can hardly fail to be impressed by the odd contrast between play and audience, by the sight of well-dressed middle-class folk gratefully applauding a bitter denunciation of bourgeois morality. The production of the Bert Brecht-Kurt Weill *Three-Penny Opera* is, it seems to this occasional theatergoer, in every respect admirable – it is pungent, electric, crisply staged theater. It is also profoundly subversive. (I think this latter characterization is true of both the staged Blitzstein translation and the printed Bentley-Vesey version in Eric Bentley's *The Modern Theater, Volume One*.)

One cannot, of course, disentangle and weigh in absolute proportion all the various elements of a popular success. It would be hard enough to separate out the accidental factors (timing, accessibility, publicity, stars) from those more basic to public acceptance (theme, music, staging, and so on). But it is impossible to forget that *The Three-Penny Opera* is a revival; in a sense it is a revival of a revival. First performed in the United States in 1933 during the depth of the depression (when one would indeed have expected it to be a smash hit given enough people with the price of admission), it had crossed the ocean from Berlin, where, with its mixture of jazziness, exoticism, and cynicism, it had been a characteristic theater success of that international headquarters for the disillusionment of the Twenties. And of course Brecht had based his play on

John Gay's *The Beggar's Opera* and the poems of François Villon, both of which have proved their viability in their own right, over the centuries.

Why should such a play, popular in an era seemingly so different from ours, be so rapturously received in the New York of the Fifties? It is worth bearing in mind that in recent years we have had other revivals of comedies and musicals of other eras by authors ranging from Shakespeare to Wilde which have simply failed to attract a substantial public, despite the fact that money and good taste (sometimes even in combination) have been lavished upon their production.

One should be able to conclude fairly from this that at least a portion of the relative popularity of the Brecht play must be attributed to its theme, its mood, its underlying attitude toward society. Of course one cannot assume that everyone who vociferously applauds this play would join the Peachum family in singing, "There's nothing we can do, For the world is rotten through and through!" any more than one can imagine General Eisenhower holding to the anarchism of Eric Hoffer, even though the press reports him so moved by Hoffer's iconoclastic *The True Believer* that he is presenting copies to the members of his official family. Nonetheless we may infer a correlation between the temper of a play, particularly when it is forthrightly and even brutally expressed, and the temper of its audiences, when they are large and enthusiastic.

It is the view of the Brecht play, mordantly if somewhat tinnily set forth, that bourgeois life is a swindle; that the crook, the cheat and the hypocrite are the true men of distinction in a world ruled by crookedness, cheating, and hypocrisy; and that the only man worth admiring is the picaresque hero who earns his pleasures by pimping, theft, and murder, who cheats on his bride and double-crosses his gang, and who sings "The Ballad of Comfort":

> . . . Poverty makes you wise but it's a curse
> And brav'ry brings you fame but it's a chore

And so not to be great's a bloody bore
But being great – my friends – it must be worse –
Here's the solution inescapably:
The life of comfort is the life for me.

But even though Captain MacHeath's sensuality brings him down (his former lady love Jenny tells us in "The Song of Solomon" that "So long as he was rational, And stuck to highway robbery, He was a Great Professional"), and even though he is betrayed by his whores, we are not spared the final irony. A ridiculous messenger enters on horseback bearing the Queen's pardon for Mack the Knife as he stands on the very gallows. What's more, he is raised to the nobility and given a ten-thousand-pound pension. To make sure that there should be no misunderstanding, Peachum steps forward to explain: "Mounted messengers from the Queen come far too seldom, and if you kick a man he kicks you back again. Therefore never be too ready to oppose injustice."

The play then closes with the words:

Do not defend the Right with too much boldness
For Wrong is cold: its death is sure though slow
Remember all the darkness and the coldness
The world's a vale of misery and woe.

It is easy to imagine the impact of *The Three-Penny Opera* on Germans living in a defeated capitalist state, where, under the shadow of a feeble and anemic democracy, there strutted the same old George Grosz caricatures – the profiteers and bemedaled goosesteppers and all their whores and hangers-on – who had brought their country down in the first place.

But what is the magnetic attraction of the drama's viciously ruthless philosophy for well-meaning and liberal-minded playgoers in a country where, and at a time when, so everyone is constantly being assured, poverty has been all but abolished, discrimination is on the way out, and soon work itself will be a thing of the past in this best of all atomic worlds? One can only speculate on the inner state of mind of the New York audiences who fill the little Theatre de Lys night after night to cheer *The Three-Penny Opera,* corrosive as acid as it gnaws its way past the comfortable pleasantries with which theatergoers are usually regaled, the paeans to gray-flannel-suited resignation and suburban garden-tending, or the hymns to up-and-at-'em *South Pacific* liberalism. This play undercuts the platitudes of playwrights and politicians alike. It goes so far underneath that it comes very close to home.

I would submit therefore that no audience which is stirred by *The Three-Penny Opera* can be stirred solely by what it reveals of the mentality of Berliners under the Weimar Republic or Londoners of the eighteenth century. I would submit further that customers who are well-heeled enough to pay three or four dollars for an evening's entertainment and then discover that the very basis of the society in which they have been earning that money is being called into question are undergoing a genuinely cathartic experience. Certainly it is true that many thousands more spend twice as much for an equivalent evening's entertainment on Broadway; but they do not come with the expectation of having the very source of their income undermined, so to speak. They do not wish to have their lives disturbed — and they sure as hell are *not* disturbed by what they are fed on Broadway.

The "cool" young intellectual of today, who, as I am given to understand, prides himself on his aloofness from emotional involvement in matters political and cultural, and who apparently feels that there is an important distinction which must be made between commitment and excitement, may have more in common than he suspects with those who are somewhat older and hence still subject to agitation over public questions, whether of engagement or disengagement. For both have reacted in common to the theatrical representation of the loathsomeness of a commercial society in decay, most particularly of the spineless and soulless hypocrisy of its ruling members. It would seem that this reaction is not confined to the young and prematurely disillusioned, or to the older, who one would have thought had mostly made their peace with the world as it is; but how would *The Three-Penny Opera* be received by union audiences, say, or by Southern farmers, if they were to encounter it at their local drive-in theater in Detroit or Montgomery?

Never fear. This "non-affirmative" play will not find its way to a really mass public. If anything is certain in this constantly surprising world, it is that *Three-Penny Opera* is one musical comedy that will not be translated by Hollywood into a Technicolor Cinemascope production starring Kathryn Grayson as Polly Peachum and Howard Keel as Captain MacHeath. Despite the huzzahs for American national culture now being emitted by those liberal intellectuals who have taken to rallying 'round the flag, there are still things which cannot be said except to the relatively restricted publics of off-Broadway theaters or to the relatively few readers of books. And *The Three-Penny Opera* says a good many of those things.

Let it be accounted cause for optimism that this play has found an audience – not a huge, mass audience, but an audience. It is an audience whose very existence had been called into question, bombarded as we have been with depressing accounts (whether favorable or unfavorable) of the mass taste of the middlebrow public. We may justly hope that it could spontaneously foregather if there were offered to it equally well-mounted native works of the theatrical and literary imagination, works which hesitated no more than this remarkable play to slash through the treacly morality of bourgeois society and to reveal yet one more aspect of that inner truth that is the heart and function of all art worthy of the name.

Anvil and Student Partisan, Winter 1957

Footnote, 1961: The matter becomes more complex when one considers, not a ghostly revival from the Twenties like the Brecht-Weill play, but the new generation of comedians and their relationship with the new audiences. The most mordant and the most directly political of the group, Mort Sahl, still returns to the "hungry i" in San Francisco in the sweater and slacks which were his trademark when he first gained his reputation; presumably his audience is still basically the same — and yet the connection between the two has altered and most importantly the performer's conception of himself has changed. Inevitably. It is one thing to stand up in a smoky cellar and establish a sense of communion with a small band by puncturing the inflated inanities of Eisenhower-Dulles-McCarthy and all the rest of the gasbags of the unlamented Fifties; the small salary paid for delighting the intimates is an honorable symbol of disaffiliation. It is quite another to poke fun at Kennedy and the liberals of the New Frontier to an audience of salaried liberals, of young academics from Berkeley and Palo Alto whose little Triumphs sport Kennedy stickers on the bumpers (to distinguish them from their students with the Nixon and Goldwater stickers), of snug young couples from Sausalito and Belvedere, on whose Danish teak coffee tables repose the latest analyses of Mort Sahl and his bank balance. No matter how hard he fights it, Sahl has become a success — which means in our American terms that his salary must be measured in four and five figures weekly, that he thereby assumes a new identity and enters into a new kind of relationship with his audience, and that willy-nilly he becomes accepted as one of their own by the very masters of mass culture whom he must regard as beneath contempt. The strain tells on his face as he returns to the scene of his early triumphs, but more important, as one observes *his* three-dollar audience queuing up to be "entertained," is the evidence of the increasing unlikelihood of there being any room in our society for the long-term existence of an independent dissenting stance in the popular arts. Worse, the more venomous one's opposition to the master trends in American life, the more certain it becomes that one will be taken up, popularized, imperceptibly assimilated, and finally defanged. It is disconcerting to think that if you attack, say, popular magazines vigorously enough, your chances are good for winding up on the cover of *Time* – you may even become the Man of the Year.

What this boils down to is a rueful admission that the assessment in the article above was probably over-optimistic.

The Cult of Personality in American Letters

Practically all judgments of recent American fiction seem to take as their implicit (and often explicit) benchmark the 1920's. Our postwar novelists are measured against the postwar novelists of the earlier era and found wanting, sometimes because supposedly there are not as many interesting novelists practicing today as there were a quarter of a century ago, sometimes because not one of our current novelists has managed to achieve the supposed universality gained by the giants of the preceding generation.

When we inquire who it was that achieved this universality we are usually referred to our Nobel Prize winners, or more specifically to our male Nobel Prize winners, Ernest Hemingway and William Faulkner. Sometimes a third is added – the gifted and doomed Scott Fitzgerald. These are the ones who are considered to have outlasted Cabell, Hergesheimer, Lewis, Buck, yes, and Caldwell, Steinbeck, and O'Hara too.

I think it could be demonstrated, however, that only one of this trio became, at the crest of his career, not simply internationally renowned, but the incarnation of the European conception of the American as artist. This was Ernest Hemingway, and while it can probably be said that he is still so regarded abroad, it must also be observed that in recent years his reputation has undergone a severe decline in his own country. And so we are left with William Faulkner, whose Nobel Prize address is regularly quoted by those who are now so proud of him as an award-winning

American, but who – we may be permitted to suspect – seldom take the trouble to read the actual novels, and were hardly to be found among his fans during those years when Faulkner was writing his best books and not selling them to any but a handful of admirers.

Obviously extraliterary factors have entered into these evaluations, as they have all too obviously in the case of Scott Fitzgerald, who has become in a way the modern equivalent of the velvet-jacketed tubercular attic artist of nineteenth-century bohemia. For the sake of clarity let me add that I am not attempting to belittle the product of these men (since my teens Fitzgerald has been one of my personal literary heroes, and as for Faulkner I do not see how it can reasonably be denied that he is our greatest living writer) but rather to insist that nowadays it is all too often not the novel which is placed in time, but the novelist.

We are suffering from what might be called the cult of personality in American letters. No doubt it will immediately be objected that this is mere obfuscation, confusing popular acclaim of middlebrow spokesmen (who – as Louella Parsons serves the movie-going public – serve their public with news of Hemingway's chest measurements and William Faulkner's alcoholic propensities) with genuinely serious appraisals of established literary critics. Let us anticipate this objection by examining some of the current enthusiasms of our literary critics, and contrasting them with several omissions.

If there are any two American writers of the current generation who have been more written about in recent years than any others, they are surely J. D. Salinger and Norman Mailer. It seems to me not at all irrelevant that the first of these has so sedulously avoided publicity that he has inevitably aroused the liveliest curiosity about himself; and that the second has frankly and unremittingly sought to gain what the metaphysicians of advertising would define as maximum exposure to his reader-potential.

Salinger, the Greta Garbo of American letters, is now in his early forties and is the author of one novel, *Catcher in the Rye,* and two books of short stories, mostly dealing with the travails of the Glass family. That is all we are supposed to know, and in all conscience it should be enough. Unquestionably he is a clever and knowledgeable writer about a somewhat restricted segment of American society, with an absolutely first-rate ear for certain mannerisms of American speech, particularly those peculiar to the young. Once this has been said, we find ourselves shifting, so to speak, from one foot to the next. And yet such has been the outpouring of articles, essays, and speculations on J. D. Salinger that the Salinger bibliography might lead one unfamiliar with his work to think that it consisted, not of one bittersweet novel and some short stories, but of an *oeuvre* comparable to William Faulkner's twenty-odd books.

What is more, this outpouring has come not so much from the middlebrows as it has from the groves of academe, and from those not accustomed to trifling with merely popular writers – although surely Salinger is popular with the younger set. Can there be a college literary magazine in the land which has not had its Salinger piece? By now it has become as obligatory as the Pound exegesis or the James explication. Why?

For one thing, these critics seem much impressed with Salinger's increasing popularity abroad as a spokesman – he begins to approach the universal acceptance of Hemingway, which in itself is awesome. Yet we have not been subjected so far to a spate of studies of Dashiell Hammett simply because he is much admired in France, or of Jack London simply because he is adored in Russia. We must be led to believe therefore that other considerations are involved. In addition to the fact of his popularity abroad, these critics are apparently much moved by Salinger's manifest and continuing appeal to youth, and by the evidence in his work that he is attempting to compose a Christian parable.

Both of these factors, the touching appeal of his work to the young and his painfully self-conscious effort to be

Deep, are of course closely interrelated. But those of us who can, if we are honest, recall all too easily our own adolescent infatuation with Thomas Wolfe because he seemed to be speaking directly to us, and speaking too of the really profound things in life must, I am afraid, be reduced in our maturity to stammering embarrassment for the author and for his apologists when we are asked in all seriousness to consider Salinger, like Wolfe, as a profoundly reflective philosophical novelist. No, it seems more likely that there exists in the minds of those who make such claims a connection between Salinger's supposed profundity and his tantalizing physical inaccessibility. The legend of mysterious private suffering cohabiting with a singularly Christian literary morality is self-generating and self-perpetuating; it is also conducive to excited appraisals of a writer's importance based finally on what must be regarded as extraliterary considerations.

Salinger's opposite number, Norman Mailer, has been so unabashed at exposing his private problems, both literary and psychological, and so adept at gaining attention for this exposure, that we need not dwell on the details of his biography further than to note that he is some years Salinger's junior, and that he is the author of three novels, some briefer pieces, and the recent omnium-gatherum *Advertisements for Myself*. It is this last which has given Mailer his breakthrough from the ordinary book buyers to the highbrow critics.

For months now it has been virtually impossible to pick up a magazine – *The Reporter, The Nation, Commentary, Partisan Review,* on and on through the spectrum – without coming upon an assessment of Norman Mailer. We have had Norman Mailer on Mailer, Norman Podhoretz on Mailer, Alfred Kazin on Mailer, Irving Howe on Mailer, F. W. Dupee on Mailer, Leslie Fiedler on Mailer, Gore Vidal on Mailer, Robert Gorham Davis on Mailer, Granville Hicks on Mailer, and certainly not least, Seymour Krim on Mailer in that organ of the itinerant poets, the *Evergreen Review*. The last-named is noteworthy in that it is in the nature of a reassurance to Norman that, though he may be neglected or misread by the squares, he is cherished by those who dig him the most.

This is a strange kind of neglect! Reeling under this flood of assessments (and there are of course many more than those itemized), one would think that Mailer had come forth, at the very least, with a big new novel. What he has come forth with instead, however, is an assertion that he will one day come forth with a big new novel . . . and an extended apology for the delay.

I do not mean to belittle Mailer. If any contemporary novelist has the audacity, the courage, the inventiveness, and the bite to do something really new, it is Norman Mailer, whom I have read with respect ever since he first appeared in print. But, while this has also been acknowledged by a number of his many critics, one gains the impression that this is not why they are impelled to write about him. It is rather that they are stunned by his nerve. Uninspired by his novels — none of which, it seems to be generally conceded, has been successful on its own terms, or as a wholly realized work of art — they are overwhelmed by his *personality,* and they are driven through a series of logical gyrations to vote for him as the most likely successor to Ernest Hemingway — which is precisely what Mailer, by his own confession, has been dying to be told.

In the course of these odd intellectual exercises, some strange things get said. Several of the critics are so taken with Mailer's intensity and honesty in arguing for himself that they are persuaded that there must be more to his novels than first met the eye — as though they cannot decide for themselves, without the author's help, just what they do think — not of him or his intentions, but of his lonely, naked, published work. Others, impressed (as anyone must be) by Mailer's candor, are driven to recall that earlier searing confession, *The Crackup,* in which Scott Fitzgerald laid bare his inmost agonies and the bitter frustration of his aspirations. A strange analogy! One would think that *The Crackup* had been written by the clever young man who had turned out two glib novels, *This Side of Paradise* and *The Beautiful and Damned,* and a collection of bright and catchy short stories, rather than the mature and exhausted artist who had gone beyond that early work to complete his greatest novels. Surely it will be time enough for such comparisons when Mailer has given us his *Gatsby* and his *Tender Is the Night.*

Norman Podhoretz, in his eagerness to have his say too, has even been driven to *post hoc* justification of Mailer's naïveté in becoming associated first with the Henry Wallace presidential campaign and then with a peculiarly doctrinaire variant of Marxism: this belated infatuation with causes long since cast aside by other intellectuals, explains Podhoretz, is proof of Norman Mailer's refusal to be guided by the experience of others and of his insistence on finding things out for himself – as though this argument could not be adduced to excuse, not mere eccentricity, but any kind of extreme antisocial behavior on the part of a literary figure. Apparently anything will do, even if it is manifestly unfair to Mailer and to what he himself thinks of himself, in this haste to create a new myth and to enshrine a new personality in the pantheon of synthetic American literary giants.

This massive concentration on a handful of writers (for reasons all too often nonliterary), coupled with a massive exclusion of most other writers from consideration, can result in a ludicrously distorted picture of the American literary situation. Recently a leading editor observed at a literary symposium that the past decade's fiction had been "dominated by adolescents." Presumably what he meant was that the beats had made the most noise and had therefore drowned out such writers as Baldwin, Bellow, Malamud, Ellison, Bourjaily, Morris, and other serious novelists who have come to maturity during the Fifties. But who did "dominate" the fiction of the decade? If it was the beats, as the editor implied, and not the really serious creative people, then we may be justified in asserting that the editors and critics are, as Norman Mailer has shrewdly observed of American audiences in general, "incapable of confronting a book unless it is successful."

Before adducing the names of some writers whose books have been neglected, as I have instanced the names of some who have been written of so widely, it should be emphasized that I am not directing my primary objection to the amount of attention that J. D. Salinger and Norman Mailer have been receiving. I have, in fact, learned a good deal from some of these articles – as indeed I would hope that Salinger and Mailer have themselves. What I *am* objecting to, and as strenuously as I know how, is the imbalance on the part of the magazines which have printed them and the critics who have written them. Some of these magazines have been protesting that they lack space to include a regular examination of all current fiction – although they seem always to have space for the current sensation; some of their editors – and some of these critics – have been heard to murmur that there is nothing much worth while coming out anyway in serious fiction, perhaps because we are in a period (how critics love to generalize about periods!) that is simply not grateful to the creation of important novels. In consequence they do not trouble to acquaint the reading public with what is going on.

I offer as evidence two books which were published in the last two seasons. One was a novel, the other a book of stories. The novel was *Crazy in Berlin,* by Thomas Berger; the story collection was *The Little Disturbances of Man,* by Grace Paley. Each book was an ornament to its publisher and to the season in which it appeared. Both books were brilliant, original, insightful, and exciting – not, to be sure, to consumers of best-sellers, but surely to those in search of the new and the stimulating. Both books were utterly ignored. We need not call the roll of the magazines already mentioned, other than to note that the only one to review either of these books was *Commentary* (which ran a notice of Mrs. Paley's book some six or eight months after publication). But where were the Messrs. Podhoretz, Kazin, Howe, Dupee, Vidal, Krim, etc., etc.? (I specifically exempt

Granville Hicks, the only literary journalist aside from those affiliated with daily newspapers who has attempted week in and week out to fulfill his obligations with conscientiousness and dignity.) One could hardly expect all of them to have reviewed, or even been aware of, both of these books. But surely *one* critic, among a group so professedly concerned with American fiction, might have reviewed *one* of these books.

The truth, however, is that neither of these two authors is a "personality." They are simply writers. They were not born with, nor did they acquire, funny first names. They are not in their teens. They are not addicted to drugs or exhibitionism. They are not sexual inverts. They do not write about how hard it is to write, or how hard it is to become a Great Writer. (We might note, parenthetically, how startled, shocked, thrilled, the critics have been at Norman Mailer's perfectly straightforward assertion that he is trying to become a great writer – as if every line that every serious novelist writes were not instinct with this very desire to become great.) There are other good young writers being neglected, but for now these two will do, a novelist and a short-story writer, neither of them professors of writing or adepts at grantsmanship or members of literary sets. Because these writers simply mind their business, which is writing, they are ignored. What is more, they are insulted – or I should think they would be – by having to read time and again that nothing worth while is happening in American fiction.

We have here a situation in which it is possible for very good writers to be soured and warped through no fault of their own. It is all very well to say comfortably, In time they will find their place, in time they will make their name, in time they will be known to us all. But there is also the meantime. What if, heaven forbid, Berger and Paley, Mailer and Salinger, were all to die tomorrow? Would it be easy for the reader of tomorrow to make a just estimation of their relative merits? Could he readily discover for himself, uninfluenced by the cult of personality which has set off an avalanche of publicity for one group, and consigned the other to oblivion, that the audacity and intensity of a Thomas Berger, the wit and virtuosity of a Grace Paley, represented something as new and exciting in American fiction as the highly touted work of those public personalities, the O.K. writers?

It takes a very strong spirit indeed, a dedicated and courageous one, to turn one's back on the entire matter, to ignore being ignored. We need not look far to see the effects of the star system in American letters on those desperate for recognition. There is more than one genuinely talented writer, like Herbert Gold, who, in his anxiety to be regarded as a personality, writes obsessively about the accidents of his autobiography, and defaces a lively style with adolescent puns and verbal cutenesses in an effort to ensure that he will be heard above the others.

This, it may be objected, is precisely what separates the sheep from the goats. True. But do we really need to make it so hard on the sheep?

The fault does not lie alone with the critics: Last spring there was published a first novel, *The Coming of Fabrizze*, which for all its weaknesses (would the critics who continually beat contemporary writers with the greatness of the Twenties seriously defend the literary merits of the first books of Hemingway, Faulkner, or Fitzgerald?) was obviously the work of a sweetly gifted young storyteller. When I wrote as much to the publisher, he replied that this manuscript had been making the rounds of other publishers unsuccessfully for eight years. I do not know the author, Raymond de Capite, so I cannot be sure what went on in his mind during those eight years, but I can guess. I can guess, and I do not thereupon feel my heart warming to those publishers who make much of their cultural dedication and their nineteenth-century ethics, when in actuality they are all too often aping the behavior of the buccaneers of the mass media in everything but the ability to catch the eye of the mass public.

It should not be thought that this is a nostalgic plea for

a return to a past in which novelists were all seriously considered, earnestly discussed, and warmly appreciated during their lifetimes. Such a past never existed. But surely we have the responsibility to plead for a better future. I speak now not as an occasional critic, but as a novelist concerned about his fellow writers as well as his fellow readers, when I propose that the critics and the publishers who regard themselves by definition as the caretakers of our culture, but function in reality as drumbeaters for an arbitrarily limited galaxy of stars and hence as vulgar hucksters for the cult of personality, be required to assume what should be their true responsibility: to make more accessible and more profoundly revealing to us all, those writers who do not "look for adventures," in the words of Manès Sperber, "but for an encounter with consciousness; not for the dream, but for the awakening."

Saturday Review, October 1, 1960

The Image in the Mirror

> May fiction not find a second wind, or a fiftieth, in the very portrayal of that collapse? Till the world is an unpeopled void there will be an image in the mirror.
> — *Henry James, The Future of the Novel*

The pages that follow are an appeal to the intelligent reader, whoever he may be, to put aside the prejudices about the American novel that he has been accumulating over the years, fortified, perhaps even inspired, by the critical pronouncements of his favorite journals. What I propose he accept in their place is at least a willingness to grant the hospitality of his hearth to the American novelist, with all his reputed eccentricity, tediousness, feebleness, and senility; and if what I am going to say has any validity, he will hopefully find not only that American literary productivity is considerably less abysmal than he has been led to believe, but also that the contemporary novelist still has the power to speak to him, to touch his heart, to open for him, even in his own house, doors the keys to which he thought had been lost and which could not be forced by other locksmiths. In his turn he may discover that if all too many current novels' insights seem devoid of centrality or indeed of any significant relationship to his own inner life, this may not be due unqualifiedly to the willfulness of the novelist, but in some measure to the situation of that novelist, to the critical hostility which greets not the end product alone, but even the presumptuous act of creation, and finally to the indifference of the general public, himself included, toward the problems of the novelist.

It is not without significance that some of the severest

fire with which the novelist has been raked comes from just those quarters where one would expect to find, if not a last-ditch defense of the artist, certainly a receptivity to his work in a time of more than ordinary confusion and difficulty. Naturally both the novelist and the intelligent reader whom he presumes to be waiting somewhere as his putative audience are taken aback by this phenomenon: the novelist can only begin to wonder where his friends are and whether they really exist, the reader to wonder whether he is not a fool for caring at all about what is in the new books that are still (despite everything) being published, when it would be so much less demanding to turn to the consolations of the popular entertainments. Since it is my contention that the current attack on the American novel is based on false premises and faulty reasoning, I shall have to devote more space in the following paragraphs to a consideration of its expression in certain periodicals than might otherwise be considered profitable.

In the summer 1956 number of *Partisan Review,* Mr. Steven Marcus concludes an appreciation of Evelyn Waugh with some observations on "why writers in America have shown so little capacity for development. It is a truism of our culture that the majority of serious American novelists are 'one book' writers; they either write one large good book and then almost nothing else, or spend their careers writing the same book over and over again. . . . What we sense in the typical American 'giants' who fail is an enormous talent that is dying unexpressed, a latent richness that can find no means of articulating itself. We regularly produce novelists who seem just on the point of writing really first-class works, while what we get from them are large, unwieldy failures, evidences of an inability to harness or express themselves with any kind of grace or economy. . . . Until the conventions of the written language have become more accessible to our daily speech, America will continue to present us with writers who, though of the highest talents and intentions, are largely brilliant and inspired amateurs . . ."

Let us pass over the question of why an essay in praise of the virtues of an admittedly minor English novelist should conclude with two pages devoted to minimizing the virtues of admittedly major American novelists. Let us pass over Mr. Marcus's apparent unawareness that the problem of lifelong fecundity versus repetitiveness or early silence — crudely, Titian versus Rimbaud — cannot be explained by contrasting European fertility and American sterility. It is an unsolved and perhaps insoluble problem in the relation of artistic productivity to psychic energy, still puzzling critics, historians, and psychiatrists. Let us even pass without comment the question of taste involved in mentioning by name such writers as William Faulkner, Mary McCarthy, Thomas Wolfe, Robert Penn Warren, and Saul Bellow just prior to the above-quoted lines with no attempt to document the attack or to remove the implication that at least some of them are "one-book" writers, "failures," or "amateurs." Let us note rather that as we turn the pages of the magazine we come immediately upon another assault on the novelist, this time in what purports to be a review of current fiction by Leslie Fiedler, which opens like a direct extension of Mr. Marcus's closing remarks, and which I should like therefore to examine in some detail.

"To read a group of novels is these days a depressing experience. . . . after the fourth or fifth, I find myself beginning to think about 'The Novel,' and I feel a desperate desire to sneak out to a movie." In its fashionableness this complaint is characteristic of a certain group now busily proclaiming to all who will listen its disaffection and disappointment with the modern novel. Mr. Fiedler is depressed by the novel because (1) it is "respectable" and "predictable"; (2) "the consumption of novels has become a dull public observance like going to church"; (3) "the *avant-garde* novel has become a tradition"; (4) "the novel of the last twenty years remains largely sterile" and "there has been no general sense of a new breakthrough";

(5) "the First Novel has become so rigid and conventional in form that it seems an icon."

By his own testimony, Mr. Fiedler belongs to what Henry James called "the group of the formerly subject, but now estranged, the deceived and bored, those for whom the whole movement too decidedly fails to live up to its possibilities. There are people," James went on to add, "who have loved the novel, but actually find themselves drowned in its verbiage, and for whom, even in some of its approved manifestations, it has become a terror they exert every ingenuity, every hypocrisy, to evade."

If James could render such judgment at the turn of the century, what would he say today, after the great novelists of the fifty years succeeding him have told us at least as much about ourselves and our world as any comparable international body of philosophers or social scientists? Those who turn from the novel for Mr. Fiedler's reasons are exerting more than hypocrisy, they are actuated by precisely that "deep-seated contempt for literature" with which Granville Hicks has sternly but, I believe, justly charged Anthony West, book reviewer for the *New Yorker*.

Mr. Fiedler assures us that he admires the achievements of the twentieth-century masters, that indeed what he is objecting to is that "our novelists in general fight the old fights" and that the contemporary first novel is dismaying "by its bondage to the accidents of biography, its exploitation of the tenderness the young feel toward themselves, its dissolution of form into feeling." But this sighing over a falling-off is nothing more than the stock response of those who always oppose the trivia of the present to the glories of the past, those who assure us that they were, like the hypocrites of James's day, formerly subject, but are now estranged.

The crude conception of culture as consisting simply of a chain of triumphant *avant-garde* masterworks, and the consequent conception of the critic's task implicit in Mr. Fiedler's remarks, rings strangely in the columns of a literary review that has earned a reputation both for seriousness and literary hospitality. For Mr. Fiedler what lies below the peaks is fit only to be ridiculed because the old fights are still being fought, or haughtily ignored: "I have decided not even to discuss any of the current first novels."

It seems never to have occurred to him that, as André Gide put it, "if there were no names in the history of art except those belonging to the creators of new forms there would be no culture. The very word implies a continuity, and therefore it calls for disciples, imitators and followers to make a living chain; in other words, a tradition."

If Gide's words are true, does it not follow that one of the primary responsibilities of the critical intelligence should be the conscientious examination of the living chain? This entails not simply a bibliographical listing of the new novels, but a consideration without superciliousness or patronizing of what is being done that is most interesting by the disciples, imitators, and followers – if it is true that no one else is producing anything worthy of note. It would seem an elementary rule of critical conduct that one not make unfulfillable claims on what one examines; the critic who approaches the work of others with venom and envy rather than with love and devotion (not necessarily for the work under discussion, but for the culture of which it is a tiny link) is not only going to be unable to infect us with the enthusiasm which should arise from the discovery of a moving artistic achievement, he is going to be unable to tell us precisely why a new work is overvalued or valueless, because inevitably he will confuse his own passion for fashion with a historical sense of the continuity of culture.

Harold Rosenberg put the matter succinctly enough when he wrote (in *Art News,* February 1956), "Admiring inherited masterpieces in order to saddle contemporaries with the responsibility to equal them is a trick of totalitarians and busybodies." The statement is applicable to book reviewers, even though Mr. Rosenberg was writing about the situation in painting, and was concerned with the attacks on contemporary painting by vulgarians in

Congress and in other seats of power and influence, and even though the novelist, unlike the painter, has not been the object of Congressional attack, nor has the exportation of his work been questioned by Presidents or State Department officials or envious fellow craftsmen working in an earlier, more conservative tradition.

Perhaps it would have been simpler if the attack on the novelist *had* come primarily from such quarters rather than from within the ranks of his "friends," for then the novelist would at least have felt that he could call upon his allies to support him in a battle for cultural freedom — instead of discovering that the bricks heaved at his head come from those who continue to protest that they love him most. Nevertheless it remains his responsibility to identify and dissociate himself from the totalitarians and busybodies who would prescribe for him, whether their voices are raised in the *Congressional Record,* the *New Yorker,* the *New York Times Book Review,* or the quarterlies.

But when we examine the stylish attitude toward fiction expressed in Mr. Fiedler's essay, we cannot merely reject his strange conception of the critic's function. I would submit also that what he has to say specifically about the recent first novel in America is quite simply not so.

We have heard before the charge that our writers were obsessed in their first novels with formless, overemotional, sentimentalized autobiographical material, and if we look back at the period when many young writers, reacting against the proletarian formula, embraced the mood of Thomas Wolfe, we should have to agree that there was a time when there was a basis for such a charge. But for a supposedly serious critic to make such a statement in 1956 betrays either ignorance or the kind of malice with which noisy ignoramuses attack abstract art by characterizing it as indistinguishable from children's and lunatics' scrawls.

I have myself done considerable reviewing of fiction, and can recall without difficulty a substantial group of first novels of the past few years which were in no way sentimental portraits of the artists as young men. In no particular order, I should list Herbert Gold's *Birth of a Hero,* about a middle-aged Cleveland businessman; William Styron's *Lie Down in Darkness,* chronicle of a Southern family; A. M. Klein's *The Second Scroll,* allegorical drama of Jewish exile and fulfillment; Stephen Becker's *The Season of the Stranger,* a picture of China in transition; Ernst Pawel's *The Island in Time,* a study of Jews in an Italian D.P. camp; Bernard Malamud's *The Natural,* mythical saga of a baseball hero; James Baldwin's *Go Tell It on the Mountain,* the story of a Negro family seen through a poet's eyes; William Gaddis's *The Recognitions,* a symbolic panorama of counterfeiting in the worlds of art, money, and religion.

And those are only books which I myself have reviewed for various publications. Readers who follow new fiction with any degree of attentiveness can of course add to the list at some length.

No one would claim that these first novels are all extraordinary (although certainly two or three of them are just that), that they are all of equal merit, or that they are sure to be read fifty years from now. What can be said is that for one reason or another they stand out from the ordinary, and that in not one case do they correspond in intention or execution to the absurd conception of the American first novel as an adolescent portrait of adolescence. They move in space from the Orient to the Middle East, in characterization from the Chinese peasant to the American businessman to the Israeli pioneer, in style from neo-realistic to fanciful to frankly experimental, in tone and temper from passionately affirmative to unyieldingly pessimistic. Their very existence in print casts an interesting light on Mr. Fiedler's solemn warning that "if one is looking for even the hint of something new, he must avoid the First Novel."

Staring at himself through Mr. Marcus's spectacles, the novelist sees himself as the endless experimenter, hopelessly attempting to achieve compression, grace, and facility in a language that is not really his; turning to squint through Mr. Fiedler's bifocals, he sees himself alternatively as a traditional teller of dull tales, or as a second-rater feebly imitating the innovations of his predecessors.

(While with one hand Mr. Fiedler deplores the undocumented prevalence in the first novel of gratuitous autobiographical data, with the other he submits to the readers of *Perspectives USA* his own autobiography. This is in an article *about Partisan Review,* and the *curriculum vitae* is presented as the credentials of a more or less typical *Partisan Review* reader and/or contributor. He tells us that he is Jewish, an ex-Trotskyite, a professor of English, and the father of six children. He does not tell us that he is writing – although the inference seems likely – a novel – not, Heaven forbid, a first novel, but a novel nevertheless; nor does he tell us how he would react if and when his own book were published and went unnoticed in *Partisan Review* because its book reviewer took nose between thumb and forefinger at the very sight of a pile of new novels and hurried out instead to his neighborhood movie house.)

What I have said thus far has been intended primarily not as an attack on Leslie Fiedler, but rather as a criticism of the mood of which I think he is not unrepresentative and as an examination of the kind of writing about novels that is currently all too common. Of course, it is always tempting to think that it was not ever thus, that there was a time when book reviewing and literary criticism stood in a somewhat closer relationship, just as book reviewers think back nostalgically on a nonexistent time when much of what was published was new and exciting and little of what was published was dull and worthless.

But if Henry James conceded in 1900 that fiction "has been vulgarized, like all other kinds of literature, like everything else today, and it has proved more than some kinds accessible to vulgarization," if he asserted that "the high prosperity of fiction has marched very directly with another 'sign of the times,' the demoralization, the vulgarization of literature in general, the increasing familiarity of all such methods of communication, the making itself supremely felt, as it were, of the presence of the ladies and children — by whom I mean, in other words, the reader irreflective and uncritical," he also wrote about criticism: "The review is in nine cases out of ten an effort of intelligence as undeveloped as the ineptitude over which it fumbles. . . ."

This is not merely to say that the more things change the more they remain the same, but to indicate that present problems are not always unique but can often be seen as grotesquely magnified versions of older problems. Fifty years and fifty million tons of paper pulp after James's comment, concurrently with the remarkable discovery of a new public for good novels in cheap reprint editions, there *is* a certain weariness with the novel among the formerly subject, now estranged, and if the disillusioned are not all turning to the movies (the disconsolate captains of Hollywood surely wish that it were so), it may be that they are turning to television, inspirational texts or personal gossip for the values and satisfactions formerly obtained, supposedly, from the novel. We do know that in recent years, even while new thousands have been eagerly buying everything from Faulkner to Spillane in paper covers, the published total of hard-cover fiction titles has been diminishing; we do know that the sales of these titles, even while paperback fiction proliferates, have hardly risen in proportion to the zooming population curves.

Why? Has the writer really failed the reader?

I do not think so. Since the turn of the century mankind has been subjected to a series of cataclysmic shocks unparalleled since the great plagues. It has been tricked and trampled by totalitarian tyrants. It has been dragged into a series of catastrophic wars which have dwarfed in their destructiveness and annihilation the combined effects of all previous military adventures, and which have culminated in the planned and methodical murder of some six million human beings. Obviously the novelist has now to deal with the human heart pushed to such extremities as would have been beyond the most horrid imaginings of a Jane Austen or an Anthony Trollope, or even a Henry James. Can we honestly charge that the novelist has funked his obligation, or that he has utterly failed in its execution? It seems to me that in comparison with what the poet and the playwright have managed to say about the twentieth-century world, the novelist comes off very well.

I must confess that I am baffled by V. S. Pritchett's assertion that novelists "have not observed and defined a characteristic man of these years." If he means a characteristic Nazi, one might perhaps agree. But who has told us more about the characteristic Italian peasant, the characteristic Spanish peasant, the characteristic Russian Communist, the characteristic American expatriate, than Ignazio Silone, Ralph Bates, Victor Serge, Ernest Hemingway? Can we not say that we have learned as much of what we know of twentieth-century man from the novelist as from any other single source, historic or scientific? And if we have suddenly stopped learning about post-Hiroshima, post-Dachau man, may it not be for reasons other than a sudden inexplicable failure of the novelist to come to terms with his world?

Presumably Mr. Pritchett is referring mainly to British and American novelists of the postwar years. Without involving ourselves in the *cis*atlantic literary scene, we may point out that novelists like Wright Morris have been doing as much to present us with a gallery of characteristic Americans as have any other creative artists on the American landscape. Without claiming that Wright Morris is a supremely gifted innovator, we can say that he has a unique vision of American life and of the American character which is in the nature of a pleasurable revelation. If he goes virtually unread in the United States today, after having published ten or eleven books, this can hardly be laid solely to his own inadequacies, but must be a function of (a) the attitude of the reading public, (b) the failure of the critic in an age of criticism, and (c) the topsy-turvy situation in the publishing business.

A public which ignores a novelist like Wright Morris in favor of its drive-ins or its television screens is hardly in a position to protest that its writers are giving it nothing nourishing to feed on. We are not yet faced with a situation like that which prevailed in Russia under Stalin, wherein all writers but the foulest sycophants were silenced, wherein those capable writers who remained at large had to devote themselves to translating the classics, wherein the public turned in disgust from the trash authorized by the regime to the great writers of the past. The American public is not turning from officially sponsored "affirmative" propaganda to the great voices of the nineteenth century; it is turning from — or passing by — the Wright Morrises in favor of the Paddy Chayefskys.

The reading public, much of it "new" and consequently self-conscious, is being ill-served by even the most "advanced" critics. (I have no intention here of discussing the New Critics, who are often either determinedly soporific or unintentionally comical, and who in any case rarely stoop — with honorable exceptions — to the textual examination of current fiction.) We know that the readers of the nineteenth century were mostly leisure-class ladies, many of them producers as well as consumers of fiction. We know that these ladies are still the backbone of the book clubs and the circulating libraries; in short, that they are still the principal steady buyers of novels, although they are being joined each year by increasing thousands of young college graduates of both sexes anxious to keep up with what is new and thus be considered in some sense as intellectuals (these are apparently the big new market for paper-cover novels, about which I shall have something to say a little later).

The new novel-reading public grows daily more sophisticated. Yet this is not always to the good, for since like most new audiences it is unsure of its developing tastes, it tends to turn for guidance to those book reviewers who express their supposed sophistication, like the *New Yorker's* stable of reviewers, by parading their own erudition and unintentionally revealing the depth of their own contempt for the novel and for what it sets out to do. The review of current fiction which I am afraid I have already treated at unpardonable length concludes, after some highly unflattering remarks about John Hersey and Nelson Algren, with a favorable notice of a new novel by Iris Murdoch, young English writer. The tone of the favorable comment is so guarded and *dispirited* in contrast to the vigor with which Hersey and Algren are demolished that one may legitimately doubt whether a single reader will remember the name of Miss Murdoch's novel – much less be set aflame to read it or – horror of horrors – to buy it.

Those few critics who, like Alfred Kazin and Granville Hicks, are secure enough in their own taste to be able to praise a *new* book (the woods are full of critics who know how to appreciate *old* books, particularly when the authors are dead and incapable of disrupting considered judgments by bringing out something else) without communicating a feeling of acute embarrassment and unease are unfortunately rare indeed. As an example I would point to Mr. Kazin's brief but highly laudatory review in the *New Republic* of J. F. Powers's collected stories: I mention this particular review precisely because, in addition to the fact that I am not always an admirer of this critic's manner, I do not share his enthusiasm for the work of Mr. Powers. Nevertheless, Mr. Kazin's intensity of feeling and his generous warmth moved me to re-examine my own response to the Powers stories; had I not already read them, the review would certainly have impelled me to do so. In short, Mr. Kazin was here exercising one of the basic functions of the critic of fiction, one currently ignored when it is not scorned.

"When a literary journalist comes upon a good novel," Granville Hicks commented recently in reviewing Adele Wiseman's *The Sacrifice* for the *New Leader*, "his first obligation is to say so. Afterward he can try to explain why it is good and, if he sees fit, why it is not so good as it conceivably might be. These are important matters, but they are not so important as that an act of creation has taken place."

If the book reviewers for such magazines as the *New Yorker* and the *Partisan Review* think it vulgar to betray enthusiasm even for those few novels of which they approve, can we expect their readers to step out in advance of them? Those readers are aware that *Marjorie Morningstar*, for example, does not advance their understanding of themselves or their contemporaries – but instead of moving from Mr. Herman Wouk to other novelists who are digging deeper and coming up with purer ore, they dismiss the medium as moribund or obsolete, fortified by the obiter dicta of the reviewers. Can it be that this audience's very desires are ambiguous, that even while it eagerly absorbs the more easily assimilable products of our culture, as purveyed by slick-paper weeklies and book clubs, that major portion of it which is mass-oriented nervously rejects without examination those more searching statements of the individual mind, because it senses that the best-written and least-sold novels of recent years would raise questions of identity and purpose upon which it is unprepared and unwilling to reflect in the fat years of the Fifties?

In any case, we can observe the spectacle of more than one very young man "going into" literary criticism as years ago they would have gone into medicine or law. Seeking quick access to the attention of the new audience, they direct all of their newly acquired vocabulary of invective and derision at those novels whose merits they are, if not blind to, firmly determined to ignore. They have learned that critical names are made not by praise, not even by judicious appreciation, but more commonly by hatchet jobs on the work of their betters.

"In a world in which criticism is acute and mature," wrote Henry James, ". . . talent will find itself trained, in order successfully to assert itself, to many more kinds of precautionary expertness than in a society in which the art I have named holds an inferior place or makes a sorry figure. A community addicted to reflection and fond of ideas will try experiments with the 'story' that will be left untried in a community mainly devoted to traveling and shooting, to pushing trade and playing football." One is tempted to add that talent will not find itself trained, nor public taste elevated, by careerists who treat literary criticism as another means of pushing trade.

As I have indicated, I do not think that the novelist's external problems end with an uncultivated and unreceptive public and a body of venomous or disappointed men serving as his critics. There is also the situation in the publishing world, so ludicrously stacked against the writer that one may marvel that there are still young men and women with the temerity to write and submit first novels. The publisher tells us that he *must* charge four and five dollars for a novel because of his economic position, that the novel today must sell from five to ten thousand copies if it is to show any profit at all, and that it is becoming increasingly more difficult to publish a novel with a predictably smaller market. But he does not tell us where there is to be found a steady market of ten thousand Americans who will spend four or five dollars at frequent intervals for the best fiction he can find to publish.

The position of the New York publisher is becoming more and more like that of the Broadway producer. He is gambling on smash hits, and he can less and less afford to take chances on a newcomer whose work is merely promising, or is more than promising but less than commercial. What is more, in many cases he is frightfully sorry, but he can no longer afford the luxury of carrying on his list a writer who — no matter how highly regarded he may be by critics, editors, and a small but faithful body of readers — does not make money for the firm. He can still publish as a gamble or an investment a prestige book by a promising new writer; but that new writer's next book had better give proof that it shows some understanding of the requirements of the larger literary market, or in all likelihood it will be politely but firmly rejected.

The effect on the American playwright of this unrealistic cost-price situation is already painfully apparent. Except for one or two Big Names, who are still almost as much box-office draws as the Hollywood stars regularly co-opted to help insure Broadway success for their new shows, the American playwright is now little more than a minor member of a collective, endeavoring to manufacture a product salable to the largest possible public; his function may be compared to that of the speech writer or idea man on the team of the campaigning politician. By the time directors, producers, and play doctors have finished processing his work, he is only a name in small print on the advance advertising, to be dropped and all but forgotten during the run of the play.

This can hardly be predicted as the inevitable fate of the novelist. But surely the pressure on him to create a marketable product acceptable to those on whom the publisher is increasingly dependent, the book-club and reprint firms, if not the Hollywood producers, is bound to increase. Just as the young dramatist nowadays bends himself to the task of pleasing not himself but the grimly harried real-estate manipulators who may award him an option, so the apprentice novelist, faced with the choice of publication or oblivion, may very well tend to adapt and adjust himself by gradual stages to the needs of his publisher and to what that publisher assures him are the tastes of the waiting public. After all, is he not currently assured from all sides that commercial success and literary achievement are no longer mutually exclusive, but positively complementary in this "affirmative" age?

The publisher who perceives and perhaps fosters the emerging parallel between his speculative endeavors and those of the Broadway producer may not stop to think that the unrealistic economic state of the theater, unlike that of the publishing world, is underpinned by one of the peculiarities of our tax structure. The double factors of the expense account and the entertainment allowance actually represent a concealed federal subsidy of the preposterous Broadway ticket system in which fifty or seventy-five dollars is gladly paid for a ticket to a hit musical show because "nobody" is actually paying such a ridiculous price out of his own pocket. According to *Fortune* magazine, between 30 and 40 per cent of all theater seats are sold to expense-account customers. There has not yet been a comparable generosity on the part of the Internal Revenue Bureau toward fiction consumers, nor has anyone yet even claimed a deduction for his annual expenditure on novels, so publishers cannot, like producers, count on the cushion of an assured minimum of expense-account customers.

While doubling the price of their product, they have not doubled their authors' royalties. They cannot afford either, so the story goes, to pay substantial salaries to their younger editors. Although this does not result in their having to make do with inferior help – apparently there is always an adequate supply of young men of private means and of young ladies from female colleges for whom the glamour of the publishing world is an adequate substitute for a living wage – it does effectively close off for most writers an avenue of comparatively undemanding employment that was formerly frequently utilized by writers on their way up.

Caught in the inflationary squeeze, the writer whose books do not sell at least partly because they are priced too high, who cannot support a family in New York City on the salaries paid by publishers, who no longer finds a low-cost bohemia or indeed any interstices of a daily more highly organized society in which he can nest, is being pushed into the college towns in increasing numbers as, we are told, his British cousin has been forced into the employment of the BBC. There has been a good deal of worried discussion about this recently, to which I hesitate to add, but which is so intimately bound up with the current situation of the novelist that I cannot pass it by without comment.

Some of the complaints that security-minded writers are fastening themselves like barnacles to university faculties come from people who are themselves attached to universities or who have private means, and who seem genuinely perturbed that writers who have in the past lived as splendidly enviable bohemians are now concerned with such vulgar problems as making both ends meet. Their perturbation has not as yet taken such a constructive turn as the issuance of suggestions for the solution of these problems without resort to the consolations of college salary checks and their concomitant insurance and pension funds, tenure and long vacations. What is more, the fear that writers who have been drifting back to the campus will cut themselves off from the main currents of American life would appear singularly inappropriate when measured against the background of the writers: depression, war, world-wide cataclysms often lived through at first hand. Those writers who have lived in the world for the last thirty or forty years need have no shortage of usable experience for their individual undertakings, no matter how they earn their livings.

But there is a situation in which these fears for the insulation and isolation of the American writer do have a good deal of point. We do see now the beginnings of a trend which can only be reinforced by the economic factors already touched on. A good many young men who are determined to become writers are already going directly from college to graduate school, from graduate school to teaching and writing, in many cases without ever discovering at first hand the existence of any world other than the academic – with the occasional exception of a European Fulbright year, and that all too often lived through in a little American community scarcely distinguishable from the college town back home. They seem not merely content at spending their lives in such a predictable manner, but terrified at the idea of spending them in any less predictable manner (if envious of those who do somehow manage to). The cult of experience, so castigated as one of the literary fallacies of the Thirties, is apparently being replaced in the Fifties by the cult of inexperience.

A sheltered existence, from undergraduate adolescence to emeritus retirement, may be a matter of indifference (or indeed of positive benefit) to lecturers in topology or medieval history; to storytellers, romancers, writers of novels, may it not prove disastrous?

We are not speaking here of individual cases, for obviously there may be imaginative writers who will mature and flourish in a cozy academic environment, who will find in it materials for anything they are impelled to create; we are speaking of a tendency. We need never worry about the individual genius, whether he sits in a wheat field or a seminar; but we have already noted that a culture is more than the sum of its geniuses, and we may wonder as to the prospects for a literature emerging from the universities in the next decade that will not be ingrown, precious, or desiccated, that will evoke in some way the spiritual climate of two hundred million Americans far removed from the academic atmosphere.

The new writer may with justification retort that the economic situation already described makes it almost impossible for him to play, read, and dream (all of which it would seem that a novelist must do, in his youth if not later) without the sheltering arm of the university, the meal ticket of the Ph.D., and the security that will alone free him to write unprofitable novels. This complaint has already been answered far better than I could by the brilliant young journalist Dan Wakefield, in an article in the June 23, 1956, number of *The Nation* entitled "Sailing to Byzantium: Yeats and the Young Mind." Replying to those members of his own generation who opt for security, crying that it is no longer possible for those now coming of age to go forth and encounter the reality of experience as it was, for example, after the First World War, Mr. Wakefield asserts: "But it has always been impossible. It was just as impossible when Hemingway lived on potatoes in Paris. The difference today is that the young are so willing to accept the impossibility."

Without attempting to dictate to my juniors, I should like to conclude my own brief consideration of this problem by noting that just as the problem is different for men of twenty and men of forty, so it assumes different aspects for single men and married men. No aspiring young writer has yet given convincing reasons why it is impossible for him to exist marginally, from one job to the next, while he learns something of the world, nor an incontrovertible statement of the absolute necessity for digging in at a university before marriage and dependents ultimately force the issue of security and stability.

Obviously, however, if young writers are obsessed with security, that obsession is a function of the society in which they live as much as their choice of theme, comparative unpopularity, consequent separation from their audiences, exploitation by publishers, and mishandling or neglect by critics more ambitious than devoted; and it can no more be wholly exorcised by exhortation than can the other ills we have been compelled to categorize.

If it were possible for the novelist to take his place as a productive and accepted member of society, most of the complaints we have been analyzing thus far would doubtless recede into their properly trivial proportions. It was not Karl Marx but Henry James who asserted that "the future of fiction is intimately bound up with the future of the society that produces and consumes it." In a society which babbles interminable platitudes about battling for the minds and hearts of men even while it demonstrates in a thousand ways that it values the football coach and the sales engineer above the novelist and the poet,* we

* *Footnote, 1961:* On August 16, 1959, both Admiral William F. (Bull) Halsey and Wanda Landowska died. Admiral Halsey had been responsible for the World War II slogan, "Kill More Japs," and Mad-

can expect nothing but a continuation of the circumstances which drive the novelist not only into a marginal position – bad enough in itself – but into marginal utterances. So arise the false dichotomy between "affirmative" and "negative" writing and the vicious spiral of neglect, in turn isolating the writer even further and forcing him yet further to feed on himself and his similars instead of on the social body for his material. The impossible economic situation resulting from his isolation forces him into the insulated little world of the university, from which he produces work received by the critics not with interest, attention, or even compassion, but with envy and malice, treated as an object of scorn and seized on as an opportunity for self-aggrandizement.

In these circumstances it would seem all the more creditable that such works as those I have mentioned by name have recently appeared, testimony to the vitality of the form and the unlikelihood of its absorption by new mass media or of its dwindling into a hobby of hyper-intellectual academicians. Mr. Gore Vidal, a novelist as well as a television playwright, has expressed (in the *New York Times Book Review*) an honest fear: "After some three hundred years the novel in English has lost the general reader (or rather the general reader has lost the novel) and I propose he will not again recover his old enthusiasm."

It is Mr. Vidal's thesis that "the general reader" is now

---

ame Landowska had been responsible for the revival of the harpsichord and for a severe interpretation of the work of J. S. Bach. Presumably, it would be an easy task for a moderately well educated American to assess the relative permanence of the contributions of these two people. Yet in the newspaper of record, the *New York Times* of August 17, 1959, Admiral Halsey's death was announced on page 1, and Madame Landowska's death on page 23. . . .

the general looker, and that "the fault, if it be a fault, is not the novelist's (I doubt if there ever have been so many interesting and excellent writers as there are now working) but the audience's," which has turned from the mediocre novel to the television play. The mediocre novelist, says Mr. Vidal (more gracefully than my paraphrase), is already in the process of retooling for the better-paying production of television plays, leaving to the genuinely creative men the miniscule audience that has been the poet's in recent years.

Mr. Vidal's question is a fair one: are we witnessing the decline of an individual art form concomitantly with the birth of a collective art form? Is the highbrow novel destined to join the poem as the property of a handful of intellectuals while the journeyman novelist hastens to provide the mass audience with speaking shadows for their twenty-one-inch screens?

This is somewhat different, and surely of more moment than, say, Frank O'Connor's assertion that with D. H. Lawrence "the period of the novel has gone by," since technical definitions which would exclude from the realm of the novel some of the greatest fictional achievements of the past thirty years are – however entertaining and provocative – hardly germane to the broader problems under discussion here.

Mr. Vidal bases his somewhat depressing conclusion on his interpretation of the tastes of the mass public today, as expressed in the purchase of paper books, "consuming haphazardly rather than reading." But can we not come to an opposite conclusion on the basis of a different interpretation of the same evidence? Just as it is difficult to share Mr. Vidal's optimism about the future of the television drama ("ten new 'live' plays a week: from such an awful abundance, a dramatic renaissance *must* come" – but must it? What came from the awful abundance of radio but the sonorous dramas of Norman Corwin and Arch Oboler, and an enormous increase in the power of the detergent manufacturer and the advertising agency to corrupt and debase the public taste? What has come from this new abundance thus far but a gluey, patronizing portrait of the "little guy" acclaimed as bold and courageous playwriting because it is couched in a liberalese rhetoric at once defiant and meaningless?), so it is difficult to share his pessimism about the future of the novel and of the public which consumes it in its new paperback format.

The fact is that the novelist has not lost his audience. The paperback industry has demonstrated incontrovertibly that the public for the modern novel is from ten to twenty times as large as one would have gathered from its hard-cover sales: good novels which sell from five to twenty thousand copies at three or four dollars sell from fifty thousand to five hundred thousand at thirty-five or fifty cents. This is not simply because the reprinted novels are disguised with misleadingly vulgar covers for people who haphazardly consume rather than read, for many of them do not have such covers, and many could not compete textually with those leafed through by consumers on the prowl for titillation. Nor is it simply because they form part of an undifferentiated mass of westerns, mysteries, and science fiction, for we know now that certain paper books do not sell, and that certain others draw appreciative correspondence from readers who would never write letters about hard-cover novels – and perhaps never read them.

It would seem elementary that good modern novels sell in large quantities in paper covers to a public of hitherto unsuspected size for two perfectly good and obvious reasons: first, they are within the price range of people who want to fill their shelves but cannot afford to spend fifty dollars a year on novels; second, they are available. The well-stocked bookshop is in all seriousness one of the glories of Western civilization – but there simply are not enough of them to fill the vast American spaces, nor are the twelve-hundred-odd that we do have accessible to fast-moving, suburban-spreading commuter Americans.

Granted that the, say, 300,000 actual readers of Saul

Bellow or Carson McCullers in paperback editions are scarcely a fraction of the millions who are nourished solely by the television playwrights; granted even that a portion of these thousands are haphazard buyers who consume rather than read; nevertheless we can fairly assume the existence of a substantial fraction as regular readers of serious novels – provided that these novels are easily accessible and cheaply priced. In absolute numbers they may be small, indeed tiny in comparison with the agency-estimated millions who watch any given television play; still, they are more than the two or three thousand who buy four-dollar novels (if they were not, both the novelist and his audience would truly be disappearing and undiscoverable in a country of one hundred and seventy million people).

What is more, their number is increasing. Just as America has more autos every year, more electric blankets, more people, so also it has more intellectuals. Of course, most of these are going to be mass-oriented and in that mood for liberal self-congratulation already noted, but a by no means negligible number of the rising total are demonstrating their receptivity to what is new and upsetting: if the number of buyers of Van Gogh prints rises in direct ratio to the number of college graduates, so does the number of those disturbed and excited by abstract-expressionist American painters, although these latter are few in comparison with the Van Gogh discoverers; so with the new publics for the fiction of both the best-seller and the more ambitious varieties. It is the responsibility of the intelligent reader to determine which public to identify himself with, and having determined, to broaden its base among those he likes.

The more rational approach, it would seem therefore, would not be to consign the novelist and his reader to the ranks of a radical and hopelessly shrinking minority, but to begin to attempt (as Knopf, Doubleday, Ballantine, and a few other publishers have already done somewhat abortively) to connect the new writer and the new reader by making the economic leap and bringing out new novels in cheap editions of twenty-five and fifty thousand rather than in expensive editions of twenty-five hundred and five thousand.

We have to consider, in addition, and finally, just what it is that this rather special public expects of the novel—which raises the question of the position of the novelist in our society. One of the first critics to place this question in its contemporary context was Van Wyck Brooks, who, in an essay entitled "The Silent Generation" (in his *The Writer in America*), has opposed "curative" to "diagnostic" writers, and has pleaded with American novelists to "break the evil spell that weighs upon their minds."

Mr. Brooks asks:

> Do not most contemporary tastes suggest that people read now for help in the solution of their problems, their predicaments and plights, rather than for the objective interest that readers in so-called normal times found in Shakespeare or Molière or Goethe or Dickens? . . . In short do not people nowadays read mainly for aid in the quest for security, which has become the general quest of our time in a world that has come to seem as irremediably evil as the post-Roman world of the early Middle Ages?

I trust that by now my own attitude toward these questions has become clear, if only by implication. The best American novelists today are not invariably the least popular, but they are surely not the most popular, and the odds are that most of them cannot earn a living from their books. The most popular novelists in the United States today, the Sloan Wilsons and the Herman Wouks, are the "curative" writers, the novelists who do in striking fashion "offer aid in the quest for security." A critic as extraordinarily erudite and sensitive as Mr. Brooks would surely not take Mr. Wouk and Mr. Wilson as his literary examplars in preference to some of the writers I have mentioned earlier. But it is the Wouks and the Wilsons who are not even aware of a spell weighing upon their minds, who are deliberately engaged in offering their readers a "solution of their problems"; these, and the television playwrights who, as Gore Vidal implicitly concedes, are destined to be the purveyors of the second-rate.

If our best writers are "diagnostic" rather than "curative," it is not because an evil spell weighs upon their minds (at least, no more than other creative minds have always been oppressed by an evil spell), or because they deliberately choose to write for the coterie rather than for the mass audience, or because they are turning their backs on their historic function. It is rather, I am profoundly convinced, because they are paying the penalty for working in a society which has never granted the creative artist a legitimate place in its communal life.

The unfortunate truth is that the novelist in America has never been either an accepted member of a closely knit intellectual elite, as has his English counterpart, or a culture hero and intellectual leader, as has his French counterpart. There are no American novelists who speak regularly on radio and television to their fellow citizens as, for example, V. S. Pritchett does in England. There are no American novelists who write regularly on matters of national and international interest for the daily newspapers as, for example, François Mauriac and Albert Camus do in France. When Robert Penn Warren speaks his mind as a novelist and a Southerner on the question of segregation, the publication of his remarks is regarded as a special coup by *Life* magazine instead of as a logical part of the literate and intelligent intercourse on the question, and must be placed between covers before it can be soberly evaluated. When William Faulkner is invited by Dwight Eisenhower to form a committee of writers to propose ways of making the United States better liked, the invitation is not taken for granted as would be a similar request to a network executive or an advertising agency official: questions of motive inevitably arise. Even those writers who have agreed to participate in the program must wonder whether William Faulkner's name would ever have occurred to Mr. Eisenhower's advisers (that it is unthinkable that it would ever have occurred independently to the President is only another symptom of the condition I am describing) if Mr. Faulkner had not received international publicity attendant upon his acceptance of a foreign award.

There is no logical reason why American novelists should not be invited to participate in the formation of public opinion as they are in other countries; nevertheless they are not. There is no logical reason why the pronouncements of novelists on such questions as the control of international waterways, the control of atomic energy, or the control of race prejudice would be any more ridiculous than similar pronouncements by industrialists running military establishments, generals running industrial establishments, financiers running scientific establishments, and lawyer-theologians running diplomatic establishments, all of them eagerly sought after on all occasions and reproduced in all mass media; nevertheless novelists' opinions even on cultural and humanitarian matters are sought after only when a propaganda point is to be scored.

The novelist in America is not only negatively regarded as a man unfitted by background or training to contribute to the formation of intelligent attitudes on public affairs; he is positively regarded as a kind of freak unless he retreats to the university or hits the jackpot in the mass media. Inevitably what he *does,* too, is regarded as freakish, unless his book strikes it rich.

In a commercial culture in which the writer is held in so little esteem, in which his craft is not respected, in which there is no sense of kinship between writer and reader, we can hardly expect that his will be the loudest in the chorus of affirmative voices.

I hope that what I have said in the foregoing pages is not interpreted as either a cry of pity for the poor novelist or a plea for absolute indulgence for every piece of fiction he publishes in this country. In actuality if we view his task with eyes unclouded with ennui, venom, or anger that he is not repeating the work of the eighteenth- and nineteenth-century masters, we must see that he is faced in America with the most dreadful obstacles and the most challenging raw materials, the most clamorous competition and the most singular expectations, the most dangerous pitfalls and the most extraordinary potentialities. I venture to suggest that the coming decade's frenetic rate of technological development, mass-media expansion, and suburban growth will make the novelist's America of the Sixties more different from Scott Fitzgerald's America than Fitzgerald's America was from Edith Wharton's. Increase in difference will mean increase in difficulties, but we have no reason to fear that the artist of the future will prove any more cowardly than the artist of the past.

With every passing year there will be not less, but more people anxious to learn what he has to say. With every passing year there will be an increasing conviction that all of the answers are not necessarily to be gotten from the findings of groups, committees, boards, and teams, or from punch cards fed into machines, or even from the efforts of men pooling their crafts and skills in the theater, the movies, and television, but that awareness and understanding of doubt, complexity, anguish, and triumph may still be gained as one man listens to another, as one man reads the words that another has written to him and to all his kind.

If the novelist clings to that most unselfish (in its ultimate effects) of all selfish beliefs, faith in himself, then even in a world seemingly more than ever aimless, irreligious, and trapped in its own confounding contradictions, his voice will have to be heard. In the confused meantime, let him inscribe on his banner the words of the great artist whose lines inspired and hence are to be found at the beginning as well as at the close of these reflections:

> The more we consider it the more we feel that the prose picture can never be at the end of its tether until it loses the sense of what it can do. It can do simply everything, and that is its strength and its life.

New World Writing #12, 1957

Footnote, 1961: Since the above was written, the situation has changed considerably in the publishing industry, in some ways for the better, in others for the worse. For writer and reader of fiction, it has altered too. "An average first novel that once sold 3,500 copies," the *New York Times Book Review* quotes Evan Thomas of Harper's as saying, "now maybe reaches 2,000." A Chicago bookstore is quoted as saying that it "can't even give away a novel." A year or two ago the sour joke used to be that if William Faulkner were to come in to a publisher, unknown, with *The Sound and the Fury,* he would be thrown out of the office. This year I think it can be added that if, through some fluke, *The Sound and the Fury* were accepted, its publisher would "decline" the writer's subsequent unsalable novels. I would not myself have admitted several years ago what I now know to be true: that, in addition to the published writers who can no longer feel any sense of commitment by their publishers unless they show signs of becoming big winners, there are good young writers who find it difficult or impossible to find publishers, even after years of submissions.

But even while the market for serious novels is shrinking to the size of the poetry market, the publishing industry is booming as never before. Thanks in large part to a swelling school-age population and a concomitant surge in the demand for textbooks, publishing has been transformed from small, dignified, family-owned enterprise to Big Business. Its stock has been put on the public market, it is attracting substantial investors, mergers are proceeding at a dizzying pace. The novelist John Brooks, discussing these matters in the Authors Guild *Bulletin,* and noting that textbooks rather than trade books have been traditionally the big moneymakers, finds that "it is perfectly obvious that trade departments are in danger of suffering under the impact of public stock-ownership. The investors who buy publishing stock — and thereby enter the publishing business — may or may not be 'gentlemen,' but in either case, as investors they have no opportunity to share in the pleasures and satisfactions of trade-book publishing, and are concerned only that their investment pay dividends and appreciate in value. They are bound to ask the question, 'Why not curtail or eliminate entirely the unprofitable trade department?' and the firm's management is bound to listen to them and give them some kind of answer." Mr. Brooks goes on to ask a pregnant question: "Is the quality of trade books destined to decline because of a stockholder-induced tendency to play safe, avoid introducing risky new talent, and stick to frankly commercial items and established best-sellers?"

In this uneasy situation, editors, publishers, and booksellers close ranks. The villain of the piece is once again the novelist. Mr. Harold Strauss of Knopf, according to the *Times Book Review*, says that "the mature people aren't writing fiction, and the youngsters have retired to some private world of their own." Though I am painfully aware of the amount of bad fiction being written and even published, I must say that this strikes me as somewhat broad.

And the bookstores, the supposed link between writer and reader, all assure us, so we are informed by the *Times Book Review*, that "they could sell good fiction, if they had it." But the unhappy truth is that 90 per cent of the bookstore proprietors wouldn't know good fiction if they saw it. They refuse even to stock it; surely they do not read it, any more than do the publishers' representatives, the traveling book salesmen, read most of the fiction that they attempt halfheartedly, with less and less success, to peddle to the bookstores. The notion of the bookstore proprietor as dedicated to the life of the mind and to urging his clientele forward on the pathways of culture bears about as much relation to reality as does the AMA public relations image of the modern physician, that competent technician-businessman, as a simple, selfless, small-town Albert Schweitzer. I have met bookmen who were such dedicated culture-bearers in unexpected places like Colorado Springs, and I salute them. Unfortunately there are not very many of them in the thousand-odd American bookstores, which are doing so well on sick greeting cards, cookbooks, dictionaries, and other items which sell themselves and need not be read before being purveyed. When these merchants say they could sell good fiction, they mean they could sell best-sellers, a task which could as readily be discharged by an illiterate as by a lover of fine prose.

The fact is that the bookstore no longer has a significant role to play in the dispensing of serious fiction. With the exception of the occasional good book that "catches on," serious fiction simply does not sell in bookstores in hard covers. Nor is there any reason why it should, when under a rational order of things one ought to be able to buy any decently recommended new novel in a perfectly substantial paper cover for about a dollar and a half.

Those of us who retain our belief in the vitality of the novel and our confidence that there is an audience for it larger than that represented by those few thousand who pay five dollars for a novel must turn our attention from the traditional trade-publisher-bookstore channel to the potential of the paperback. There are now available to us, it is true, more good titles in reasonable paper editions than anyone could read in a lifetime; but no one in this country has yet successfully published serious original fiction in cheap paper editions. The reasons are complex: paperback originals are often ignored in the reviewing media; display space is all but unavailable in the new paperback bookshops; trade-book publishers who venture into the field are defeated too by their lack of experience with the distribution problems involved in merchandizing this different kind of commodity.

What is more, the inexorable pressure of our economy is exerted on the paperback industry as it is on every other section of the mass-entertainment industry, which is dominated by the cult of numbers and the hunt for the lowest common denominator. Robert Alan Aurthur, the television playwright and producer, recently described to the readers of *The Nation* how several ambitious and successful television programs were forced off the screen because it was found that they were reaching only ten million viewers, and not the twenty, thirty, and forty million who were staring at competitive programs. Similarly, a novel or a paperback magazine may be well received and even critically acclaimed, but will be considered uneconomic by the new magnates of paperback publishing because it will predictably sell "only" a hundred thousand copies in contrast to other, inferior books which can be fed into the pipeline in larger quantities at a larger profit.

As a result, all too many good novels are still not being made available in cheap editions. If it took fifteen years for Jean Stafford's *Boston Adventure* to be made available in paper, it may very well take that long for a number of unusual novels of the last few seasons to be reprinted in cheap editions. (And let us bear in mind the feedback: inevitably, the unlikelihood of a trade publisher's being able to realize his 50 per cent of the reprint rights to a serious novel is going to color his judgment as to whether he should accept the book for his list in the first instance.) Mass paperback editions of good new fiction therefore still seem out of the question.

I suspect that solutions to this dilemma will be found only by men bold enough to bypass completely the obsolete trade-publisher-bookstore roadblock, and imaginative enough to make use of newly evolving techniques in both quality paperback and book-club publishing. The novelists are here, and more good ones are on the way; so are the readers. It may very well be that a book-club kind of distribution of good new fiction in paper, in editions of ten or fifteen thousand and priced at a dollar or two, could succeed in making the connection which is essential if writer and reader are to profit mutually. I think we are at the threshhold of an age of intense literary productivity; the extent to which it will flourish may quite possibly be determined by what we do to forge new links between those who write and those who are refreshed and stirred by what they read.

3.

Popular Taste and *The Caine Mutiny*

In the months that have passed since the publication of Herman Wouk's *The Caine Mutiny*, it has become something of a phenomenon in the publishing business by climbing slowly to the top of the best-seller lists without fanfare or ballyhoo, and then staying there week after week, month after month, until it begins to look now like another *Gone With the Wind*. Why?

I should like to suggest that the answer will reveal a good deal about the changes that have recently taken place in the reading taste of the American public as well as in what is known as popular culture. The best-seller, unlike the movie or even the musical comedy, is still the work of one man, a creative craftsman of greater or lesser skill responding directly to his sense of the public taste. In the case of Mr. Wouk, this skill is pressed into the service of a mythmaking that more or less corresponds to certain ideas currently dominant in American middle-class life. *The Caine Mutiny* is in every aspect a faithful reflection of the morals, fears, and intellectual aspirations of the new middle class, that proliferant white-collar segment of the American community that is basically responsible for "progressive" movies praised because they deal – no matter how – with the problems of minorities, musical comedies praised because their songs are filled with "social significance," and radio programs praised because in the recent past, before television, they evolved a kind of rhetorical statement that passed for poetry.

This new middle class, many of its members the successful sons and daughters of struggling and bewildered immigrants, is yearly producing larger and more avid audiences of high school and (increasingly) college graduates with more leisure time than working people ever had before. Impatient with traditional pulp stories, Western movies, and show-girl musical comedies, they want to feel that their intelligences are engaged by the programs they hear, the movies they see, the books they read; and they take it as an act of social piety and, by extension, of artistic integrity, when these media feature favorable stereotypes of minorities once represented by unfavorable caricatures. At the same time they participate in a kind of mass snobbery of which they are all but unaware, on the one hand rejecting in angry frustration those whom they instinctively fear and admire — aristocrats, millionaires, and serious-minded intellectuals — and on the other hand patronizing the underlying population with pseudo-democratic verbiage about the "average Joe" and the "common man." To a large extent they are responsible for the new trends in popular taste because they are themselves the very begetters of our leading practitioners of popular culture, the Dore Scharys, the Stanley Kramers, the Irwin Shaws.

Consider how *The Caine Mutiny* meets the needs of this great audience. The American wartime experience is refracted through the eyes of Willie Keith, who might be described as the average American rich boy whom we have come to know from the writings of J. P. Marquand and even F. Scott Fitzgerald (there is in some ways a remarkable similarity between Amory Blaine or Anthony Patch and Willie): a home on Long Island, another house in Palm Beach, four years at Princeton, a small talent for versifying and piano playing, a domineering mother, a love affair with a poor but honest Italian nightclub singer, and finally a leap into Navy officers' school to avoid the draft. In the Navy, however, he is simply a reserve officer, a member of that middle segment of wartime society that lords it over the enlisted man and lives in fear, admiration, and bewilderment of the regular Navy career officer. Willie accepts assignment to a rusty old minesweeper, the *Caine*, which is commanded by Captain Queeg, an Annapolis man. It is soon apparent to everyone that Queeg is at best a tyrannical martinet and at worst a psychopath. A series of small but nasty incidents, described in lengthy and convincing detail, persuades Willie and his fellow reserve officers that Queeg is a coward, an unbalanced disciplinarian, and finally a madman.

In some of the most interesting pages of the book, the officers of the *Caine* discuss Captain Queeg in an attempt to decide whether he is mad or simply vicious. It is Lieutenant Thomas Keefer, intellectual, playwright, and budding war novelist, who first discovers the obscure naval regulations providing for the replacement of mentally or physically incapacitated commanding officers through a kind of legal mutiny. He plants in the mind of Lieutenant Maryk, a stolid and competent peacetime fisherman, the seed that grows into a conviction of Queeg's insanity. But when Maryk gets Keefer to accompany him to Admiral Halsey's office to plead for Queeg's replacement, Keefer begs off at the last possible moment with the explanation that their proof is insufficient and subject to misinterpretation. Neither Willie nor any of his fellow reserve officers from whose point of view Captain Queeg is observed can think of him apart from his role as Navy officer. A fine line divides them from Queeg and his Annapolis clubmates, who are described as either fantastically tyrannical (Queeg) or infinitely wise, experienced and compassionate (Queeg's superiors).

No effort is made to portray the enlisted men of the *Caine*, except in so far as they advance the story and play their little supernumerary roles in the mutiny. We see them vaguely, through a veil of sympathy, although a good deal of the action takes place in the confined quarters of the *Caine*. As for the messmen, who appear only to pour coffee, they are simply good-humored, yassuh-ing

Rastuses. Not that there is anything of vulgar anti-Negro prejudice in this. Here is a different kind of vulgarity, not unlike the blind "liberalism" of the Hollywood movie makers who attempt to represent a cross section of America by showing us Army companies composed of bragging Texans, tough but sentimental Brooklyn Jews, quiet and brave Westerners, oversensitive but essentially courageous rich men's sons, and Negro boys who are almost like everybody else. . . .

When the *Caine* is caught in a violent storm and seems doomed, Queeg freezes on the bridge, unable to issue the orders that would save the ship. At this crucial point Maryk takes command and does save the ship, with the passive consent of Keefer, Willie, and the other officers. After the storm the ship returns to the United States and Maryk is court-martialed for his unprecedented behavior; and Willie, knowing that he, too, must stand trial if Maryk is convicted, supports his fellow officer to the best of his ability. Keefer protects his own career by equivocating and refusing to swear to Queeg's madness. But Maryk is finally acquitted, thanks to the brilliant courtroom tactics of his counsel, Lieutenant Commander Barney Greenwald, a crack Jewish lawyer from Albuquerque, who is recuperating from severe burns received on active duty as a carrier fighter pilot. Greenwald is convinced that Maryk and his mates are guilty, but he is equally convinced that he can get Maryk off, and he finally succeeds, by harping on Queeg's instability and by appealing to the Navy's pride in its officer caste.

Keefer throws a champagne party to celebrate the sale of his novel together with Maryk's acquittal. Greenwald is invited, comes in drunk, and stays just long enough to deliver an impassioned speech to the shocked officers of the *Caine* and to throw his champagne in Keefer's face. In his speech Greenwald indicates that for him the war has been a struggle to save his grandmother from being melted down into soap like the Jewish grandmothers of Europe; in that struggle the Queegs – regardless of their brutality or stupidity — have played an essential role by contributing their skill to the maintenance of a vital core of defense in the years when military people and military expenses were belittled. The Keefers have sabotaged these defenders of freedom with their mocking cynicism, says Greenwald, and in Captain Queeg's case, Tom Keefer not only incited Maryk to an irresponsible, if well-meant, act of disloyalty (for he could simply have covered up for Queeg during the storm and then returned the ship's command to him), but compounded his guilt by his cowardly testimony at Maryk's court-martial.

Here we must be struck by the correspondence between what Mr. Wouk is saying and what the public wants to hear. It is his thesis that the Second World War was worth while if only because it put a stop to the enemy's slaughters; that it was won by a devoted and previously trained officer caste, despite the incompetence of individual members; and that the most insidious enemy is the man who works to destroy confidence in his country's military leadership.

It must be noted first that this is a thesis which can be — and has been — upheld by fascist as easily as by democratic theorists. Second, and perhaps even more important, is the identification of the intellectual as the villain of the piece, with his cowardice and his shameful sniping at the regular officer class. Here again it is necessary to point out that the middle-class reading public would almost certainly reject such a brutal assault on the intellectual (against which one might have expected intellectuals to rally, just as undertakers or chiropodists rally to meet unfair representations of their professions in the movies) if it were made by a boor or an obvious philistine. It is symptomatic of Mr. Wouk's shrewdness that he puts his assault on the intellectual in the mouth of Barney Greenwald, who speaks with the voice of authority, from the "inside." For in addition to embodying civic virtue as a wounded hero, he gained enormous financial success in the law, a field popularly associated with the regular exercise of the higher faculties; he is also a member and fighting representative of a minority group, and a passionate defender of an even smaller minority, the American Indian! And it follows, therefore, that Greenwald's opposite number, the cowardly intellectual who conceals his inadequacy beneath a surface charm that temporarily captivates the susceptible Willie Keith, should not be a shabby Greenwich Village Jewish bohemian but a handsome and successful playwright named Thomas Keefer.

If we reverse the roles, conceiving of a clean-cut Tom Keefer charging a degenerate and decadent Barney Greenwald with being an irresponsible intellectual whose writing and preachings have had a devastating effect on American youth, we can imagine the justified protest that *The Caine Mutiny* would have aroused.

After he returns to the *Caine*, Willie, who had admired Keefer, is forced to concede that Greenwald was right. Keefer is now captain of the *Caine* and Willie his executive officer. In the closing weeks of the war, the ship is hit by a Kamikaze, and Keefer, to his own shame and disgust, hastily abandons ship, leaving Willie to save the *Caine* and the men who have remained aboard, and returns only when the danger is past. Willie is given command of the *Caine* after Keefer leaves the ship in Japan, and he sails home to New York a man, a hero, prepared to cut loose from his mother and to fight for the hand of the Italian girl who had seemed beneath him at the beginning of the war.

It must be noted that Mr. Wouk is an exceptionally good storyteller. Willie Keith's adventures, travails, and loves are handled with a directness and a swiftness that bear the mark of the practiced professional writer. But this is true of a good many other novels, even novels dealing with the Second World War, that have not had a tenth the success of this book. What we must consider is the special quality that has made *The Caine Mutiny* seem important to so many people.

It is a quality not to be found in many best-sellers that

depended for their popularity simply on romance, swordplay, décolletages, and civil wars. For those books, despite obvious attractions, cannot possibly involve the modern middle-class reader's deepest feelings about sex, war, and society, in a way that flatters him into the belief that he is participating in a thoughtful intellectual experience.

Let us turn to Willie's love affair. It is one of the novel's main themes and also serves technically both as counterpoint and relief. When Willie first meets Marie Minotti they fall in love, but are kept from intimacy by the bittersweet realization that their social backgrounds are worlds apart, for he is still under his mother's domination and she is only the daughter of a Bronx immigrant. So far their relation has a certain comfortable familiarity – tragedies have been written on just this theme and innumerable soap operas, too. There is, to be sure, a certain flavor of the archaic in tracing the difficulties of a love affair between two young people who come from utterly different milieux; when J. P. Marquand treats it, as he does so often, he removes the love affair a generation or two from the current reality, presenting it as part of the recollections of an aging man. Furthermore, the liberal-minded middle-class reader is well aware of the impediments that have been removed from the path of true love by the withering away of the uppermost and nethermost classes in American society and the consequent expansion of the middle sector. Nevertheless he is also reminded by his parents and by columnists, whose sensible advice to the lovelorn is increasingly spiced with modern psychiatric lingo, of the dangers inherent in romance between young people whose family backgrounds are "incompatible."

In any case, Willie cannot bring himself to break off with Marie, and when he returns to the West Coast from his first Pacific cruise, he impetuously goes to bed with her. Here the reader is brought from the world of impossible romance into a world that he knows perfectly well exists. The author makes it quite clear that the couple have transgressed, although they are young, healthy, and heedless; thus the reader has the double advantage of feeling that the love affair is realistic while protecting his moral sense. Marie, however, refuses to repeat the experience with Willie, who appreciates her new-found reserve, but begins to wonder if he can possibly love a girl who has given herself to him so easily, even if only once.

Although the reader knows that Willie is still rationalizing his snobbishness, Willie goes on torturing himself until his naval experiences bring him maturity and the need for permanent companionship. When he returns to New York in command of the *Caine* at the end of the war, he finds Marie singing for a prominent dance-band leader, and apparently living with him too. But now Willie is no longer a boy. He stands his ground and announces to Marie that he is going to take her away from the bandleader and marry her; she, fearing that Willie is simply feeling sorry for her, reveals that she has not *really* been sleeping with the bandleader, although everyone thinks so. At the close of the book it seems fairly certain that Willie will win the girl.

Here I think is an almost perfect correspondence between current sexual morality and the realities of the American experience. For a reading public caught between Sunday school training and exposure to the Kinsey Report, the dilemma of Willie Keith, although it can add no new dimension to their lives or depth to their experience, must seem completely "true to life" and overwhelmingly poignant. Even the falsity of his hard-won "maturity," which enables him to assert his love by suddenly disregarding the profound social differences between himself and Marie, is accepted by an audience eager for a description of love more meaningful than moonlight and roses but which still does not deprive them of the consolation of a happy ending. Virtue must still be rewarded; it is only that the rules defining virtue have been modified by the economic necessity for delayed marriages and by the back seats of forty million automobiles. Willie's virtue in loving Marie despite her affair with the bandleader is rewarded with the revelation that she has not *really* slept with the man. It is as though Mr. Wouk were subconsciously attuned to the precise degree of sexual liberation which the popular mind is ready to grant to American youth, as well as to the exact amount of traditional romance with which the depiction of the liberation must be leavened.

Indeed, any analysis of the most successful components of popular culture would compel us to refer to the ability of men like Mr. Wouk to let us have our cake and eat it, to stimulate us without unduly provoking us, to make us feel that we are thinking without really forcing us to think.

Just as Willie's virtue is rewarded with the revelation of his girl's purity, so are his heroism and his steadfast support of Maryk rewarded with a medal, a command, and a hero's return. Keefer, on the other hand, is punished for his sophistry, irresponsibility, and cowardice, not by official action, but — what is worse for him — by the consciousness of his ineradicable inadequacy despite his literary success. And Maryk, in what is perhaps the neatest touch of all, is formally acquitted of the "mutiny," thanks to the brilliant defense of Greenwald, but suffers for his presumption in deposing Queeg by being deprived forever of the possibility of realizing his life's ambition — a career as an officer in the regular Navy. Thus, the lives of all the principals are composed in accordance with their just deserts, i.e., with accepted standards of reward and retribution.

What the new middle class wanted — and found in *The Caine Mutiny* — was an assurance that its years of discomfort and hardship in the Second World War were not in vain, and that its sacrifices in a permanent war economy and its gradual accommodation to the emergence of the military as a dominant element in civil life have been not only necessary but praiseworthy. More than this, it requires such assurance in a sophisticated form, allowing it to feel that alternatives have been thoughtfully considered before being rejected: in *The Caine Mutiny* ample space is given over to consideration of "psychoanalytic" motivations in Queeg and in Keefer too, and even the Cain-Abel analogy is mentioned as evidence that the title is not an unmotivated slip of the pen.

The taste of the middle-class reading public is conditioned by an increasing prosperousness in a military economy, tending to reinforce conservative moral concepts and to strengthen a traditional envy and distrust of intellectuals and dissidents. But its taste is modified by an indebtedness to its European forebears, New Deal heritage, and continuously higher level of education. Thus it is inclined toward a sophisticated and hospitable acceptance of those entertainments of the vanished European aristocracy which have flowed into the mainstream of Western liberal culture through the channels of mass production and distribution. Witness the phenomenal increase of ballet audiences and the number of people buying "classical" records. Writers like Herman Wouk will inevitably arise directly from this class to verbalize its inchoate and often contradictory attitudes. Indeed Mr. Wouk's background – he has combined a faithful adherence to Orthodox Judaism and a career as a radio gag writer with no apparent discomfort – has prepared him admirably for his task as a practitioner of popular culture.

Partisan Review, March-April 1953

Exurbia Revisited

SALES MGR
Intangible exp, must be able to move effectively at top mgmt level & effectively understand "Big Business" problems. Should be able to handle 12 martinis 12,000
— Advertisement in *New York Times*, February 5, 1956

I looked up recently after a sojourn abroad to find that a new word had sneaked into the language while my back was turned, like the 8:55 crawling into the station at Weehawken. The word is "exurbanite," and unlike the West Shore Railroad it is probably here to stay, since it fulfills what the social workers call an unmet need. Its coiner, A. C. Spectorsky, like Sinclair Lewis before him, has used it to title his book.

Mr. Spectorsky's *The Exurbanites* is both a good and an exasperating book. It is good because it is a pioneering investigation into the mores of the new middle class who have spilled out of their city apartments into the country areas beyond the suburbs and who have become commuters but remain big-city types. Mr. Spectorsky casts a wide net and inevitably comes up with many an interesting specimen. His territory includes Bucks County (Pa.), Nassau, Westchester, and Rockland Counties (N. Y.), and Fairfield County (Conn.), which means that he has under examination a variety of New York City-based salary-earners, ranging from $75,000-a-year network executives close to the seat of real power if not actually warming it themselves, downwards to impecunious young agency men desperately anxious to look as though they are on the way up. Since New York is the center of the "communications" industry, the exurbanites are inevitably associated with it in one way or another.

Mr. Spectorsky has been to these exurbs — indeed, he is frighteningly knowledgeable about the minutiae of daily life in all five localities — and he has taken the trouble to gather some figures on income, railroad commutation, and the like, so that his study is grounded in reality, even though highly impressionistic. What is more, he is not afraid to say that exurbanites are manipulators rather than producers, husbands rather than lovers, providers rather than fathers, urban-focused rather than rural-focused, middlebrow rather than individual in their tastes, ambitious rather than visionary in their aspirations, enslaved rather than liberated by their incomes. For his boldness alone, Mr. Spectorsky would be entitled to our respectful attention. *The Exurbanites* is a more original and provocative description of what is going on around us than the pronouncements of many another commentator with more impressive academic qualifications.

But I said that it is an exasperating book. This is partly because it has been hoked up to sell, although I for one prefer my reading matter about the American scene in a lively style rather than in the tone of a monograph for the *American Sociological Review*. No, what is disturbing is that although Mr. Spectorsky has lifted the curtain on a desolate new landscape, he himself insists (when not busy cheerily minimizing the desolation he has described for 278 pages: "Not only do they do the best they can at the difficult and exciting job of living, but the job they do is, under the circumstances, often remarkably good") that the desolation is limited to the five areas named above and to those people who work in mid-Manhattan between 42nd Street and 57th Street, between Lexington Avenue and 6th Avenue. I am not merely raising the petty objection that Mr. Spectorsky has deliberately narrowed his sights. Of course, when he says that an exurbanite "cannot or will not remember the time when he did not grind his pepper fresh from a small mill" he is abstracting snobbisms as common to certain Greenwich Villagers, Detroiters, Buffalonians, and San Franciscans as to exurbanites – witness the mail-order advertisements for "smart" household objects in the *New Yorker*. Far more important is the fact that this book includes a clinical analysis of certain developing traits in the national character, traits which – if there is any substance to the analysis – add up to a condemnation of the entire way of life which is producing them, while its author persistently denies that these traits are anything more than the sadly amusing characteristics of a severely restricted group.

This insistence I find unacceptable. It is of course perfectly true that a special kind of tension is engendered within families when the husband is bound to a train schedule and the wife is forced back on her own resources twelve hours a day. But Mr. Spectorsky would have us believe also that only in exurban families is one day a week given over to the children by fathers relieving their guilt at not having participated in their offspring's lives for the other six days; or that "fear, insecurity, living beyond one's means, drinking too much" are peculiar to "life in exurbia"; or that it is only exurban wives whose "most frequent complaint" is that "their husbands are sexually inadequate."

One would assume that the principal reason for Mr. Spectorsky's determination to pin these, and many other, miseries like so many badges of dishonor on the breasts of the exurbanites is that it sustains a salable thesis: outlanders – which means all other possible book buyers – will predictably read with pleasure books exposing the heartbreak behind the glamour that is Manhattan and environs; while exurbanites themselves, always eager for self-anatomizing (the advertising men among them, Mr. Spectorsky justly points out, are pathologically sensitive to criticism and hence addicted to gratuitous self-justification), will also search out anything that analyzes their life-patterns. And indeed *The Exurbanites* is a commercially successful book.

But there is also a negative reward for Mr. Spectorsky in

his special approach. Since he disclaims any general validity to his survey beyond the confines of those in the communications industry in the New York area, he is thereby absolved from the necessity of commenting even in passing on the implications of his picture of exurban life for American society as a whole. He can end on the jocular, things-aren't-really-that-bad note that I have already quoted, and he can even invite us to grin wryly at this collective portrait of a group of sad sacks, to take it not as a descriptive analysis of a snowballing tendency but simply as a compendium of lively anecdotes. And of course if that's all we're after . . . Mr. Spectorsky is a first-rate case-history teller, and he stimulates us to circulate others that he has not included: one hears, for example, of exurbanite wives in Nassau County who have formed a car pool to commute to their Central Park South psychoanalysts . . .

But some of us may be stubborn enough to go on believing that social problems demand social solutions rather than individual solutions, or at least consideration of possible *common* avenues of progress. Implicit throughout Mr. Spectorsky's book is a recommendation of the course he appears to have followed himself: "If you don't like it where you are, why don't you go back to the City?" Which is like saying: "If you don't like what you see and hear on television and radio, why don't you turn them off?" The drift from City to Suburb and beyond is not confined to the New York area; it is nationwide. The drift is not temporary; it is irreversible. The new stratum of white-collar technicians and idea men is *not* confined to the New York area; in the Los Angeles and Chicago areas, and indeed in every sizable American community, the communications industry is burgeoning – branch offices as well as local advertising agencies, TV stations, newspapers, department stores, public relations outfits are claiming an ever-larger proportion of the ever-growing white-collar community. If these people do not live like the New York exurbanite it is not for lack of trying.

What is more, there is an intimate interrelationship between the problems of the exurbanites and those of the proletariat. Just how much difference is there between the worker enslaved to the time clock he must punch twice daily and the exurbanite enslaved to the train he must catch twice daily? Between the worker alienated from his tools, his craftsmanship, and a genuine relation to what he produces, and the communications industry operator dealing in "intangibles," able to handle twelve martinis but with no more proof than the worker at the end of the weary day that he has actually produced anything at all? Between the debt-burdened worker, oftener than economists know shouldering two jobs at once or relying on a second family wage-earner to help pay the freight on his mortgaged TV, car, washer, house, and kids, and the living-beyond-his-means exurbanite, taking his work home at night and swearing that he could break even on just three thousand more a year? Between the worker's prematurely aged wife, with her backaches and her notorious lack of sexual fulfillment, and the exurbanite's isolated and overworked wife, with her fifteen-hour day and her (according to Mr. Spectorsky, at any rate) notorious lack of sexual fulfillment? Between the worker who has become, as we used to say, bourgeoisified, whose main conversational topics are the soldier's staples of cars, women, and spectator sports, who is becoming transformed into a TV-passive mass man, and the exurbanite who mistrusts, envies, and ridicules the "egghead," who is ahead of the highbrows "in everything but the most intellectual aspects of life," and who lends himself so easily to caricature as a faceless type?

What I am suggesting is that, even as the sheer numerical mass of the proletariat — or at least its percentile proportion to the rest of the population — is shrinking, its stigmata are perhaps being transferred to the swelling millions of suburbanites and exurbanites. Are we actually becoming a nation of tense, anxious, and wretched white-collar proletarians, with nothing to lose but our uninsured TV antennas? I am grateful to Mr. Spectorsky for having provoked me, through his trenchant and admirably organized book, to raise this question, even though he himself has thus far backed off from considering it.

Dissent, Spring 1956

Popular Taste and the Agonies of the Young

Within recent months, the Leopold-Loeb murder case has served as the theme of a movie by Alfred Hitchcock; novels by Meyer Levin, James Yaffe, and Mary-Carter Roberts; a paperback case history; and a Broadway dramatization of Mr. Levin's most successful and fascinating *Compulsion*.

Superficially, it would seem obvious that this terrible murder and its aftermath – a sensational courtroom trial involving two wealthy, brilliant, wayward boys, the most successful criminal lawyer in the country, and a battery of conflicting psychiatrists – should prove magnetically attractive to writers. But thirty-three years have elapsed since the kidnap-murder, and we are surely entitled to wonder why the novelists of the Twenties, the Thirties, or the Forties did not seize on the drama. Inevitably, too, a parallel question arises: why now the Leopold-Loeb case rather than the Sacco-Vanzetti case?

The answers to these questions are interrelated. For many of us, both Leopold-Loeb and Sacco-Vanzetti have come to represent two crucial illuminations of American life in the Twenties. And if numerous writers and their publics are currently intrigued with that era (for reasons beyond the scope of this brief discussion), the fastening on one sensational trial rather than on the other should be fairly clear to us in the Fifties.

The Sacco-Vanzetti trial was an ending; the Leopold-Loeb case a beginning. It is not just that Sacco and Vanzetti were in all likelihood completely innocent and were revered as martyrs throughout the civilized world, while Leopold and Loeb were admittedly guilty and were the universal objects of fascinated loathing – although that is not irrelevant. It is not even that Sacco and Vanzetti were poor and Leopold and Loeb were rich – although that, too, bears on the problem.

It is, most importantly, it seems to me, that the Sacco-Vanzetti case is the *last* instance in recent history in which the American people were stirred in great numbers to protest an apparent and gross miscarriage of justice. The issues were clear-cut, the verdict appalling.

Just so, the Leopold-Loeb case may be viewed as one of the *first* instances in contemporary American history in which official cognizance was taken of the vast murky areas beyond such deceptively simple words as guilt and insanity. The issues were as clouded as the motives of the boys, the trial – heard by a single judge – an admission of the inadequacy of jury democracy, the judge's verdict an uncomfortable compromise between revenge and therapy dictated by psychiatric testimony.

It is just this ambiguity, just this realization – indeed, at times this reveling in the fact – that there are no simple answers, that has proved so appealing to readers and writers of the Fifties. In an age which prides itself on its sophistication, its appreciation of complexity, even, at times, on its impotence, it is only natural that Sacco-Vanzetti should be scanted in favor of Leopold-Loeb as a key to understanding the Twenties.

Perhaps one day our bolder novelists will see in the Rosenberg case the usable tragedy of still another famous pair whose travail illuminates certain aspects of American life not revealed by the two earlier trials, each of which might be said to expose one side of the Rosenberg coin, counterfeit as it was for both accusers and accused.

I mean by this that questions accepted as given, or at least questions accepted by both parties in the America of the Leopold-Loeb and Sacco-Vanzetti trials, became – in the America of the Rosenberg trial – public relations materials, to be manipulated by counsel for both the accused and the State:

The question of race and religion. There was no felt need in the Twenties to prosecute Leopold-Loeb with Jewish lawyers, or Sacco-Vanzetti with Italian lawyers, or to hear the trial of either pair with a Jewish or an Italian judge. Nor was there a concomitant necessity for either defense counsel or the various defense committees to proclaim the loyal Jewishness or Italian-ness of the defendants of the Twenties, as was done with such nauseating thoroughness in the case of the Rosenbergs.

The question of politics. There was no felt need in the Twenties to deny that Sacco and Vanzetti were committed and dedicated anarchists. Nor was there a concomitant necessity for the defense to portray the two as innocent liberals who preferred not to spell out their beliefs because the climate was currently somewhat unfavorable to anarchists, because nobody had the right to ask them such personal questions, and because they weren't anarchists at all but just patriotic liberty-loving Americans.

The hypocrisy – or the counterfeit, as I have called it – of *all* sides in the Rosenberg case, from the sanctimonious judge who heaped on the heads of the wretched couple the onus for Korea and World War III, to the advisers of the defense show, insistent on portraying the two (with their solemn approval) as flag-waving, Sabbath-observing innocents who had never heard of international Stalinism, was so horrifying as to make the Leopold-Loeb case seem in retrospect a model of well-balanced jurisprudence and honest grappling with presently insoluble problems.

The American mass public, however, is not currently intrigued with Meyer Levin's presentation of the Leopold-Loeb case solely because of the honest bewilderment of the judge, or the impassioned humanitarianism of old Clarence Darrow. If the symbolic attitudes of these men, and the fathomless depths they attempted to plumb, help to account for intellectuals' fascination with Leopold-Loeb, there is another aspect, not so far touched upon in the preceding paragraphs, that may explain the rapt attention given by a wider audience to productions like *Compulsion.* I refer to the fact that Nathan Leopold and Robert Loeb were what we call in the Fifties teen-agers. A special kind of lost teen-agers, in fact: juvenile delinquents.

The lost souls whom the readers, the general public, of the Twenties cared about were the Jake Barneses and Lady Bretts, the Jay Gatsbys and Daisy Buchanans. The youngsters were busy, as always, having fun; it was the adults who were in deep trouble. (It is interesting to observe in passing how stolidly the audiences of the Fifties gaze upon the spectacle of a thick-waisted Tyrone Power and a wrinkled Erroll Flynn earnestly and capably portraying those doomed young comedians of *The Sun Also Rises,* in contrast to the enthusiasm with which they greet movies of, by, and about teen-agers.)

What has happened in the intervening thirty years is that the country has been turned over not to the wives, the widows, and the moms, but to the young. Reading *Life* magazine and the slicks, from *Woman's Day* of the A&P to *McCall's,* The Magazine of Togetherness; seeing the movies of the Fifties, from the big-screen Technicolor jobs like *Rebel Without a Cause* to the modest black and white films like *The Young Stranger;* glancing at the frightened newspapers, one cannot but be struck by the emphasis placed on the dress, the doings, the designs for living of the young.

It is understandable that manufacturers and distributors should concentrate on the fastest-growing market in the country. What is somewhat more worthy of consideration is why in the Fifties the one big problem whose existence is universally admitted and discussed in the United States is that of adolescent disturbance. More than disturbance, domination of the American scene.

In the Twenties, Leopold and Loeb were *exceptional:* their comfortable situation, their college cleverness, their social ease, were in themselves so striking as to aggravate the passions directed against the boys and their crime. Today those qualities could be described as almost typical of a substantial segment of American youth.

Is it not extraordinary that during the very period when immigration to the United States slowed to a trickle, during the very period when the last immigrant generation was frantically assimilating itself into the American way, it should have been the immigrant attitude toward children which triumphed over the traditional Yankee attitude?

The immigrant faith, often the first article of that faith, was that one must sacrifice all for the children. One came to America in the first place for the children; one labored in sweatshops, coal mines, steel mills, in order that the children might have the American opportunity. One broke one's back, burned out one's eyes, even yielded one's ideals, in order that the children might have the chance at a college education, a firm grip on the success ladder.

So today the first article of faith is that everything that carries contemporary sanction, from togetherness to religious revivalism, is being done for the sake of the children.

The parents move from city to suburb not for themselves but for the sake of the children (I speak now of explicit justifications and rationalizations which may not always coincide with actual reasons); the father commutes to work not from choice but so that his children can grow up in the fresh air; the mother becomes a chauffeur not to fulfill a secret desire but because there is no other way, even with the car pools, for the children to get to and from public school, Sunday school, ballet school, music school; and finally the parents hand over their inner selves to the ministration of the community church, not because they believe, or because they expect the act of capitulation will help them, but because they think the children must have "something" in which to believe, even if they themselves need not.

The kind of children emerging from school, church, and station wagon in the Fifties would seem best exemplified by their heroes and the heroes of their parents too: Elvis

Presley, Sal Mineo, Natalie Wood, even James MacArthur, and – the apotheosis of the entire generation – the late James Dean. The face of each is eloquent of the tormenting discontent of an American youth for which everything is being done, to which everything is being given – except a reason for living and for building a socially useful life.

The face of each is one facet of the composite faces of the rich, handsome, gifted, doomed Leopold and Loeb. The sullen sulkiness of the speed-hungry Presleyan, whose motorcycle is his religion; the liquid-eyed wretchedness of Mineo, the immigrant's son, who cannot belong; the bouncy emptiness of Natalie Wood, who would die like Joan if there were an ideal worth dying for; the clean-cut loneliness of the unloved MacArthur, whose Dad has a closetful of suits but no time for Son; and the astonishingly tortured and grief-ridden countenance of the Dean of them all, dead in his Porsche at twenty-four – these speak more eloquently of the essential quality of American life in the Fifties than once did Andy Hardy, Harold Teen, Our Gang, or Shirley Temple for their day.

Is it any wonder that the terrible story of Leopold and Loeb should return to challenge us more potently today than ever before, a ghost returned to haunt our uneasy consciences?

Dissent, Spring 1958

Footnote, 1961: Depending on the angle of vision, there have been head-shaking and huzzahing in comment on the San Francisco student riots, the young Freedom Riders, and the student demonstrators around the U. S. protesting the Bomb, capital punishment, segregation, Cuban aggression. But all of these students taken together constitute a mere fraction of those who were engaged this spring in a different kind of coast-to-coast protest movement. In Fort Lauderdale, Florida, in Galveston, Texas, in Santa

Monica, California, thousands of college students have battled police, not for the dignity of their fellow men or the inviolability of human life, but for their own inalienable right to invade these beach areas during their vacations, to carouse, to neck en masse in public, to litter the ground with the beer cans that are the vessels of their ambition, their esthetic sensibility, their rebellion. So far there have been no newsreel propaganda films made of these riots, nor have any Congressional committees announced their relentless determination to get to the bottom of this violent defiance of constituted authority. As long as it is possible for thousands of young people to call themselves college students, and to demonstrate to the world that they have nothing more important to do with their time, nothing more important to do with their lives, than to foregather for weeks on end at public playgrounds in order to commit a public nuisance – for just that long our society will stand condemned as one which, as I said above, gives American youth everything except a reason for living and for building a socially useful life.

Popular Music and the New Men of Skill

Not long ago there took place in my neighborhood a most exasperating – and illuminating – debate on the effects of popular music on musical standards, between Donald Waxman, an uncompromising young composer, and Mitchell Miller, the distinguished oboe virtuoso, and presided over by Robert Rice, who had written a profile of Mr. Miller for the *New Yorker*.

Mr. Miller's remarks and the attitude toward popular culture that they reveal are deserving of a wider audience than that afforded by the roomful of his neighbors and admirers whom he addressed in Rockland County, and I should like to make them available here in somewhat abbreviated form. Mitch Miller has not been content to be a "working classical musician," his own modest description of a career that has won him international recognition as one of the great oboists of our day. He is also "A & R Man" (Artists and Repertoire) for Columbia Records, which means that as director of that company's popular music recording division he has been responsible for the phenomenon of Johnny Ray and for a considerable amount of the music that we hear over the radio and on juke boxes.*

* *Footnote, 1961:* Mr. Miller has since, of course, gone on to become a familiar star and personality in his own right. Those who do not Sing Along with Mitch have surely seen his smiling countenance in the vodka ads.

It was perhaps unfortunate that Mr. Waxman chose primarily to demonstrate how popular music has declined in basic melodic themes since the Twenties and Thirties. Mr. Miller was consequently freed from the necessity of addressing himself directly to the subject. He countered Mr. Waxman's playing, with acid comments, of such records as "The Little White Cloud That Cried," with his own company's recordings of popular hits, also punctuated with irreverent and amusing remarks.

But to Mr. Waxman's complaints that everything is now geared to the juke box, that artificiality has replaced spontaneity, and that current musical sentimentality is a hybrid of Salvation Army brass and youngsters screaming for more, Mr. Miller had a seemingly endless variety of glib and picturesquely worded retorts.

There was the incontrovertible assurance that the record companies are giving the public what it wants. That this may evoke memories of similar pronouncements by bordello operators and publishers of sado-masochist "mystery" books should not consequently render it nugatory. For, more than that, thanks to LP, the record companies are now giving the public *everything* it wants, from wailing balladeers to Beethoven's chamber music. The manufacturers, men of taste though they are, simply grapple with reality when they proceed from the incontestable truth that the public prefers Johnny Ray to the Budapest Quartet. They are consoled in this unhappy situation by a keen awareness that the sales of pop recordings are a thinly disguised blessing in so far as they make it possible to produce recordings of classical or modern music which will predictably be unprofitable . . . or comparatively so. (Here again the similarity of the argument to the suave Sunday-supplement press releases of paper-book publishers and movie producers – indeed of all businessmen who seem to conceive of themselves as colossi with one foot in mass media and the other in class media – should not be interpreted as necessarily weakening its validity.)

But Mitch Miller's most sophisticated defense of the

kind of music now being manufactured for mass consumption was almost lost in the shuffle of those who wanted the floor to air their own prejudices and confusions. Music, he observed, is the most transitory of all the arts; it whizzes past the ear and is gone. Those who play classical records, as well as those who drop their nickles into juke boxes, often do not even *listen* to it, but merely allow it to fill the air while they drink, dance, eat, talk. Obviously, then, the general response to music is basically emotional. The listener who does not know counterpoint can only respond emotionally to Beethoven's *Great Fugue,* regardless of how much more highly he may value his response over that of the hillbilly-music enthusiast. Even the musically educated listener, technically trained to follow Beethoven's fantastically inventive convolutions of counterpoint, is in the end having an emotional experience too, for what else is an intellectual appreciation that is so deeply felt as to be moving in itself?

Having thus aroused the guilt feelings of the entire audience (all of whom must surely at one time or another have listened with only half an ear to good music, or regretted the lack of training which effectively precludes the higher appreciation), Mr. Miller was able to press forward unchallenged to another level of discourse. Who is to say whether one type of emotional response is superior to another? In a free society, no one has the right to deprive his fellows of a variety of emotional experience which he may disapprove of or find distasteful. Popular music serves the masses who work for a living; the novelty hit enables the workingman to "have a ball" after a hard day's work; the lyrics of "I Believe" put into singable words the philosophical banalities which the proletarian feels but cannot express (and is therefore, we are assured, the biggest hit in the world, even played in churches); the recording of "Ebb Tide," complete with sea gulls and flowing water, is released during the hot weather, and makes stifling humanity feel cool; Miss Doris Day's singing of "Secret Love" appeals not only to adolescent lovers but to reminiscent ones as well, to all who are receptive to a nostalgic evocation of their first inarticulate romance.

One cannot help but suspect that such a leveling, "democratic" defense of meretricious music, when made by a renowned performer of discriminating musical taste, must conceal a boundless contempt for the mass audience. Essentially it is the semiaffectionate contempt for the sucker, of the pitchman for the rube, of the procurer for his customer; here we find it extended to encompass not only the lowbrow, but the middlebrow and highbrow as well — all, in short, who consume music but are not so fortunate as to make it . . . or to promote it.

One of the promoters happened to be in the audience, a prominent disk jockey who took irate exception to Mr. Waxman's pointing out that in current popular music the melodic line is thin and the emphasis is on audio-technology. Himself a musician, trained at several of our leading institutions, he had left WQXR (America's outstanding middlebrow radio station) because, as he put it, he could no longer bear to listen to the endless repetition of the same forty albums of classical music. (There was no mention of money. Nor had there been by Mr. Miller.) He was satisfied, however, when he heard Mr. Waxman admit that he did not listen to the radio (although he too had once been associated with it professionally) and then utter the heresy that he did not believe unqualifiedly in recordings, that Mr. Waxman had thereby disqualified himself as a commentator on the musical scene. The implication was that departure from the intolerable middlebrow world was morally sanctioned if it took one to the democratic (and profitable) precincts of the lowbrow, but had to be condemned as an atrocious manifestation of snobbism if it led to the segregated area of the highbrow.

The arguments of the disk jockey, undoubtedly a man of sensibility and taste, paralleled those of Mr. Miller. Both defended popular music against the attacks of those who had no *right* to attack it. Why no right? Because they expressed reserve as to the inherent value of phonograph records, because they could not listen to popular music on the radio without becoming ill and hence could not be *au courant,* or simply because as laymen they were intimidated by the superior technical qualifications of the defenders. After all, you can't buck success in the U.S.A., whether in business or in high art — and Mitch Miller has it both ways.

But the appearance of the disk jockey served as a reminder that Mr. Miller is not merely a successful middleman, peddling a commodity already in existence and already in demand. He is an important part of a vast apparatus devoted to the manufacturing of public taste and to the conditioning of that taste through constant reiteration (the disk jockey and the juke box), and he cannot escape responsibility for his share in the creation of a mass demand for mediocrity and worse.

The salesmen of popular culture are anxious for the aware and the educated to believe what they would apparently like to believe about themselves: that they are merely filling a need. The exigencies of mass production of the mass media and the attendant necessity for carefully calculated programs of saturation must surely compel them to devote an increasingly large part of their business lives to the stimulation of a desire for junk among the impressionable young and among millions of ordinary citizens who, while they may be receptive, have not been observed taking to the streets in demonstration of their demand for greater quantities of that junk. They would be less than human if they did not readily subordinate this aspect of their activities in favor of an emphasis on the obvious proposition that their junk finds a market.

But this is an old complaint. It has been brought against the popular-culture merchants with depressing regularity, and there appear to be no grounds at present for hoping that it may be safely abated as the cultural level rises. Yet the terms of the complaint may have to be revised as the ranks of the culture businessmen are infiltrated by the new men of skill, who are more adept at the art of self-justification without the aid of a corps of public relations experts hired to mediate their case to an increasingly knowledgeable public. Mitch Miller can be seen as the musical counterpart of Dore Schary; as Schary supplanted Louis B. Mayer, so Miller has supplanted an earlier generation of cigar-chewing Tin Pan Alley vulgarians — and additional examples could be adduced from fields other than popular music and Hollywood movies.

With the gradual shift of control of the mass media to the hands of educated technicians there is a concomitant shift in the defensive rationale of the culture merchants, and in their resentful mistrust of the egotism and superciliousness of those who still proclaim their belief in the primary importance of the individual, self-centered creator in the arts. The most heartfelt attacks on the "irresponsibles" and the "esthetes" as subverters of the democratic diffusion of culture are coming not from those who have traditionally sought the honor of sniping at highbrows, but from the new men of skill, who regard themselves — not without a certain justification — as both liberal-minded and cultivated.*

It was hardly to be expected that these new men of skill would seek to justify their conduct in the terms of their predecessors, who could speak bluntly about being in business to make money. What was not foreseen, however, was the contempt for the consumer that would lurk behind every platitudinous protest of faithful service to the mass

* *Footnote, 1961:* Such an educated mass-media executive of the new generation as Robert Sarnoff, writing for the *Saturday Evening Post* and testifying before the Federal Communications Commission, believes that a good offense is the best defense: Television, it appears, is if anything too intellectual and too far ahead of the masses. The argument must be read to be believed.

spectrum of mass taste. Can it be that this contempt serves to screen from the very ones who harbor it a self-contempt so deep that to reveal it would be unbearable?

Dissent, Summer 1954

Be Happy, Go Liberal

In recent years there has been an increasing tendency on the part of certain of my contemporaries (roughly, those who were undergraduates in the Thirties) to regard international communism as one vast scheme designed solely to make them look ridiculous. Indeed, they sometimes give one the impression that their resentment against Stalinism was originally aroused not by oppression, violence, and subversion, but by shame at the temporary success of the Communists in hoodwinking them during the Thirties. This resentment, far from resembling the dull anguish of the East European directly overborne by Communist tyranny, seems more akin to the anger of the man who finds out, after he has bought it, that the Brooklyn Bridge was not for sale. And since ours is an age when political judgment becomes more acceptable when couched in the vocabulary of theology, we find those who have been "had" describing their common experience not as gullibility, early error, or youthful naïveté, but in terms of guilt, penitence, and absolution.

There are two principal aspects to this concern with the question of political guilt, particularly as it is being codified in the writings of critics like Diana Trilling and Leslie Fiedler (*An End to Innocence*). First, it is not stated personally, in the manner of those who feel impelled to repent their youthful sins before Congressional committees, but instead aims at including an entire social category (e.g., the liberal intellectuals) in its denunciation of past guilt. Second, it is circular to the point of effectively paralyzing any legitimate social action on the part of the condemned group.

Since the imputation of guilt is seldom personal, it would seem a primary duty to make it quite clear who is being whipped for the "great evil" (the words are Mr. Fiedler's). Mrs. Trilling, in an essay on "The Oppenheimer Case" (in *Partisan Review*, November-December 1954), underlines the absurdity of Dr. Oppenheimer's having been granted clearance when he was a pro-Stalinist and refused clearance when he was just as demonstrably an anti-Stalinist. "In effect," she says, intimating that just the *opposite* course should have been followed, "this tragic ineptitude . . . constitutes a projection upon Dr. Oppenheimer of the punishment we perhaps owe to ourselves for having once been so careless with our nation's security."

Granting Mrs. Trilling the saving "perhaps," who are the "we" who are hereby charged once again with sinning? The American people? Surely not all of them. Surely not the FBI? Surely not the Republican Party? The Democratic Party, then? Or perhaps only its "left" wing? And with that "left" or "liberal" wing, the liberal-intellectuals who were so pro-Soviet throughout the Thirties?

One can only guess. Just as one can only guess at what is meant by "our nation's security." The context would lead one to conclude that Mrs. Trilling is not referring to questions of the United States Army's being either too large or too small, nor to bombers being contracted for at the expense of fighters, or vice versa, nor even to the manufacture of atomic bombs being carried forward at the expense of research into the possibility of hydrogen bomb construction. No, the apparent meaning of this deadly charge, meriting "punishment," is that the liberal attitude of pooh-poohing the Russian Communist danger led directly to the employment — in government and in scientific research laboratories — of men who were either, like Dr. Oppenheimer, temporary dupes of the Stalinists, or, like Rosenberg, Greenglass, and the rest, deliberate foreign agents. If this interpretation is correct, Mrs. Trilling is asking us to assume with her that "our nation's security" was so endangered by these termites that punishment must be assigned even to those not formally guilty of legal crimes.

But there are other voices than Mrs. Trilling's, voices which seem with a little reflection to present a more balanced picture of recent history. There is for example the eminent mathematician Norbert Wiener, who, speaking (in *The Human Use of Human Beings*) of the demand for "the utmost of secrecy for modern science in all things which may touch its military uses," noted: "This demand for secrecy is scarcely more than the wish of a sick civilization not to learn of the progress of its own disease." It may be disappointing to those seeking to relate crime and punishment to science and research, but Professor Wiener summed up without so much as a nod to the question of liberal guilt, pointing out that "the dissemination of any scientific secret whatever is merely a matter of time, that in this game a decade is a long time, and that in the long run, there is no distinction between arming ourselves and arming our enemies."

These words were first published in 1950, a remarkable tribute to Professor Wiener's prescience, given what we now know and did not know at that time about hydrogen bombs. But since there may be those who feel that Professor Wiener has disqualified himself as a commentator by virtue of his very standing as a heterodox scientist, it may be illuminating to consider what the distinguished conservative observer Walter Lippmann has learned from recent scientific developments.

It is in connection with "the spying out of secrets," wrote Mr. Lippmann in his column of August 28, 1955, "that informed opinion is changing. The Geneva conference on nuclear energy has proved conclusively what scientists have long been saying — that scientific secrets do not last long because what one scientist can discover, others — since they deal with the same natural world — will discover too. It is also plainer than it was a few years ago that what you can hide temporarily from the Russians, you must hide also from your own scientific community.

The net of it is that the preservation of scientific secrets is not nearly so important as it once seemed because there are so few real scientific secrets."

This statement would seem not merely a triumphant vindication of Norbert Wiener's warning, but a practically incontrovertible statement of the spying-science-secrets question vacating the whole liberal-guilt mythology of any practical significance. Seen in this light, Mrs. Trilling's argument seems probably untrue, and certainly foolish and unimportant.

Let us return therefore to the question of the identification of the liberal "we" and to the further guilt of this group. Mr. Fiedler is somewhat more precise than Mrs. Trilling: "I use the word 'liberal' (and 'intellectual' is, for better or worse, historically synonymous with it in America) to mean all those who believe or believed Sacco was innocent, who considered the recognition of the Soviet Union not merely wise strategically but a 'progressive' step, and who identified themselves with the Loyalist side during the Spanish Civil War."

It is worth pointing out that Mrs. Trilling, who comes to conclusions somewhat similar to Mr. Fiedler's, uses different criteria in defining her "liberal-progressive" or her "intellectual." Mr. Fiedler will have his Sacco, while Mrs. Trilling tells us that in the days of Sacco and Vanzetti "nothing could be more typical of [*Dr. Oppenheimer's*] time than the intellectual's separation from the concerns of his nation and the world." I mention this not to prove that two literary critics have different conceptions of who belongs in the liberal-progressive-intellectual grouping that is still so poorly aware of its guilt that it must be continually reminded of it, but to demonstrate the ultimate irrelevancy for them of all liberal attitudes other than that toward the Soviet Union. *There* is where the guilt lies, we are told over and over, not in how "we" felt about Sacco or Haywood or Mooney or Dreyfus or other ultimately secondary concerns. The Soviet Union is the touchstone; the international Communist conspiracy is the arch-menace; those who at any time harbored illusions about the Soviet Union or co-operated in making the Communist agents respectable are guilty as hell and must acknowledge their guilt before they can make so bold as to present themselves again to the public as worthy of serious consideration.

Mr. Fiedler drives the point home in a reduction that must be quoted precisely if one is not to be accused of misinterpretation: "The unpalatable truth we have been discovering is that the buffoons and bullies, those who *knew* really nothing about the Soviet Union at all, were right – stupidly right, if you will, right for the wrong reasons, but damnably right." Who were wrong, and therefore guilty? "We."

What Mr. Fiedler is saying here can hopefully be made more clear by analogy. Suppose that a heterogeneous group of citizens, all cigarette smokers, were gradually to become convinced that cigarettes cause lung cancer. These citizens, idealists of one sort or another, had previously been identifiable primarily on the basis of their enthusiastic enjoyment of cigarettes and on their insistence that their fellow citizens learn to enjoy the weed. Now, however, a series of medical studies appears demonstrating irrefutably that the cigarette is a deadly poisonous enemy of mankind – even more deadly when one considers its smiling disguise. The basically reasonable idealists, convinced – some sooner, some later – by the evidence, give up cigarettes, in accordance with their individual capacities urge others to stay away from the deadly poison, and concern themselves with other pressing problems.

Surely this is enough? Not so, says Mr. Fiedler. It is not enough to condemn the cigarette manufacturers and the advertising agencies, and to dissociate ourselves from them. We must recognize that each of us who ever offered a friend – or, worse, a stranger – a cigarette, shares in the guilt. More: *Before* concerning ourselves with other pressing problems, we must publicly affirm, painful as it may be, that every crank and health nut who ever thundered against tobacco as an agency of Satan was right — stupidly right, accidentally right, right for the wrong reasons, but damnably right. Never mind that Satan has very little to do with lung cancer. Never mind that the cranks had centered their fire on tobacco precisely because it seemed to many mistaken people to offer pleasure and relief from tension, nor that "we" had touted tobacco for just those generous but mistaken reasons. What counts is that they warned against it and "we" didn't.

Well, maybe. Some of us can remember a time, after "we" ourselves had gotten good and scared of tobacco, when the cranks suddenly began selling it on a tremendous scale because it had become politic to do so — not for long, and from the highest of motives, but still . . .

They were "right" and we were "wrong." The Hearst press was "right" when it condemned the Soviet Union, if somewhat inaccurately, as a pesthole of nationalized women run by bearded bomb-throwers; and the liberal press was "wrong" when it presented Stalin's Russia with varying degrees of sympathy, based on wishful thinking, misinformation, and occasional distortion of the facts. Is that *all* we have learned from the Thirties, the Forties, and the Fifties? Is that the sole lesson the liberal must draw from the Moscow Trials, the Spanish betrayal, the Nazi-Soviet pact, World War II, the Berlin blockade, and the atom-hydrogen bomb race — that "we" were wrong, wrong, wrong, and they were "damnably right"?

Small wonder that for Mr. Fiedler other problems, such as the behavior of the liberal (read: ex-Communist) on the witness stand, inspire a knowing grin at the stupidity of the "we" who persist in being shocked when one of them names friends of a generation ago as Communists. "When such a witness . . . identifies for the investigators the utterest scoundrel in the pro-Soviet camp, he finds himself scorned and ostracized by the kind of 'sincere' liberal who gasps horrifiedly: 'He named names!' — as if to 'rat' were the worst of crimes. It is not, however, really the boys' code of not squealing which is at stake, but the whole dream of an absolute innocence." Mr. Fiedler is so enamored with this little conceit that he uses it also in his essay on "Hiss, Chambers, and the Age of Innocence": "Hiss, sensing his inestimable advantage in a society whose values are largely set in boyhood when snitching is the ultimate sin, had traded on his role as the honest man confronted by the 'rat.' "

Let us set aside the question which seems never to have so much as occurred to Mr. Fiedler: "From where is the boys' code received, from Heaven or from the adult world?" and consider instead a more important matter. This political moralist, so concerned with guilt and shame and ambiguities and ambivalences, dismisses airily, as unworthy of consideration *nowadays,* the problem of "snitching," "squealing," "ratting." Apparently it is more congenial to mull over other nuances than to define the motivation of the man who saves his own career and earns the praise of a Congressman Walter at the expense of those who were his comrades in the Thirties and may now be no more Communists than he . . .

Just so, the man who persists in using such old-fashioned expressions as "selling out" is nowadays regarded as hopelessly naïve and behind the times – after all, selling out would imply that there is still an enemy to sell out to (other than the perpetually useful Communists, who if they no longer existed would surely have to be invented); but "we" should all know by now that the enemy has been "damnably right" about the central problem, that he is therefore not really an enemy any more when we are all menaced by Stalinism, that the real enemy is probably the "we" who have been so damnably wrong.

One finds more understanding of what is going on in America on any page of Louis Kronenberger's *Company Manners* than in the whole of Mr. Fiedler's collected prose, for all of the latter's praise by his fellow authority on liberal guilt, Mr. Irving Kristol, as a "brilliant and imaginative" social critic. Mr. Kronenberger observes that there is a logical result of our outgrowing such gaucheries as selling out: the new breed "don't sell out at 40, they sign up at 20. One can even at moments understand why there are now, along with so many shameless young careerists, so many tight-lipped young prigs: they are sitting full-time, in judgment on a society that cries out to be judged."

I should like to make only one further comment on Mr. Fiedler's method of political analysis. In each of his political essays he assumes what is presumably the standard liberal posture: in "Afterthoughts on the Rosenbergs," he argues that these spies should *not* have been executed; in the Hiss piece that "there is no magic in the words 'left' or 'progressive' or 'socialist' that can prevent deceit and the abuse of power"; in "McCarthy and the Intellectuals," that Joe McCarthy is a scoundrel and McCarthyism "a psychological disorder." Obviously, however, there is no flavor to such dull stuff; and so the spice of neo-liberalism is added – the running condemnation of the liberal "we," the discovery that it is "we" who are as much to blame as anybody for what Hiss did, for what the Rosenbergs did and what was done *to* the Rosenbergs, and for what Joe McCarthy has done. That being the case, since "we" are partially responsible not only for how far the Communists managed to get before they were stepped on, but also for such consequent excrescences as McCarthyism, what is the point in our going on at all? Why not turn the whole show over to those who were "damnably right"?

"The fight against McCarthyism," Mr. Fiedler informs us with a turn of phrase that might well leave Arthur Koestler writhing with envy, is among other things "a war for the truth we cannot help betraying even as we defend it . . ." Elegant; but will it do for those who really want to fight against McCarthyism and not against the straw men of the Thirties? Let it be noted that practically every anti-McCarthy statement is qualified (or "balanced") with an attack on his liberal critics, that the condemnation of the death sentence for the Rosenbergs is stretched to include those who protested that death sentence *before* it was carried out: why on earth should a man still want to consider himself as a liberal after reading these exercises in self-scorn, unless he wishes to gain happiness through the purifying flames of suffering?

"It is not necessary that we liberals be self-flagellants." The words are Mr. Fiedler's — their denial is his book. Since he has been joined in this denial by Mrs. Trilling and a host of others to whom abasement before the errors of the past and acknowledgment of the wisdom of those who rule at present seem to obviate any possibility of their concern with our future, perhaps it may be as well for the impatient to leave them in full possession of their liberalism.

For there are problems demanding the attention of serious and articulate idealists, people who are not satisfied with the world in which we exist so precariously and who believe that the expression "a better world" is neither sinister nor old hat. Let those of us therefore who are going to be grappling with these radical problems call ourselves radicals, and leave liberalism to those who claim possession, but warp its militant elements to fit a passive literary pattern of fashionable nuances serving only to conceal their own utter emptiness and prostration before the status quo.

Anvil and Student Partisan, Fall 1955

Footnote, 1961: It is unfortunate that the questions discussed above should still be live in 1961 — how much better for us all had this piece become thoroughly dated and irrelevant. But our tragedy is that we have not learned from the McCarthyite era that reaction must be aggressively countered, not with groveling or penitence, not with liberal rhetoric, but with programmatic realism. The ailment is upon us again in the Sixties as it was in the Fifties; in fact, McCarthyism never died, as the liberals wishfully thought – it was only comparatively dormant until new demagogues could arise. Inevitably they do arise to service those who live in a nightmare world of impotent frustration, their real or imaginary possessions – homes with green lawns, daughters with fair hair – menaced by bearded Cubans, boorish Russians, exotic Chinese, uppity Negroes, violent Puerto Ricans, and slippery intellectuals.

What is more, the demagogues and their allies, the rightist generals whom Senator Fulbright now charges with politically indoctrinating young Americans at public expense, do exercise an effective veto over the feeblest efforts to revamp foreign, domestic, or military policies. They and their subalterns, the cool young characters who call themselves conservatives, in State Department, Pentagon, and extremist wings of both parties, may not themselves take power in this decade; nevertheless they inflict a creeping paralysis on those who do hold power, by their blackmail ability to empoison the very air at the merest suggestion that the United States may attempt to accommodate itself to reality. To take but two examples, one foreign and one domestic: The Kennedy Administration dares not recognize Communist China, much less support its admission to the United Nations, even though both courses are regarded as vitally necessary by our allies and by our own leading foreign-policy students, because the rightist cranks threaten to befoul with renewed charges of treason those whom they force to deny repeatedly any thought of revising our China policy. As a consequence of this cowardice, the extremists are emboldened, and the nation drifts nearer to isolation and ultimate catastrophe. At home the Kennedy Administration declines to present civil rights legislation to the Congress in the vain hope that the minority Southern demagogues who still dominate that body will reciprocate by supporting other legislation deemed more essential to the public welfare. As a consequence of this kowtowing to the worst elements in American public life in the name of that kind of political "realism" which always proves illusory, the know-nothings and the hysterical defenders of a dying order of things are encouraged, and the Negro is driven to believe that there is no place for him in a hypocritical white world. So at home too we drift nearer to the most terrible kind of racial warfare, and no one comes forward with anything more than liberal mush horridly combined with a continued cringing before those animated by nostalgia for the past, hatred of the present, and fear of the future. No one comes forward with a radically rationalist program which would respond invigoratingly to the real problems of the real world, and would thereby finally isolate and render impotent the neo-McCarthyites in their nightmare world.

The Dilemma of the Educated Woman

One of every three college graduates in the United States today is a woman. Of these hundreds of thousands of girl graduates, 92 per cent enter the labor market immediately after getting their degrees.

Anyone who glances at such statistics, and penetrates no further, might assume that the millennium has arrived – at least for those women who yearned and fought for absolute equality with men. It is true, to be sure, that, like our college graduates, one of every three American workers is a woman, and that more than a third of all women of working age are to be found in the ranks of the labor force. But intelligent women are asking pertinent questions about home and career in the overorganized society, questions which imperiously demand answers; and those answers which are forthcoming are both misleading and inaccurate. If we reframe some of these questions we may succeed in clarifying the problem and in focusing public attention upon a variety of proposals, the implications of which have not been carefully examined even by ardent feminists.

The most cursory glance at the Labor Department's figures on women at work suffices to destroy the more vulgar of the petulant plaints that ours has become a republic of women, with the cowed and castrated males dominated by mindless moms with big busts and bigger portfolios. What percentage, for example, of the coeds who will be receiving their B.A.'s this June will go on with the men to the graduate schools where the real intellectual digging goes on? What percentage of the girls who major in philosophy or math or history or science will wind up with a lifetime career in their chosen field? The fact is that it is the new white-collar proletariat which is overwhelmingly female (68 per cent of all clerical and kindred workers are women, 97 per cent of all stenos, typists, and secretaries are women), just as are those industrial drudgeries traditionally dependent upon the meticulous repetitive labors of a docile work force (canning, wiring, sewing, and the packaging of everything from foodstuffs to antibiotics). Turn the matter around: what percentage of the commanding positions in the arts and sciences, in college teaching, research, medicine, government, is occupied by women?

It should not be surprising that this question is still met with bland generalizations about the mental, physical, or biological inferiority of women — as if the Scandinavian and Russian women who play leading roles in their respective technical and medical communities were creatures from another planet. What *is* perhaps surprising is that so many otherwise intelligent American women, "emancipated" though they may be in other areas, will passively accept or even themselves participate in the perpetuation of a pernicious and degrading myth. Nevertheless, we need not assume that when they are silent, or confused, their particular problems do not really exist.

Their dilemma is not — like that of their nineteenth-century New England great-grandaunts — that in a man's world they cannot find men. Almost any woman who so desires — whether she is thin or fat, young or old, beautiful or homely — can usually find herself a husband. Their dilemma is not — like that of their mothers during the Great Depression — that in a society dedicated to work they cannot find work. Almost any able-bodied woman can usually find some sort of work, more readily in fact than her unemployed husband or brother. Their dilemma is rather, quite simply, that they cannot combine satisfactory work with a satisfactory marriage in such a way as to lead truly fruitful and harmonious lives.

The irony is that instead of its being ameliorated, the situation is becoming more aggravated, as year by year more and more bright girls are exposed — temporarily, tantalizingly — to the exciting vistas of the life of the mind. Anyone who has taught at a girls' college cannot but be moved by the intensity and eagerness with which the best of them hurl themselves into the world of books and ideas: they fervently believe that they can learn anything, that they can achieve any goal; they take pride in the swiftness with which they can absorb new ideas, unhampered by the distraction of male classmates. But anyone who meets these girls as ten- or twenty-year alumnae will also be moved . . . but very differently. Here, all too often, are women who reveal in their faces the wretched uncertainty of those who feel they have somehow been betrayed, or have themselves betrayed their own best possibilities; or who expose the utter and absolute dissipation of their adolescent intellectual enthusiasm and its replacement by a supposedly mature, but really mindless, busyness.

Some who speak for our women's colleges claim that it is an absolute positive good for the community, as well as for the individual woman, that she be exposed for four years to the noblest reaches of the human spirit, regardless of whether thereafter she benefits personally from this exposure beyond gaining the confidence to propagandize effectively for the Community Chest or for the regular and persistent exercise of universal suffrage. This may be so; perhaps it is good in the most general sense that the generality of housewifery be leavened with those who at one time were personally involved with Thucydides, Dante, and Tolstoy. But that in itself will not eliminate the frustrations engendered in the bosoms of all those who dreamt briefly of great things.

Suppose that all discriminatory barriers, whether racial or financial, were to be removed from all of our colleges and universities so that any young Negro who desired might attend them. Suppose also, however, that the barriers to his subsequent useful employment in the arts, industries, professions, and sciences, were simultaneously maintained and intensified. It is quite possible that we would thereby produce a generation of thoughtful Pullman porters, redcaps, and janitors, better equipped to exercise their sacred prerogatives as citizens, and leading richer inner lives than earlier generations of porters, redcaps, and janitors. But isn't it also possible that we should have bred a caste of discontented and embittered intellectuals, as has happened in some of the less developed nations?

The analogy is not necessarily farfetched. One need hardly be a research sociologist to determine that American women – and most particularly those who have been to college – are restless and dissatisfied, that in fact many thousands of them feel cheated of the bright promise that glowed so briefly in their teens and early twenties. Our periodicals are flooded with articles on the "disenchantment syndrome," our library shelves are stacked with bad novels (and even a few good ones) about the miseries of the college-trained housewife, which supposedly range from melancholia and alcoholism to promiscuity, and even the TV networks are running programs with titles like "The Trapped Housewife." When the mass media put their paws on the trap, we can be reasonably sure that it exists, in one form or another.

The young woman in the trap is typically in her early thirties, with a commuting husband, several small children, and some happy memories of undergraduate days when teachers and classmates treated her as something more than an ambulating cookbook, with more on her mind than formulas and feeding schedules. Most likely she worked at an office job for several years after college and after marriage, until the down payment was in hand and the first baby was on the way. Now she discovers, some years later, that she is hideously bored, that the babies do not fill her life, that the coffee sessions with her female neighbors consist not of intelligent discourse but generally of inane babble, and that while she may look forward to the day when she can return to the labor market, she is not prepared to take a job which will compensate her decently or make worthy use of her college training or her atrophied mental equipment. A few years ago the *New York Times* ran a series of promotional advertisements in suburban newspapers; one, soliciting subscriptions from culture- and conversation-starved housewives, asked shrewdly whether they weren't sick and tired of having no one taller than three feet high to talk to day in and day out.

Many of these women do go back to work, or hang on to their jobs – after all, almost twenty-three million American women hold down jobs, and about an eighth of these have children under six (almost half of our working wives have children of school age). But when they do they must set up makeshift arrangements for the care of their children, and thereafter they are often as uncertain that they are doing the right thing, and as filled with guilt about their maternal and wifely responsibilities, as are their nonworking sisters about the gradual degeneration of their intellectual faculties. Who has not had to listen to the laughing – but not very funny – complaints of working mothers that they are paying practically as much for baby-sitters, servants, carfares, and clothes as they are bringing home in their pay envelopes?

So the debate rages; suburban symposia are held, with both working and nonworking wives protesting too much in support of their particular individual solutions; ax-grinding lady educators and earnest male psychiatrists leap into the fray, all too often with pseudo-psychoanalytical claptrap about the traumatic effect on American males of involvement with intellectually superior women; and the house organ of the educated housewife, the *New Yorker,* has developed an entire subculture of wearisome jokes about the servant problem.

In all of these endless discussions, the solution to the dilemma of the educated woman is invariably posed in individual, and usually in hortatory, terms: Recognize your psycho-environmental problems. Glory in motherhood. Teach your husband not to fear brainy females. Prepare for the nonchildbearing years. Take extension courses. Join book clubs and reading groups. Adjust to reality.

It is worthy of note that these adjurations and entreaties are not addressed to matriculating coeds, perhaps because those who fill the air with them are dimly aware of the depressing effect that they would have on girls still so naïve as to believe that they are stretching their minds to become useful members of the intellectual community at twenty-five and not (doubtfully) at forty-five.

In short, what is basically a nationwide social problem is treated as though it were a private or a family matter, susceptible of resolution by each woman in her own way, in accordance with her own personal dictates.

This is a peculiarly American habit. Already over half a century has passed since Herbert Croly observed, in *The Promise of American Life:* "The way to realize a purpose is, not to leave it to chance, but to keep it loyally in mind, and adopt means proper to the importance and the difficulty of the task. No voluntary association of individuals, resourceful and disinterested though they may be, is competent to assume the responsibility. The problem belongs to the American national democracy, and its solution must be attempted chiefly by means of official national action."

The observation is even more pointed today than it was in 1909. We are still so reluctant to concede the objective external social reality of supposedly personal problems that, advanced as we are technologically, we lag behind much of the rest of the world in an entire spectrum of public concerns. Instead of recognizing that individual health is inseparable from public health, we assume the eternal nature of nineteenth-century customs of medical care and content ourselves with makeshift family insurance schemes; we are only now beginning to concede the necessity of public responsibility for the medical care of even a restricted segment of the populace. Instead of recognizing that the education of our own children is inseparable from the education of all American children, we move our families from place to place in search of better schools, or put them in debt to send our children to private schools, or dissipate valuable energies in the mothers' clubs ludicrously miscalled Parent-Teacher Associations. Instead of recognizing that the American landscape belongs to us all and should be tampered with only by those who can be socially accountable, we settle for family havens on 60′ × 100′ bits of grass separated one from the other by wire fencing. Indeed, we are even reluctant to conceive that peace may be attainable by common national—and international—action: we throw up our hands at the enormity and complexity of the problem and allow ourselves to be persuaded to invest in family bomb shelters so that we may bury not just our heads but all of our beings beneath the ground.

Is it to be wondered then that we should flinch from the admission that the locus of the dilemma of the educated woman is in the nation at large and in the nature of our social organization, and not just within the confines of her own family?

But suppose we were to concede that we must go beyond the family situation to the very structure of American society in grappling with this as with other problems. What good would it do the intelligent American girl? For one thing, surely it is in itself salutary to arrive at an understanding that one's problems are not always unique, not always the result of some peculiar twist in one's psyche, but may very well be grounded in the earth of our common social landscape.

In addition, it would release for reasoned discussion and debate an entire series of possibilities. Once it is accepted, even for the purposes of argument, that the current family unit–supermarket complex (personal shopping, cooking, child-raising) is neither divinely ordained nor necessarily ideal in promoting both the general welfare and the individual's realization of his full potential, then a number of lively questions pose themselves.

Would it be in the national interest, and in that of a generation yet unborn, to establish a uniform network of infant, child-care, and family cooking centers so that the girl undergraduate could prepare herself for a profession, secure in the knowledge that she would not have to postpone practicing it until her middle years? Would it be feasible to establish in the midst of the tract houses, the subdevelopments, and the housing projects, a decentralized parallel system of adult education so that the young mother could pursue directed graduate studies? Would it be worth while to extend the scholarship and graduate assistantship programs of our universities to provide young professional women with assistance in the care and feeding of their babies as they arrive on the scene?

I can anticipate the objections which would be raised to the implementation of such suggestions; and I believe that there are as valid responses to the inevitable objections as there are to all the resistances to concerted public attack on the other social problems already instanced. But this is not the place to detail the arguments pro or con. I shall be satisfied if these lines will serve to stimulate the recognition – even if agonized or outraged – that the pressing problems of living human beings, of unfulfilled and underutilized American women, are at least as urgent public concerns as are the problems of our highways, our food surpluses, and our water shortages.

1961

Exercise and Abstinence

At ten twenty-five on the rainy tumultuous evening of June 26, 1959, Constantine D'Amato, manager of the heavyweight boxing champion of the world, clambered into the bleak white ring at Yankee Stadium and disposed himself casually in the champion's corner. With his arms outspread along the ropes on either side of him, he crossed one leg over the other and paid no attention as Floyd Patterson was eased into the ring and fussed over by his seconds. He was as serene and contemptuous of his surroundings as he had assured me a week earlier that he would be.

Ten minutes later D'Amato, tears in his eyes, was assisting the beaten, helpless, and dazed Patterson from the ring, and 25,000 shrieking spectators were congratulating each other on having been present at a minor historic moment – the defeat of a 5–1 favorite, the consequent collapse of D'Amato's alleged aspirations to take over the entire boxing business, the emergence of a new kind of fight promoter in Bill Rosensohn, an inexperienced but personable young Ivy League publicist, and the enthroning of a most unorthodox young Swede, Ingemar Johansson, as the first European heavyweight champion since the days of Carnera and Schmeling.

It was my first impression that the crowd was happy primarily because they would be able to say that they had been there. People always like to recall that they were themselves present at a great triumph or catastrophe. And as far as I could tell, the historic event in this case had no racially symbolic overtones, as did the knockout of

Joe Louis by Max Schmeling, or the victory of Jesse Owens in the 1936 Berlin Olympics with Hitler furious in the audience. If there was tragedy this evening at Yankee Stadium, it was a personal tragedy for two strange partners — a shy and intelligent young Negro athlete, and a supremely confident and ambitious Italian student of human nature.

When Joe Louis knocked out a challenger, the black belts of New York, Buffalo, Detroit, Chicago, went wild. Their boy was better than any white man, he was blasting away for all of them — and the whites knew it. I remember the summer night in 1937 when Tommy Farr, the Welsh white hope, stood him off for fifteen rounds. I was working the night shift in a Michigan radio factory with several hundred hillbillies, and we all had little radios at our workbenches, courtesy of the management. The tension whipped through the three floors of that factory, conveyed by electricity — they were *dying* for the black bastard to be beaten — and when he triumphed once again the frustrated fury of my fellow workers was close to terrifying.

I remember too going to the fights in New Orleans some five or six years later as a member of an all-white audience, watching an all-Negro card of fighters pummel and bruise each other to the savage delight of their supposed racial superiors. It was so vile that I never went again (and rarely watched the fights even on television) until the rainy humid evening of the Patterson-Johansson match in New York.

What has happened in the intervening years is that the position of the American Negro has changed so greatly that it is no longer necessary for a Negro heavyweight champion to be a hero to his people; when he is beaten it is no longer inevitable that the defeat will be regarded by Negroes as a racial setback (or by whites as a white conquest). Those Negroes who still crave athletes as heroes have likely gotten more satisfaction out of the ballplayers who have moved into a formerly forbidden sport traditionally dominated by small-town boys and Southerners, and out of the exploits of Althea Gibson on the tennis courts of the international leisure class (Dr. Ralph Bunche, reputedly regarded as something of an Uncle Tom, Nobel Peace Prize and all, by more aggressive Negroes, hit the headlines last year when he revealed that he had been denied admittance to membership in a posh tennis club). But more and more the Negro appears to look for leadership, or for heroes to worship, among those who have been conquering newer worlds in Hollywood, on Broadway, or on the civil-rights front — to the Sidney Poitiers, the Harry Belafontes, the Martin Luther Kings, and Daisy Bateses.

Things haven't reached the point where fighting is no longer attractive as a quick and comparatively easy way for a poor Negro boy to make a buck. But the boy who makes good at it nowadays, like Floyd Patterson, is no longer under the obligation to regard himself as a kind of Walking Symbol. He can simply be a man who has chosen a particular method of getting rich, given the right physical equipment and sound management. And with sufficient progress on the economic front, it is conceivable that fighting will one day seem as senseless a way of getting rich to the poor young Negro as it has come to seem to the poor young Jew and to the youth of other minority groups for whom new doors have opened in the last twenty years. When that day comes, the Puerto Ricans will probably dominate the fight racket until such time as they too are supplanted at the bottom of the economic heap. Or, when the roughest edges of poverty have been worn off for everyone in this country, something entirely different may come to pass — something foreshadowed by the momentary appearance of Bill Rosensohn and the triumph of Ingemar Johansson.

I have been thinking about the fight, and about those three unusual men, Cus D'Amato, Floyd Patterson, and Ingemar Johansson, for some time now, and I begin to suspect that Johansson's victory may indeed symbolize the beginning of a new era in more ways than those I enumerated at the outset. More of this a little later.

Like most readers of the sports pages, I was sucked in by the *expertise* of the boxing writers, who were positive practically to a man that Patterson would beat hell out of Johansson, a big bulky playboy and very possibly a coward (as an amateur he had been disqualified and disgraced at the 1952 Olympics for refusing to fight). So I didn't go up to Grossinger's, where the dimpled young Swedish sportsman had installed himself and his entourage in a one-hundred-thousand-dollar ranch house to prepare for the championship fight. Instead, I went out to Jersey to watch the champ work out and to have a nice quiet talk with Cus D'Amato.

Ehsan's Training Camp has seen better days. Great fighters have trained there in the past, and the champ had chosen it as his headquarters, but still the cluster of buildings at the side of the road had the seedy aspect of a run-down Catskills summer colony. The white clapboard could have used some fresh paint, the grass was more trampled than barbered, and a very motley crowd was hanging around as I drove up. There was an expensive-looking woman with dark glasses in a Cadillac, there was a uniformed New York cop chatting with D'Amato in the driveway (wherever there are fighters there seem to be cops), there was a fellow in a wheelchair. A colored girl relaxed near a wooden playpen as her youngster toddled tentatively on the lawn. Cooks sang in the kitchen.

D'Amato himself is a compact, bullet-headed little man of fifty-one. He wears his thinning white hair so closely cropped that from a slight distance his crew-cut head appears shaven; his cheeks are as smooth and unscarred as those of a man twenty years younger, and he has a humorous and piercing eye. He is also — or was on that relatively innocent day — a hugely self-confident and persuasive human being. A lot of fools run around loose convinced of their own profundity and intellectual superiority – the man like D'Amato who can persuade others of it is worth taking seriously.

I asked him to reveal to me the background of the national fight picture from his angle of vision. He was happy to oblige. It is his view that fighting, like any other profit-making business in this country, has come to be dominated by the men with the most money. The monopolistic combination of multimillionaire Jim Norris, the Interstate Boxing Club (the I.B.C. was broken up several years ago following an extended antitrust court action), resulted from a power vacuum into which moved the money of Norris, D'Amato's arch-enemy. D'Amato is convinced that he would have beaten Norris even without the aid of the Supreme Court: "I almost felt sorry for Jim Norris – he was so rich he never had to think, whereas I was so poor that I *had* to exercise my mind. In consequence I always knew exactly what Norris and Truman Gibson would do next – I knew them as a man knows his own brother. It was pathetically easy for me to foresee their every move."

D'Amato disdains to conceal his belief that Norris – the only member of his set not indicted last fall when the federal government moved in on lawyer Truman Gibson and hoodlum Frankie Carbo and charged them with intimidation and blackmail of fighters and managers – has a warped mind. "How else could you characterize a man with all that money and background who chooses to operate as he does and to associate with gangsters and hoodlums? I know that they call me a psychopath – they're the ones I would characterize as psychopaths."

He has been called not only a psychopath, but a man himself hungry for the monopolistic power he attacks in the hands of others. In his eyes, however, he has been a poor man crusading for the right of the horde of nameless fighters to earn a living without paying tribute to a cartel. And what about the gangsters?

"I have pity for those men. They're ignorant, they grew up in bad environments, they never learned how to get the good things out of life. They're cowardly, dominated by fear, and worshippers of force. And they're only hangers-on, on the fringe of the fight business, as they are in almost every business in the United States."

This is not exactly the way New York District Attorney Hogan sees it; Hogan has spent a lot of time interviewing gamblers and others supposedly involved behind the scenes with the allegedly clean-cut and innocently inexperienced Bill Rosensohn in his promotion of the Patterson-Johansson title bout, a promotion now revealed to have been more farcically complicated than a Wodehouse novel. But then if Hogan were to investigate with equal assiduity the relationship of gamblers and mobsters to other varieties of business enterprise, he would no doubt be the most exhausted district attorney in American history.

And D'Amato himself proved somewhat less than eager to philosophize about immorality in his profession when he was invited to do so, some months after our conversation, by the New York State Athletic Commission. Instead, he betook himself to Cuba under the name Carl Dudley, to look after the affairs of another fighter, and did not return in time for the commission's deadline to refute accusations of improper finagling, because of what his attorney explained as an aversion to flying. His pal, one Charley Black, a former fight manager, did turn up, and volunteered the interesting information that "Cus is a lot smarter than I am." He also admitted that he was acquainted with such types as Fat Tony Salerno and Trigger Mike Coppola, as well as with D'Amato. "But he said," according to the *New York Times,* that "he never had told D'Amato of his associations with Salerno and Beckley [*a gambler also involved in the Runyonesque Patterson-Johansson fight arrangements*]. Had he done so, he said, 'D'Amato would have had nothing to do with me.'"

Be that as it may — and D'Amato may already have had something to say about it by the time these lines appear, if only to contest his suspension as a fight manager in New York State and his own subsequent indictment — the matter of fear brought us to one of D'Amato's favorite topics. He said to me: "I love fighting, despite all this dirty business, for the same reason that you love the profession of writing: I am a student of human character as you are, and fighting enables me to see people raw, with their emotions on the surface. Where else would I see fear so readily exposed as in fighters?"

From here on he spoke in the accents of the thoughtful military man. Indeed he tends to think of himself as would a staff officer in a military academy or a staff sergeant in a combat situation. This self-image is fortified by his bachelor's dedication to his profession (the cooks behind the screened porch where we stood were teasing him, and he remarked, mildly amused but still sharply: "Women are tormented by the idea of a single man") and by his Prussian hairdo and positive address.

"I can stand at the head of the stairs in my gymnasium in the city and watch a new boy climbing up the stairs for the first time, and from the way he mounts those steps I can form a pretty good estimate of his character. Of course, he is afraid – everyone who fights is afraid – but what I am interested in is the quality of his fear and how it expresses itself. I tell every single one of those boys that I have fears too, as every intelligent human being does, but that I consciously train myself to overcome those fears, and that part of my job as a manager is to teach fighters how to overcome their fear by facing it and learning to live with it."

I got the impression that he conceived of himself as a molder of men. I asked him about this, and he glanced at me quizzically, surprised, as if the answer was self-evident.

"Yes, I can change a man's personality and his character, definitely I can. I studied just that for twenty-five years, I had to in order to be successful with fighters. If I changed my own I can change others'. I was the calmest man in the crowd the night that Floyd took the title from Archie Moore – I was so calm I remember being worried for an instant that I didn't feel any other emotion – and then I realized that it was only a matter of logic, it was only because I had known all along that the victory was inevitable."

Maybe so. Up until June 25, 1959, D'Amato believed and proclaimed that if one of his fighters didn't win it wouldn't be the fault of the fighter but of D'Amato: "It would be because I had miscalculated. It would mean that I'd have to recalculate."

The moment of recalculation has arrived. Because with all the talk and all the publicity and all the lectures on the psychology of fear, the fact remains that D'Amato's power and distinction rested on his being in the corner of the world's heavyweight champion. Now he has been driven into another corner. Without a champion as proof of his shrewdness, with his friends testifying to having been the friends of gangsters, he now has the opportunity to demonstrate how much he himself has absorbed of his own lectures. It seemed to me that day that he had very nearly hypnotized himself into a belief not only in his own prescience, but also in his fighter's greatness.

He has a number of stories about Floyd Patterson that he likes to tell, as illustrative of the qualities that attracted him to the boy and convinced him of his mettle. One is particularly charming, even if almost as pat as an incident in an authorized campaign biography. Floyd Patterson was a troubled Brooklyn kid, and was finally shipped off for rehabilitation to the Wiltwyck School for disturbed boys at Hyde Park, the same institution depicted in James Agee's beautiful movie *The Quiet One* (Patterson not only knows the movie well, but is a faithful old grad of Wiltwyck, which he supports in a variety of ways, as does D'Amato). There he was taken under the wing of a teacher who invited him one evening to her home in recognition of his improvement in behavior. At the end of his visit she presented him with a box of candy and said: "Floyd, this is for you. But I want you to promise me to keep it just for yourself and not to pass it around among the other boys, because they're not supposed to have any." The boy replied: "Then I guess I'd better not take it. Because my buddy and I talked about my coming here, and about your giving fellows candy when they visit you, and I promised him if there was any I'd share it with him. Now I'd have to lie and hide it from him, and I'd rather not do that."

"When the woman herself told me that story," D'Amato said, "I was confirmed in the opinion that this was a remarkable boy. I've had it demonstrated to me since in many ways, and we're going to prove to the world that Floyd Patterson is the greatest champion in the history of the ring. Come on, it's nearly time for his workout."

Things were livening up when we went outside to head for the gymnasium. A clot of neighborhood high-school boys bunched before the closed doors waiting for the champ and peering hopefully at the arriving autos in search of celebrities. Two men behind me were greeting each other in French. A pink-cheeked English reporter in bell-bottomed slacks joined two ruddy young Swedes in asking D'Amato for prognostications, prophecies, and an opinion as to the prowess of Johansson.

D'Amato smiled slowly. "We have the utmost respect for Johansson. We have never believed those stories about his refusing to fight at the Olympics. If Floyd has never seen movies of Johansson or studied accounts of his style, it's only because that's his principle, to train and prepare himself for anything, so he won't be surprised the night of the fight."

Now the limousines were rolling into the driveway. Big-stomached men in dark suits with summer straws shading their white faces and their long cigars emerged to greet and be greeted. They comported themselves with the ponderous dignity of men accustomed to respect and flattery. Invariably they were addressed by title, "Commissioner," a rich word that rolls off the lips with the luxurious grandiloquence of "Your Excellency" or "Mr. President." These were members of the New York State Athletic Commission, and I refrain from identifying them by name because they were such peerless specimens of the politician presenting himself to the populace.

Finally the press, sport-jacketed and cynical, arrived together in a rented limo. They had come to watch Patterson work out, but until the champ was ready to feed their remorselessly hungry typewriters, D'Amato was there to be baited. It is easy to see why D'Amato and the sports writers should rub each other the wrong way. Although he does not strike you as an essentially humorless man, D'Amato does combine a fanatic's devotion to his trade with an unswerving conviction of his own eternal rectitude. It is a conviction that is going to need substantial reinforcing after last fall's testimony by the seedy and sheepish crowd that surrounded D'Amato in his backroom deals, and it is obviously irritating to men who are paid not only to collect statistics for adults about basically juvenile activities, but to be oracular themselves about those games. In consequence they tend to characterize him in print as a nut, an egomaniac, or a would-be monopolist; while interviewing him, they addressed him as if he were the not quite balanced Governor of Louisiana and they were needling him in an effort to produce quotable copy for *Time,* The Weekly Newsmagazine.

When the doors opened we trooped in and disposed ourselves around the ring, which all but filled the gym—housewives in cotton dresses, boys playing hooky, floozies, stage-struck would-be pugs, commissioners, sports writers with dead cigars, excited foreigners on the home stretch of an athletic junket. Ralph Cooper, who broadcast nightly tidbits to Harlem direct from training camp, took the center of the ring to introduce everybody to everybody else, requesting applause for and bows from commissioners, sports writers, transatlantic visitors, and nonentities. It was just starting to get embarrassing when Cooper ran out of names, and the champ came out to box five rounds with a variety of sparring partners.

Patterson was solemn, unsmiling, and ferociously concentrated on his work. His slim long-muscled body, dart-ing and glistening as a porpoise's, but darker and more menacing, was the most perfectly conditioned I had ever seen. Some of the men who opposed him in the ring were well built and husky, some even handled themselves with a certain grace, but all looked incompetent and pathetic in the same ring with Patterson, who labored grimly, with inhuman intensity, on defense, on footwork, breathing, timing. He danced, snorted through his nostrils like a stallion, grunted every time he let go with a punch.

All the while Dan Florio, his little gray-haired trainer, stood leaning against the ropes in T shirt and slacks, also unsmiling, thumb between his teeth as if he were a dancing master observing the *premier danseur* at the *barre*, occasionally murmuring through his thumb: "Lift your head. Hands up. Break."

When the five rounds had been duly tolled off, Floyd pranced alone around the ring in a lunatic's pantomime of passion, bobbing, weaving, stabbing, grunting, flashing here and there like an animal suddenly released from a cage, almost incredibly fast. He cooled off slowly before his shower by punching the little bag for the benefit of the photographers and exhibiting himself in various other ways – touching his toes in sit-ups and doing bending exercises.

It was only when I went into his little dressing room with the sports writers that I saw him as a human being and began to sense the conditions of his life. He sat almost huddled on the side of his bed, wrapped in a torn and stained white terry-cloth robe, and sipped at a mug of sorry-looking broth while he attended politely to the tiresome questions asked of him by the reporters.

"The whole art of training," William Hazlitt wrote in 1822 in his classic piece of reporting, "The Fight," "consists in two things, exercise and abstinence, abstinence and exercise, repeated alternately and without end."

I had seen the exercise, and now I was looking at the abstinence. Patterson sat at bay, picking at the towel he held in his hands, separated from his wife and family, in this grubby little room furnished with one chair, army blankets on the twin beds, and a rosary hanging from a corner of the bureau mirror, as he waited patiently for the questions, and for the fight from which he was to earn half a million dollars. Always there lurked the shadow of a smile at the corners of his mouth, and his gentle and intelligent features revealed to me a man who was willing to put up with all this not because he was incapable of imagining anything else (which might have been said of Joe Louis), or genuinely enjoyed it, or was a sharp operator with an eye to the main chance (like Sugar Ray Robinson), but simply because he wanted the amenities of a quiet middle-class life badly enough to suffer fools and undergo physical indignities.

And yet, even with the sparkle of self-awareness that glowed in his eyes as he smartly parried the reporters' probes, his solemn and mystical belief in his own future as a great champion seemed unwarranted by his record (he had been defending his title against second-raters, some of whom had at least succeeded in dropping him to the canvas). When I got home that evening, I jotted down the following question: Patterson seems almost hallucinated by his own ability — has he been mesmerized by D'Amato into believing not only in his own supremacy, but also in his historical position as a great athlete?

The next time I saw him was on the night of his title defense. It had been raining ferociously, steadily, for some hours, and as it tapered off, the air, instead of cooling, steamed muggily. The preliminary fighters went through the motions mostly unnoticed by a listless crowd that milled moodily about the vast spaces of Yankee Stadium; the Stars and Stripes and the World Series Championship flags hung draggily like worn-out dishrags; behind everything the Eighth Avenue train slid by every few moments, gliding in and out of the wet vaporous fog that billowed in and out of center field, half-illuminated by the batteries of night lights.

The people who had paid anywhere from five to a hundred dollars for tickets didn't look very different from the crowd you'd find at the Stadium watching a ball game: ordinary stiffs for the most part, salesmen, plumbers, repairmen, guys who would like to be big spenders on occasion; very few women. Two priests heading for the expensive seats (separated from the cheaper ranks on the infield by bright red cloth) stood out naturally, as did the young sports in Bermudas and their lady friends attempting to look crisp on a wet wilting night. All through the final half-hour before the main event they wandered with apparent aimlessness while the prelim boys pushed each other around.

The ring in the center of the ball park, hooded overhead – I was reminded of a *chuppeh,* a Hebrew bridal canopy – was adorned with flags at each of its four corners, and focused on by three TelePrompTer cameras. The ceremonial aspect of the show was heightened by the stately parade around the ring at the end of each round of a gentleman bearing a numbered card above his head in the manner of a Ziegfeld showgirl. There are all kinds of ways of making a living.

It wasn't until Patterson came up out of the visitors' dugout and Johansson from the Yankee dugout, each surrounded by their retainers and a cordon of cops to ward off the shouting horde of well-wishers, that the evening came to a focus. Then, as I said, D'Amato disposed himself first of all of them in Patterson's corner, almost as if he wanted to show his man how cool it was possible to be on this night of all nights.

At the end of the uneventful first round the Stadium lights were extinguished, and thousands sucked in their breaths at the suddenness with which the ring sharpened to dead white and the two fighters were so keenly silhouetted. Patterson looked as I had expected him to, poised, quick, and beautiful; as he darted around the bigger Johansson like a speedboat buzzing a steamship his swift tension was accentuated by the Swede's bulk and air of stolid reserve. Johansson did little but hold his right fist cocked and wait for the moment he had predicted: he had been referring to his right as though it had a frightful power of its own, but had not once displayed it in training, as though again it were a beast whose vicious strength he had to curb. Now it seemed almost ludicrous in its ponderosity. Surely it was only a matter of time before Patterson would break through and pulverize the meaty façade of his challenger.

Then the third round began, and the Swede's right flashed sharply through the air directly into Patterson's oncoming mouth. The magnificently tempered champion tottered, exactly as though he had run full tilt into a massive wooden mallet, and fell straight backwards, sickeningly. When he arose from the canvas it was apparent that he was half senseless. Thereafter, as all of us arose screaming and howling with the pure frenzy of disbelief and delight at our own presence, Patterson was systematically beaten into helplessness by the bigger man. Moments later, his carefully nurtured career in ruins, he was assisted from the mobbed ring by his tearful manager.

The middle-aged, ruddy, shirt-sleeved Englishman on my left, who had remained throughout as silently unacknowledging of my existence as if we had been fellow passengers on the L.M.S. Railway, leaped up and down, slashing delightedly with his rolled-up air-mail edition of the London *Telegraph* and shouting at me: "You didn't believe it was going to happen, did you? Well, I did! I did!"

He was right, I hadn't believed it. And it wasn't just because I had been conned by the sports pages into thinking that Johansson was hardly any better than the others who had challenged Patterson – that was true enough. Mainly it was because, hardly realizing it, I had identified with both the bemused champion and his obsessed manager. Both men had been straining, each in his own way, after goals I could understand.

And Johansson? He was an enormously popular conqueror that night, and not merely because the modest and manager-dominated Patterson had never succeeded in capturing popular favor as a champion. He is a popular champion, too, in demand as a passable singer on TV and a hopefully charismatic actor in Hollywood. But in addition to his dimple (he is the kind of man girls call "cute") and his aplomb, he has what is basically an amateur's attitude toward the sport. I say this despite the patent fact that this hardheaded young man, already worth a reported quarter of a million dollars from other enterprises, is in boxing solely for what he can haul out of it, and is the kind of person who, as one admirer has it, "counts his own money." What matters is his utter lack of hesitation in indicating that for him there are other things in the world besides boxing.

People thought that the stories of Johansson's high life were hoked up to heighten public interest in the fight. They may very well have been, but what is more significant is that the young Swede's unprecedented training routine in the luxurious atmosphere of Grossinger's, surrounded by mother, father, brothers, girl friend, brother's girl friend, and Platonic friends, and punctuated by rich smorgasbord dinners and periodic excursions to the pleasure domes of Manhattan, represents the hidden dream of a very new generation not for fleshpots and houris, but for the private pleasures, before it is too late, of a substantial middle-class existence.

Johansson had, now, the things that Patterson was denying himself in hopes of having later on. And he had them because his attitude toward his temporary profession was — and is — that of the middle-class man of our era toward his work, whether it is medicine, engineering, or athletics: it's one way to earn a living, but it mustn't be permitted to stand in the way of life's real pleasures.

It is true that Johansson comes from comparatively humble people in Sweden, but there are really no poor in Sweden as there are in Africa, Asia, or Latin America. Sweden represents what America — and therefore the world — wants to be. It was only fitting that a Swede with no noticeable feelings of inferiority or inadequacy to overcome, and who photographs like an ad agency's beau ideal of the young middle-class man about town, should have been the one to bring into question not only centuries of accepted practice in the conditioning of an athlete, but an entire attitude toward work and discipline.

Lest it be thought that I am trying to construct a fancy theory out of one brutal evening's brutal entertainment, consider the reaction of Rocky Marciano, who retired undefeated as world's heavyweight champion. Marciano, the son of poor Italians in Brockton, Massachusetts, could have earned another million dollars if he had gone on fighting, but he couldn't see the sense in indefinitely deferring a comfortable life in favor of leading a wretched celibate existence as a dedicated athlete. When he visited Johansson on the night of his victory, he told him: "I wish you would have been my trainer when I fought. I'd still be fighting."

Marciano (or his ghost undoubtedly, but no matter) informed the readers of the New York *Journal-American* that the Patterson-Johansson fight was "the most radical thing to happen to boxing in this country. I don't mean the K.O. There have been bigger upsets. I mean in what it will do to our attitude toward conditioning a fighter. I said Ingemar trained all wrong. He never boxed hard. He lived with his family, particularly a lovely, but distracting, fiancée. Floyd did everything correctly, while Johansson was the worst, take-it-slow training camp fighter I've ever seen. . . . All I could think of was me waking up in Grossinger's when I trained. I'd see Charley Goldman – before he shaved – and Allie Columbo, and then go out on the road. When I'd get back from running, Al Weill, also without a shave, would be up and ready to give orders. . . ."

Am I wrong in thinking, then, that we may possibly be on the verge of a new era in boxing, in which the sport will come to be dominated, not by poor boys drawn into it from an inability to conceive of themselves as proportionately successful in other fields, but by that new breed of cool young men who see all forms of human endeavor simply as alternate modes of buying leisure?

I realize that particularly at this moment, with the first Patterson-Johansson shindig being fine-toothed by the law for evidence of malefaction, and with more slobs exposed to public contumely in every sports final that hits the streets, it may seem ludicrous to suggest that boxing will become more rather than less respectable. But since when has the periodic apprehension of embezzling bank tellers in Buenos Aires or Bahia deterred an ambitious young man with a head for figures from going into the banking profession? We tend to be amused, rather than indignant, at the crooks and sharpshooters in other areas of American enterprise (at least in all except labor unions), and it may very well be, may it not, that when the gold dust blows away, our institutions of higher learning, which have been replacing the moribund minor leagues as a training ground for professional baseball, basketball, and football players, will also replace the slums as breeders of rich and respectable fighters?

In that case, the tragedy of Floyd Patterson will be seen in his having been – needlessly and regardless of his impending return bout – one of the last figures of a dying era, rather than as one of the first of the new. And that of Cus D'Amato, in his overweening ambition, single-mindedness, and pride finally being unavailing, simply because they were outdated and hence overmatched against the button-down-collar boyishness of a far more relaxed bachelor manager, Ingemar Johansson. I suspect that it is the man who manages himself, Johansson, who will be seen – together with whatever temporary buddies he may gather about him as successors to the in-too-deep and already sunk-from-sight Bill Rosensohn – as riding the wave of the future.

The Noble Savage, No. 1, March 1960

Footnote, 1961: Since the above was written, Floyd Patterson has whipped Ingemar Johansson, not once but twice. All too obviously I am no expert on the fight game. Those who criticized me for this, or for not writing with the knowledgeability of an A. J. Liebling, mistook my intention.

The article tries to point up a tendency for which there would seem to be evidence throughout American life, even though one ought not to bear down on it too hard – only the sports writer, making bum guesses about his play world, can stand the strain of being wrong year in and year out!

For another thing, it *was* Johansson, after all, and not Patterson, who really capitalized on his title. It was Johansson who became the crooner, Johansson who became the movie actor (in a war movie, with Mort Sahl, of all people), Johansson who became the dimpled TV personality alongside America's Current Sweetheart, Dinah Shore. No matter how long he retains his title, no matter how many plump and passive playboys he knocks cold, Floyd Patterson will never be able to sell American youth on his life as a model of exercise and abstinence – not as long as the living is easy, and there is no longer anything much worth fighting for.

The Pilot as Precursor

If you want to talk to a pilot today, you have to make an appointment. He does not frequent bars. He cannot drink anything alcoholic for twenty-four hours before he flies. He does not congregate at the union hall. He regards it not as a hangout but rather as a technical headquarters. And you cannot watch him at work, because nowadays it is easier to watch a surgeon performing a brain operation than it is to check in with a flight crew and follow them through a routine run, say, from Salt Lake City to New York.

The "typical" pilot, seen through the spyglass of a survey, is a white man of about thirty-seven, who owns his own home and has a wife and two children. He has had three years of college, belongs to a union (the Air Line Pilots Association), and earns about fourteen thousand dollars a year.

Fourteen thousand dollars a year is a lot more than the ordinary union member makes. For pilots' salaries to average out to this figure, many of them have to earn up to $25,000 a year, and do. But high earnings are only one of the factors which mark the pilot as different not only from his AFL-CIO brothers, but also from the vast middle class, of which he considers himself to be a fairly representative member. These differences are really more suggestive than superficial similarities.

For one thing, pilots represent an elite group psychologically as well as physically. Drawn for the most part from the high-standard Air Force (45 per cent, with perhaps 35 per cent coming from the Navy and the Marines), they have to start all over again through a battery of examinations in order to qualify for the big new jets. Only one applicant in sixty makes the grade. The man who is cleared at last to fly these planes is not merely an A-1 physical specimen; he is, as Ed Mack Miller, who teaches him how to fly them at United Air Lines' Flight Training Center in Denver, puts it, "a very highly developed human being."

This human being, whose vision and reflexes and heart and blood pressure and nervous system must be such as to place him in the top 1 per cent of the population, can never rest on his good fortune at having once passed both government and private examinations, like the doctors and dentists who can coast after their state boards, or the professors who can vegetate after acquiring their Ph.D.'s. He is subject four times a year to a test of his flying skill and twice a year to a severe review of his physical condition. At any time he may be debarred forever from air line flying. This boils down to the fact that a pilot of sixty has to meet the health and proficiency standards of a pilot of thirty. Obviously, only a selected group of a selected group can stay on the job until sixty. His union itself figures the average rate of attrition to be about 3 per cent a year. Of a given group of one hundred copilots all twenty-five years old, only 10 per cent have a mathematical chance of flying until age fifty-five. Of the group, 89 per cent will have been separated before sixty years of age.

But there is something about these pilots that is even more special than their physical and psychological qualifications: They love their work. By and large it would seem (although it can hardly be proved) that fewer and fewer of us are happy with our work. When you come upon a group of men who are fanatically devoted to what they do for a livelihood, it is a remarkable phenomenon. There are so few pilots who have voluntarily quit the air lines that they can be called up by name by their fellow fliers, as eccentrics or misfits.

This is worth a little examination. Some years back we

might have waved it away by writing off the pilots as perpetual adolescents who loved to court danger, who craved glamour, easy dough, and the thrill of thumbing their noses at death, like racing drivers or soldiers of fortune. But now that air line operations have become as routinized as railroads or buses, pilots can buy life insurance at the same rate as office workers. These healthy, responsible, cautious men are a good risk.

Then why? What is there about flying that continues to enthrall them? The answer has to be divided into three parts. First, what they are doing is necessary. Second, it can be performed only by a highly selected elite group. Third, it is fascinating.

In inverse order: Every pilot with whom you speak insists that he likes to fly because every flight involves a series of swift and important decisions. Even the most routine and presumably boring milk run must have a takeoff and a landing; the slightest shifting of wind can make either the takeoff or landing a singular and dramatic experience. The closest analogy might be to the riverboat or harbor pilot or to the master of an ocean liner, whose job may often be boring or exhausting but also has the potentiality at any moment of intense excitement and rapid decision-making. It is this potential of great demand on the individual's skill, ingenuity, and resourcefulness that is the source of the enormous pull of commercial flying for pilots, replacing the old charge that the daredevils used to get from contact flying in planes made by hand. This potential has not been at all diminished by the development of the jet airliners. Quite the contrary. The technical work in flying the new airplanes, despite (or perhaps because of) the fact that they are actually easier to fly than the old piston aircraft, is awesome to a layman. As Ed Miller explains it, the new pilot has to be "a computer with legs." Miller, who trains pilots in the simulators, and who is himself a successful writer as well as a pilot with twenty years' experience, details a dizzying series of computations and decisions that have to be made almost automatically, and with split-second precision, by the pilot of the jet as it is leaving the ground or returning to it.

The pilot takes a natural pride in the fact that not many men can qualify to fly a commercial jet. There are thousands of competent pilots, in the military services as well as civilian holders of various classifications of licenses, who would not be permitted near the flight deck of a DC-8 or a Boeing 707. Inevitably the fraternity remains closely knit – a fact of which the Air Line Pilots Association has taken intelligent advantage. The air line pilot has a highly developed sense of exclusivity as well as of command.

He knows too that what he is doing becomes increasingly important, increasingly essential, with every passing hour. If it was hair-raising fun to fly the mail thirty years ago, letters could always be delivered by rail if you were killed or went on strike. But all passenger travel today is practically dependent on the scheduled air lines; if all of the 15,000-odd air line pilots in the country were to walk out at once (a situation which is not practically possible) the country would be in the grip of a national emergency more immediate and far more irksome than that gradually brought on by a strike of half a million steel or auto workers.

The pilot is different from other Americans in some other ways that are even more interesting, perhaps because they are unexpected. He is more worldly and somewhat more sophisticated than the average citizen, particularly if he is flying an overseas route. He tends to read more newspapers and magazines than his neighbor, and by virtue of the fact that one day he is in Karachi and another in Bangkok and another in Berlin, he is more aware than are most Americans of the true size and shape of the world and of his native land's place in it. At its best, this concern can issue in the kind of constructive selfless action taken by Captain Charles C. Dent, who donated all of the $5500 bonus awarded him for a safe crash landing to the United States Committee for the United Nations to help promote its program.

If he is a more concerned American, the pilot is also a more stable one. It should hardly be surprising that his home breaks up so infrequently that most people in the industry find it hard to name offhand any pilot who has been recently divorced. (He is not *always* a model husband. One learns from ex-stewardesses that the "key game" flourishes as a weekend diversion among flying families in the upper Midwest. Although there is no corroboration of this gossip that in certain communities blasé pilots and their wives play switch, like other bored suburbanite couples, there are others to assure you that when one air line based its pilots and stewardesses in the same Honolulu hotel a few years ago, the shack-up incidence and the subsequent marriage breakup rate were so high that sexual segregation had to be instituted.)

In the main, though, the pilot does tend to participate more wholeheartedly than his neighbors in somewhat more respectable neighborhood activities, such as scout leadership and civic affairs, maybe because he has more free time at home than they do. Surely most surprising about this middle-class man so jealous of his position in the community is the extent of his active participation in a tough union, the Air Line Pilots Association. But of this, more later.

There are pilots who in their free time are insurance salesmen, aviation consultants, travel agents, ski instructors, novelists, sail-plane enthusiasts and fliers-for-fun, teachers, cattlemen, cow-punchers, farmers (from potatoes to oranges, depending on locale), dog fanciers, aircraft brokers, ministers, parachute jumpers, woodworkers and furniture makers, real estate brokers and property managers, executive recruiters, big-game hunters. At a guess only 5 per cent have income-producing sidelines, but many of them do become passionately interested in avocations which may possibly become full-time jobs in the event of grounding or retirement. Pilot after pilot will tell you that he goes into those sidelines not at all because he dislikes flying but because he has considerable free time and does not get the variety of satisfactions from his work or his relations with his employers that he comes to feel life ought to hold. One suspects that he is merely anticipating all of those Americans who will sooner or later be going on a four-day week, or a six-hour day, or both, and who, whether or not they like their work, will find themselves unable to spend their long lives simply staring at television or building barbecue pits.

The future pilot usually goes to college for several years and then, bored and restless, signs up for a four-year tour of duty and is sent, say, to Lackland Air Force Base. He discovers that not everyone can strap the bird to his back, not everyone can fly a hot jet. So he is proud when he earns his wings, but like most of us he chafes under rigid military discipline, and he turns to the civilian career possibilities of the commercial air lines.

Here, however, he is taught that while there are bold pilots and old pilots, there are no bold old pilots. So he becomes, if he was not to start out with, a technically minded and very careful man. In his mid-twenties, he learns to forget hot jockeying, and to value stability and the ability to avoid even involvement, if possible, in emergency situations.

He learns too that the very size and speed of the big jet has shrunk more than distances. It has also shrunk job possibilities for the men at the controls. Aside from the fact that it is a simpler plane to operate, it can take more people from one coast to the other in half the previous time. This means that the pilot who is supposed to fly eighty hours a month has to make more flights, and that as the air lines turn to jets, pilots with less seniority are being laid off. Many of those who manage to hang on find that promotion has become very sluggish indeed; in an industry from which the romance has disappeared, some are coming to terms with the idea that a man can make a life's career out of being a copilot. (If he shrinks from the thought of what will happen in the coming decade when supersonic flight becomes a reality and the ocean is spanned in an hour and a half, he knows that his work-week will have to be shortened again and that only his union is currently doing any substantial research in the multiplicity of problems that will accompany the supersonic age.)

Nevertheless, as an American he is an optimist, even if a worried one. He is more aware than are most people that although flying is as popular in this country as reading, it is just as restricted to a special segment of the population. Three out of every four Americans have never flown with the air lines. Only 2 per cent of the peoples of the world have ever been off the ground. More of them are going to want to fly, and, as living standards rise, are going to be able to; and the pilot looks forward to flying them. Far more important is the potential in the air cargo business, which can only increase, with fantastic possibilities in store not merely for inventories and business in general, but for pilots. If we reach the point in this country where, with the development of modified jets and all-cargo planes, even 2 per cent of all cargo is shipped by air, there will have to be a threefold increase in aircraft personnel.

This is why the hopeful pilot believes that the employment slump brought about by the jet age is only temporary, and that great days lie ahead, probably in the latter part of the Sixties. If right now there is a surplus of pilots, despite the substantial attrition rate, he thinks that in a few years there will be a shortage, as the older men retire and the youngsters are not attracted to the industry in sufficient numbers from the military or from no-longer-star-struck high school boys. He is convinced that it is going to be necessary to train pilots in the universities, perhaps under government subsidy, since, as the missile age develops, the services will simply not be giving flight training to many young men. He points to England and France, where the corporations themselves, while state-owned, already sponsor nonmilitary flight-training programs.

The pilot, who knows that it takes better than four

crews to keep one airplane operating efficiently around the clock, sees the air lines – like the automobile manufacturers – merging and consolidating; and he is aware too that the top money is in the Big Four, where average first-pilot earnings in 1958 were better than eighteen thousand dollars. Since he loves to fly, he is stimulated far more than he is annoyed by new developments. There is nothing like novelty, challenging one's adaptability, to keep a job interesting. As one veteran pilot turned executive says, "Even the transition from the DC-3 to the DC-4 was comparable in complexity to that from piston to jet. Every technological advance is an added insurance that flying will continue to be fascinating."

Nevertheless, although he is almost unique in having a job that pays well, that is highly respectable, and that he loves, the pilot is going to be bucking in years to come – like his friends and neighbors in the ranch houses across the country – for more pay and shorter hours. Which brings us back to the intriguing question of his union.

Captain C. C. Spencer, who flies for Pan American in addition to having served as Regional Vice-President of the Air Line Pilots Association (in effect running the New York office of ALPA), estimates that there are some seven hundred pilots who are active on a day-to-day basis in the operation of the union. This is particularly remarkable when you consider, first, that these are solid homeowners, the majority of whom probably vote Republican (or at least did until General Eisenhower appointed their bane, General Elwood Quesada, as head of the Federal Aviation Agency) and have neither a family tradition nor a compelling personal interest in a militant labor movement; and second, that their union has but two salaried full-time officers, the President and the Executive Vice-President: all of the other officials are unpaid and fly for a living. The Local Executive Council of the ALPA, its basic unit of organization, varies in size, depending on the size of the air line it represents, from six hundred down to ten members.

The councils pretty much run their own affairs. (There are fifty-two air lines in this country having separate union agreements, all separately administered.)

Naturally, you will find griping about the union, mostly apparently from the younger men who feel that they are being frozen out or ignored by their seniors who have their own cliques and their own political machine. The union's official response to this is not merely its constitution and its carefully democratic table of organization, or its well-advertised freedom from corruption and collusion, but also the practical evidence that each Master Executive Council generally has two new members serving on it during any given election period, and that there is always an active search for new-member participation in the rotating positions.

How are we to explain the fact that these individualists, who like to think of themselves as professional men, and who feel no particular bonds with the main body of the organized labor movement, participate so actively in the running of their union? The answer is not to be found by approaching this union as basically a trade or professional pressure group like the American Medical Association, primarily engaged in such monopolistic practices as locking up existing jobs, restricting entry into the field, and boosting income to astronomical heights. Other unions and associations behave like this and do not as a necessary consequence elicit from their membership the kind of voluntary effort so impressively in evidence at the ALPA.

In the union's handsome Midway Airport headquarters in Chicago, President Clarence H. Sayen, the forty-two-year-old former Braniff pilot who has headed the union since the expulsion in 1951 and subsequent death (in 1953) of its first president and charter member, Dave Behncke, is voluble on this matter. The contrast between the two is almost too pat a lesson in recent American history. Behncke was a swashbuckler out of the Roaring Twenties, a barnstorming stunt man from the hazardous early days, with a hairline mustache and a flair for theatrics, but with no administrative ability or the faintest notion of the functions of a union in the second half of the twentieth century. Sayen is an academically oriented young man with a master's degree in economics, who has been a college instructor, is sensitive to the new political and social currents, and gives speeches — substantial ones, too — with titles like *The Cultural Impact of Jets,* to commerce and industry associations. Sayen has his own theories about the wide extent of member participation in ALPA and its implications for AFL-CIO organizing efforts, abysmally unsuccessful so far, among the millions of technical and white-collar people.

His union has been so successful in engaging not only the attendance but the freely given aid of its members (some 10 per cent of whom, by his reckoning, are actively engaged in union work at any particular time) that other unions, all much larger numerically than ALPA, have been coming to his office for advice and suggestions on matters of white-collar organization. Sayen is proud of this and attributes it by strong implication to several factors.

First would be the enormous concentration of union attention to problems of safety. About five hundred pilots, or enough to operate a medium-sized air line, are engaged in union safety projects on a part-time basis. The projects are both voluntary and nonprofit. Pilots involved in them are reimbursed only for lost flight time. A brief listing may give some idea of the well-nigh fanatical dedication with which the pilots concentrate on safety work: (1) Investigating crashes. (2) Flight evaluation. (3) Aircraft evaluation. This includes at-the-factory examination of designs, mockups, etc. (The DC-6 and DC-8 have 112 design modifications made as a result of ALPA suggestions.) (4) Surveillance of airport facilities. (5) Air traffic control improvements. An ALPA group worked on airborne radar. (6) Physical standards. ALPA is a corporate member of the Aero Medical Association. (7) Special projects. One example: the centerline approach light system, enormously important for obscured landing conditions; one pilot has worked on this problem for over ten years.

This is where the second factor of member involvement enters the picture. The ALPA has apparently discovered, whether deliberately or through a series of fortuitous events, how to capture the interest of its membership, or at least of a substantial enough fraction so that it can rely upon their varied backgrounds for much of its own necessary work. Air line pilots are in all likelihood the most safety-conscious group of people in the United States; significantly, it is not their employers so much as their union which has channeled that consciousness into serious and productive achievement.

"Safety not only in the workplace but in the product as well is surely a proper prerogative of the union," Sayen says. "If the United Auto Workers were to insist on building safer cars, and to show how it could be done, not only would the public benefit, but the union would be drawing even more than it does now on the intelligence and ingenuity of its members."

The ALPA has been encouraging a number of pilots to go on to graduate school, secure in the knowledge that it can tap the brains and skills of these men when necessary. ALPA is able to set up committees of members who have degrees in law, physics, etc., and who can, as Sayen concedes, "offend the hell out of people with a more leisurely approach. They are aggressive because of what they know and want, and can experience a lot of frustration." It is his union, he feels, which is doing the job abrogated by management. "Really, we run a big management-training school."

The implication is that other unions might well do likewise. While all of the full-time ALPA staff, from legal counsel to public relations men, is professional, they co-ordinate their work with pilot committees. Pilots themselves, often with a background of study in economics or accounting, negotiate their own contracts side by side with the professional staffers. "The pilot's horizon," says Sayen with a sententiousness reminiscent of Walter Reuther (with whom he obviously has a good deal in common), "expands to total responsibility."

Maybe. Nonetheless it is true that one ALPA member has done a Ph.D. thesis on the control of air space, another a thesis on the 1950 reorganization of his union, a third, in psychology, on full-field vision (a problem allied to aviation). In each case, as well as those where pilots have been encouraged to study writing, commerce, business administration, the union has benefited from the pilot's avocation.

It is an avocation which may do more than aid the union: it may become a livelihood. Few people need a second string to the bow more than a pilot – only one out of ten air line pilots flies to age fifty. And while ALPA sponsors an excellent insurance program against grounding, it is a fact that most men are grounded – whether for a heart murmur, high blood pressure, failing vision, or whatever – not toward the close of their careers but at their very peak, during their thirties and forties. "If we can get our members through the male menopause," Sayen says wryly, "they're usually set until retirement."

Not only are pilots under the constant pressure of knowing that they may be grounded at any moment by one of the two physicals and four proficiency checks to which they are subject annually, but they are now compulsorily retired by government edict at age sixty – younger to my knowledge than almost any other trade or profession in the country.

I sat in the suburban Oak Park living room of a sixty-year-old pilot shortly after his involuntary retirement and listened (it was all the consolation I could give) while the grounded pilot returned again and again to his obsessive bewilderment at having been forced out by fiat.

"One minute I was entrusted with bringing that plane into Midway with eighty passengers, all those lives and millions of dollars' worth of property. The next minute it was past midnight and I was a menace. I was forbidden to do what I can do as well as any man living. Why?"

It is humiliating for a skilled man to be put to pasture at the peak of his performance, particularly when it is done arbitrarily and when he has demonstrated year after year his physical capability to perform like a thirty-year-old, and with an accumulation of incalculable experience and judgment simply unavailable to any thirty-year-old. But more than this, he is cut off from his livelihood just as he has gained the uppermost earning bracket of those top-seniority chief pilots in command of the new jets — and, at sixty, five years before his social security checks will start to arrive.

In the next two years about two hundred and fifty pilots will reach age sixty and compulsory retirement. Their trying situation is coming about not as a result of attempted economies by their employers, but by virtue of a non-reviewable administrative regulation presumably promulgated in the interests of aviation safety (a particularly bitter pill to men who have been seriously concerned with safety all of their working lives).

Indeed, the battles over retirement and flight inspectors between the union and the FAA, together with the maze of government regulations with which every working pilot must be intimately familiar (his union participated in the drafting of the legislation which set up the FAA), have been cited as contributing — along with the broadening effect of travel — to the pilot's high degree of sophistication. These struggles with the government over "technical" matters might, one would suppose, be taken as one more factor setting him apart from the general run of the population.

But here we may begin to draw the pilot back into the general community once again. We have been enumerating the peculiarities of his craft which tend to make the pilot special and to differentiate him sharply from the millions in the American labor force. But won't virtually every one of those peculiarities (with the possible exception of his extraordinary need for exceptional physical fitness) be increasingly true of Americans in general in the coming decades? Even that final element, the increasing tendency for resentments and consequent strikes and litigation to be located not so much between labor and management as between specialist and bureaucrat, is coming to be characteristic of the American scene, as more and more of us either work directly for the government or find our working lives and our working benefits (regardless of which party is in power) dependent upon decisions made by appointed officials of the federal government.

This holds true even in the seemingly smallest areas of the pilot's working life. Not long ago the FAA promulgated another regulation, forbidding pilots to leave the flight deck except for emergencies or bodily necessities. Aside from the fact that it struck the pilots as one more slap in the face, it served to put an end to company-encouraged fraternization between flight officers and passengers. It emphasized the godlike remoteness of the pilots in their now inaccessible control room and threw the air lines' public relations burden on two of the most unstable occupational groups to be found anywhere — sales personnel and stewardesses.

If the pilot is increasingly isolated from the passengers whom he flies, isn't this too a condition of working life which he holds in common with all those who find themselves, thanks to rationalization, mechanization, and automation, more cut off than were their fathers from patients, customers, clients — in short, from human beings? Stewardesses, incidentally, tend to look upon the pilots of their planes either as tyrants who treat them like slaveys, or as distant but kindly figures, daddies away from home; their efforts to achieve autonomy, though, for the Air Lines Stewards and Stewardesses Association, have been frustrated not only by the brevity of their employment, but also by the ALPA, which insists that it knows what is best for these less-skilled sister-unionists, apparently because it fears being outvoted under conditions of equality.

If the pilot is increasingly isolated, too, from the other members of his craft, except for those few with whom he shares the flight deck, and those with whom he is associated in union committee work, this is a condition already true of many others, and one that can only be accentuated as work place and living place become more widely separated in decades to come. His friendships, like those of his fellow Americans, will be formed less as a consequence of shared work patterns; more likely they will come from community involvement, shared hobbies, or common social or political beliefs and behavior.

Today many pilots who have the seniority to bid on the best flights, the long-distance runs, instead pick the worst, the milk runs or the up-and-down runs, only because then they can remain based near their homes. But there are many who want it both ways, and hence commute by private plane or by sports car hundreds of miles to the airports. They would seem to be the vanguard of all those – yes, even coal miners – who will continue to flee the megalopolis, but will have to come back to it for their livelihoods, and will, when commutation flying has caught up with high-speed flying, be traveling fifty and a hundred miles to work within our own lifetimes.

The consequences of all this for ordinary living, from friendships to family relationships, are incalculable and perhaps best left to the trend spotters and the sociological columnists. But one thing is sure: the daredevil flyboy of recent memory has died. In his place we have a splendid physical specimen, true, but also a skilled technician, an active unionist, a community-minded hobbyist and a concerned parent who – whether you think of him as a paragon of the American virtues or as a square caricature of responsible respectability – is as close as you can get to a living exemplar of the American workingman of the future.

Esquire, October 1961

Work and the Professions

One of the great ironies of our time: The country that achieved pre-eminence in considerable part through an almost religious dedication to work has become the land where leisure and fun are enthroned as the new gods. We Americans were so fanatically devoted to work not only as the source but as the end of life that we became the butt of jokes to our own writers, from Sinclair Lewis to H. L. Mencken, as well as to European hotelkeepers and boulevardiers, who tagged our menfolk as people who didn't know how *not* to work. But in a few short years we have not only picked up the fallen flag of the aristocrats and fainéants – we have emblazoned on it our current national motto, in the international neon language of the mass media: Work is for squares.

One day we awoke to the discovery that we had developed the capacity to produce more than we could consume with less expenditure of effort than is required in other nations simply to stave off hunger. More, we discovered that more and more people could get more and more by working less and less – or by not working at all. *Fortune* magazine was not kidding when it called "not working" the fastest-growing occupation in the United States. Consider: Between thirteen and fourteen billion dollars a year in personal income is now going to individuals in the form of stock dividends, three times the amount paid in dividends twenty years ago. Over twenty-five billion dollars a year is being paid as interest income, and over twelve billion as rental income. If you take into account the twenty-eight billions going to individuals as "transfer payments" (which means payments not resulting from current production — that is, mostly social-insurance benefits and veterans' payments), this boils down to the fact that, as Sylvia Porter, a syndicated financial columnist, puts it rather excitedly, "18 to 20 per cent of all the personal income being paid in this country today is going to Americans who are NOT WORKING for the income."

Inevitably, the news of this spreading stream of gravy seeps through even to those who aren't getting any of it. If the message is not plain even to the dullest, the mass media are in there punching to drive it home. What other conclusion can we draw from the unlamented quiz shows, their wild proliferation checked only when its cancerous nature became a national shame? The sick fascination was not in any display of brains (patent nincompoops and muttonheads shared in the swag) but in the demonstration that absolutely anyone could lay his hands legally on enormous sums of money without lifting a finger or shedding one drop of honest sweat. If the quiz shows are gone, "Queen for a Day" remains, and in the supermarkets you can now enter contests without so much as writing one jingle or completing one sentence in twenty-five words or less. To jet to Paris for two on a detergent manufacturer or retire with a lifetime tax-free income on a dog-food distributor, you need labor no longer over rhyming dictionaries. In keeping with the times, such intellectual trials are often dispensed with, and the loot is passed out on a no-sweat straight lottery basis.

Why work? You don't have to be beat to be ruefully aware that, increasingly, middle-class occupations are as phony as the title to an acre of land on the moon. I believe that not one person in a hundred who "works" in advertising, merchandising, public relations, radio, television, mass circulation magazines or movies is engaged in what was once known as honorable, socially useful labor. A growing proportion of the new middle class is being paid for putting in the hours between amusements at tasks that cannot be justified by traditional standards in terms of either public utility or personal satisfaction.

Those who are indignant at the irresponsibility of labeling practically all careers related to the mass media as non-work or fake-work jobs might think about some of the implications of the following excerpt from an undelivered speech by an advertising agency official, as reported in the *New York Times* of February 17, 1960: "As long as the object of the mass communications industry is to deliver a maximum audience at a minimum cost, cultural factors must take a back seat. Entertainment, art, culture and enlightenment are only means toward fulfilling the economic objectives of the mass media. . . . Artistry, morality and religion are permitted as part of the public relations of the field. They provide a means of avoiding serious criticism and legal action. . . ." I wish only that there were space to quote further from this confession, about which the *Times* goes on to explain, "When the official learned to his horror on last Friday that his speech was not to be private, but was to be publicized, he telephoned the school and canceled the engagement."

There are others just as frank and apparently even more shameless about what the new middle class is perpetrating to earn its fun and games. In a paper in the *Harvard Business Review* entitled "The Dangers of Social Responsibility," Dr. Theodore Levitt, marketing and economic consultant and advisor to Standard Oil of Indiana, has opined that "If what is offered can be sold at a profit (not necessarily a long-run profit) then it's legitimate. The cultural, spiritual, social, et cetera, consequences of his [*the seller's*] actions are none of the businessman's business."

Significantly, the hucksters and their hired hands, the boating enthusiasts and barbecue experts, who should be the last to complain about the laziness or the dishonesty of others, are the very people who are most vociferous at their watering holes — coffee breaks, lunch dates and cocktail parties — in their annoyance that the lower orders are not putting out as they used to.

Certainly it is true that, as millions of toaster owners have discovered to their dismay and outrage, it is almost impossible to get a small appliance honestly and reasonably repaired. And it becomes less and less likely that the instinct of workmanship will have found vital expression either in the original construction or in the repair of such enormously expensive items as a Detroit automobile or a development house. No argument here. The real question is whether this decline in pride of craft and standards of honest dealing comes about as a result of union-enforced slackness and the unlikelihood of being fired simply for sloppiness or whether, as I believe, it reflects an economy increasingly dedicated to planned obsolescence (read: short-lived junk) and dominated by types who have no aim in life beyond making a bundle (ponder the case of the recently deposed president of one of our largest corporations, currently under stockholder suit for allegedly having knowingly purchased, on personally profitable kickback terms, inferior parts for his company's product).

In our understandable frustration at struggling with a national situation dominated by lack of respect for the "pro" – the man who cares enough about what he produces to work long and hard at making it both handsome and satisfying – we find it easier to refer our irritations with bad service, rudeness, sloppy workmanship, and inferior products to a few large, easily identifiable, malign bodies. But it simply will not answer to attribute all these maddening and shameful annoyances to Big Unionism on the one hand or Madison Avenue on the other.

The unions cannot be seen as either parent or midwife to these iniquities; they are rather a mirror, reflecting a disturbed awareness on the part of their members that as their tasks are made increasingly minute and differentiated, they themselves become separated from any vital relationship to the finished product, and that in many cases the finished product is hardly worth making anyway. Not only does the same hold true for the advertising-agency employee (who is additionally burdened psychologically with the manufacture of personal enthusiasm for products of dubious utility); *his* organization reflects the enormous pressure in our society to move goods and consequently to brainwash consumers into believing that they want or need these goods — without real regard to their quality or indeed the very necessity for their existence.

Given this dual deification of production and the continuous movement of goods (no matter what kind), we should not be too surprised that an increasingly uneasy public tends to blame unions, or any other easily labeled entity, in preference to the harder task of analyzing the impersonal forces that create our new national hypocrisy. Nor should we be quite so unprepared for the personality deformations occurring as a result of grown men being bribed to spend their waking hours at tasks that mock the very possibility of a serious, professional achievement with one's hands or brain.

Not least among these deformations, along with the blind, pot-and-kettle, middle-class complaint about the falling-off of working-class performance standards, has been a virtual disappearance of our concern for those whose lives are not overmastered by the forty billion dollars which *Life* magazine happily assures us are now spent annually on "nonworking." Last year Albert Whitehouse, who runs the Industrial Union Department of the AFL-CIO, described to a public-relations seminar of the Harvard Graduate School of Business Administration "a gathering of polite people in an upper middle-income suburb. The locale could have been outside any large city in the U. S. A. The group was all-professional, of middle age and upward — doctors, lawyers, government careerists, and their wives. To hear these good people, organized labor is to blame for virtually everything from the Berlin crisis to nationalist outbursts in Nyasaland. What bothered me most was that all the disagreement was virtually as polite as the agreement. . . . These professionals seemed to have forgotten the past. . . . A strange myopia afflicted the crowd, or so it seemed to me. . . ."

Mr. Whitehouse went on, "Something seems to have gone out of American life. It's a sense of sympathy for one's fellow man, a sense of integrity, an understanding of the other fellow's right to human dignity. There was a day when the picket line of underpaid textile workers commanded sympathy. There was a time when the plight of the farm worker was of national concern. There was a day even when the nation cared about its poor, and that wasn't so long ago."

The nature of the complaint is already known. What is infinitely depressing is that, as Mr. Whitehouse indicates, the infection has spread from the much-pummeled admen to such presumably unassailable areas of selfless endeavor as the learned professions. I am particularly sensitive to the conduct of the new generation of medical men because my grandfather, my father and a number of uncles and cousins have acquitted themselves with a certain distinction in the field; and I fear that some of them would be hard put to justify the action – lack of action would describe it more accurately – of a number of their contemporary colleagues. Surely no one will begrudge a hard-working medico an undisturbed day off such as he used never to be able to enjoy – or two days off, for that matter. But now it becomes increasingly difficult to obtain the personal services of any physician after five o'clock on any afternoon, particularly if you need to have him come to you, and not vice versa.

We have all read hair-raising stories about silly women jabbering on a party line and refusing to get off so that a frantic father could reach his family doctor in an emergency. What we haven't been told is whether, when the idiots finally ran out of breath, the doctor finally condescended to come to the phone. There are doctors now who will speak to you, all right – and will subsequently bill you two dollars for having taken up a moment or two that might otherwise have been spent at the lake or on the putting green. The after-me-the-deluge attitude of some of these practitioners, together with the unrepudiated last-ditch Bourbonism of their union, the A.M.A., may very likely serve to give impetus to the passage of a national medical insurance program; in the meantime, however, it helps to carve out one more stone in the monument to greed and laziness now arising in our midst. The same has to hold true for the lawyers who are so busy making money and having fun that they cannot spare a moment to restrain the American Bar Association from sniping at the Supreme Court of the United States, simply because that body has been taking seriously the upholding of constitutional liberties.

I would hold no group immune. The college teachers, of whom I have been one in recent years, have let it be known that they are overworked and underpaid. This is generally true, just as it is true that they are entitled to more time and money for travel and research. But the hot pursuit of the gravy train of grantsmanship and the chase after cushy overseas deals must arouse suspicion as to how much these selfless scholars actually intend to accomplish in the unsullied realm of free thought and to what lengths (or distances) they will go to escape from the American classrooms they claim to be so concerned about. The effect on graduate students of the antics of these goof-off artists of academe cannot be estimated here. What we can say is that college kids smarten up in a hurry, and that by the time they graduate they know as many angles as a five-percenter or an influence peddler. You still have to work in graduate or professional school, but more often than not you labor now not to extend the boundaries of human thought but to gain admission to the club or the club-car of the gravy train.

Now if these things are true, as I believe them to be, in such rarefied areas as the learned professions, consider how much more depressing they are when we encounter them, swollen to ugly proportions, in the population at large. The counterman or waitress who cannot be troubled to remember that you asked for tea instead of coffee, the cook who cannot be bothered to drain the water from a plate of lukewarm spaghetti before dumping it in front of you, the optometrist who sells you harlequin glasses when in fact you do not need any glasses — all are demonstrating in their particular ways the deformations wrought on pride of performance and the integrity of a job well and honestly done by a culture that no longer puts any premium on such accomplishments, but glorifies instead the "instant," the "magic," the "ready mix," all euphemisms by and large for the quick, the sloppy, the careless buck.

The effects are perhaps most acutely painful in the field of popular entertainment, partly because they are most pervasive and hence most unavoidable, and partly because they catch kids — future doctors, lawyers, professors, countermen, cooks, optometrists — at their most vulnerable, and inculcate them with values (whether they accept them or rebel against them) that must color their adult lives.

For quite a while one of the handsomer attributes of the American public performer, the real pro, was grace under pressure, which might be more closely defined as a carefully developed faculty of making the difficult look easy and effortless. This kind of grace helped to endear Crosby, Sinatra, Joe DiMaggio, and Ted Williams to their fans.

But now we find many young athletes motivated less by an urgent desire to do, with grace, what has never been done before, than by an expectation of doing what has already been done by many around them. The dream of the talented as well as the hopelessly untalented athlete is to clean up in a hurry.

As for the popular singers, we can in all truth regard a number of them not as human beings aspiring to impart an air of effortlessness to their performances but, rather, quite simply, as manufactured objects, with neither more nor less relationship to the rest of the human race than the juke boxes whose glassy insides they feed with an assortment of noises. One of the current favorite singers was found, by an ambitious agent, at age fifteen with his guitar on a tenement stoop. The agent gave him a name, a wardrobe, a hairdo, some recording tests and singing lessons.

These were soon given up as hopeless because the boy was tone-deaf; but this made no difference – the agent had guessed correctly that the boy would be attractive, or could be rendered attractive, to young girls, no matter what sort of noises he made. As a result, this adolescent, who will not be of voting age for some years and who is more of a concoction than he is a developing human being, is already more "successful" than Szilard, Waksman or Salk. And although he will be more quickly forgotten, his life story (such as it is) and its implicit moral is to be found not in the sociological journals but in the daily papers and the fan magazines, and is being digested by millions of youthful Americans.

Even the modest but at least honorable ambition of learning to sing popular tunes pleasingly, an ambition which implies the development of a professional attitude of respect for one's craft and for the people at whom it is aimed, now goes by the board in favor of a willingness to be shaped into a commodity that will sell phonograph records to fill empty hours and empty heads. The test is solely in the speed of the payoff, since neither the performer nor his handlers – nor, in the final analysis, his fans – have any image of him as a man building a career; they see him instead as an ambulatory bank account. Inevitably, this shambling dollar sign is taken by millions of the impressionable young, both here and abroad, to be the true Voice of America.

Are we all getting worse? Were Americans actually better human beings back in the Thirties, that decade which seems to grow more noble in our eyes as it recedes in time? I don't think so. As one who is grateful that he grew up in that exciting period, I believe that we ought to be cautious about overestimating the extent to which most young people were caught up by unselfish and idealistic movements. After all, even in the collegiate hotbeds of radicalism at the pitch of the depression, the great majority of the student body went about their single-minded business, ignoring public problems, studying commerce and accounting, trying to pass civil-service examinations.

What differentiated the intellectually aspiring young people of the Thirties from today's was, it seems to me, that the best of them found a relationship between their private aspirations and the public needs. The boy who wanted to go into electrical engineering knew that the Rural Electrification Administration was in the process of bringing the modern era to millions of farm homes; the young law student saw that Washington needed him and wanted him; the youthful visionary felt not only that the world could be remade but that he had a vital part to play in that remaking, whether in the skill of his hands or in the exercise of his mind.

Today the best of our young people find no such relationship and in consequence are so quickly corrupted that it is horrifying. Those who do not turn their backs on the whole sell and go beat, refusing to work except at odd jobs in odd moments, abdicate by settling for those values embodied in the editorial columns and the advertising pages of the upper middlebrow magazines: a blenderized liberalism, a deep cynicism about what they do for a living and about the entire possibility of achievement through work and an intense desire for nothing more than the trips to Europe, the little cars, the liqueurs, the collecting of paintings or other objects.

It does not follow that this is what the millennium must look like. These are the people who spend about seven hundred thousand dollars every single night of the year on tranquilizers to still uneasy consciences and to bring on the oblivion of sleep after days spent in unwork. Every study that I am aware of indicates that man is a creature who thrives best on work and (at least until now) has not found means of deriving continuous personal satisfaction in a society from which work has been outlawed.

This does not mean that we need ever go back to a social order built on the backbreaking toil of millions of drudges; we are on the verge of an era in which it will not be necessary or lawful for a single human being to be so ill-used. But I would deny with all my strength the notion that young people now are so rotten with soft living that they shun work as they would the plague. From my own experience as a teacher and a writer whose work has brought him into correspondence with many young people, I must assert that the flame of idealism burns as brightly as ever, that the search for fruitful work to which one can dedicate one's life is as strong as ever. It is just that it is choked off all too soon by the cynics of a culture built on corporate profit and dedicated to the principle that nothing counts but the fast buck.

This is not the place to spell out the kinds of work that could still pick college kids up by the throat and instill them with that sense of purpose we all recognize as having disappeared from the national scene. I would only note my personal conviction that it will have to be found abroad, in friendly partnership with the new nations; and I will ask only what the effect would be if, instead of sitting around and making cheap jokes about revolutionary leaders, a few thousand trained young Americans were to pitch in and try to help these revolutions achieve their professed goals, to see if they really mean business about public health, housing, literacy, agricultural diversification, full electrification, full employment. The answer to our American dilemma, as to those different problems faced by less-developed countries, cannot be found in happy hobbies or even in the most high-flown leisure. It must still be sought in fruitful work, applied to the great and greatly challenging tasks that still confront the human race.

Mademoiselle, March 1961

Why Resign from the Human Race?

I am speaking in these lines directly to the young people of college age with whom I have been having such spirited arguments in recent months. With some of you the discussions have been face to face, with some they have been by correspondence, with yet others they have been, I confess, only in my own mind – and occasionally, I hope, in yours. I admit freely now that there is real point to your complaint that I offer you nothing positive, not a single concrete suggestion as to what you and your contemporaries might do to make this a better world. Well, I believe that now I do have a suggestion. But first suppose we review the terms of our argument.

You have always been most generous in your appraisal of "my generation"; in fact, you have been envious of the turbulent fifteen or twenty years we have on you. In your opinion life was exciting and worth while for those of us who were in college in the Thirties because there were causes worth fighting for and because the ideals with which we identified ourselves so passionately did seem not only worthy but realizable. You who are in school in the Fifties claim that those causes have either been won or are no longer worth fighting for – and that any more up-to-date ideals, no matter how splendid, are in any case unrealizable. This is a consequence, you say (and with a good deal of reason), of the centers of power – political, social and cultural power – having moved so far away from the grasp of the average citizen as to be unreachable and hence uncontrollable.

Therefore those of you whom I care most deeply about, the ones who resent the assumption that young people should unquestioningly and unhesitatingly take their places as little cogs in the big power machinery of politics, mass communication or the production of trivia, are embracing cults which attempt to turn their backs on such ugly realities. In consequence you demand that I should not take a superior attitude toward your successive infatuation with funny motorcycles and funnier automobiles, noisy poetry and prolix prose cagily characterized as "beat," offbeat religious revivalism running the gamut from A to ZEN, folk songs and guitar players, cold-water flats and J. D. Salinger, and a host of unrepaid loans from the white and Negro jazzmen of "'my" generation, ranging from jive talk to marijuana. Believe me that I am not listing these enthusiasms merely in order to poke fun at them, and that I am attempting to place them in their proper context; indeed, they are in many ways preferable to those major love affairs of the Thirties, Stalinist politics and popular-front "art." In trying to evaluate them, I think in terms of the over-all view expressed by Erich Kahler in *The Tower and the Abyss:*

The impossibility of drawing any meaning from the mass of material and reasoning assembled in our age has given rise to desperate movements, like futurism, Dadaism and surrealism, which . . . in order to start afresh, attempted first of all to destroy all meaning wherever it could still be found in the conventional uses of language and action. The existentialist experience and ensuing theory is another consequence of analysis and despair. Thus, loss of meaning produced disillusionment with illusory meanings, weariness of meaning, intentional destruction of meaning and ultimate crumbling of meaning and coherence in the very texture of daily life. All these movements herald a panicky mood which looms underground in people's minds and may one day break down the last barriers of civilization if developments are left to drift the way they are.

Professor Kahler's warning in that last phrase is the nub of my own worry. I am perfectly prepared to grant you your esthetic satisfactions, even though the best of them may strike me as minor and the worst as ugly and antihuman. But I continue to ask: After your pleasures, what?

So far your response has been, "Better these pleasures than the others. For now, better to say no than to conform, better Jack Kerouac than Herman Wouk, better the poetry-*cum*-jazz sessions and the folk-song kicks than the as-advertized-in-*Life*-magazine teen-age parties. For those who are sick of guff, better Mort Sahl than Senator Dodd; for those seeking love, better J. D. Salinger than Norman Vincent Peale. For those who want to be counted out, not in, better the cold-water flat than the split-level suburb."

I could not agree more. But the road to the suburb is paved with your pleasures. For every girl living rebelliously in the Village with cats and slacks, there are two who have tired of it and settled for a commuting husband, with kiddies and station wagon. For every boy reciting bad poetry and talking of shipping out to sea with his guitar, there are two who have called it a day and gone back to graduate school or on to motivation research. You must understand that I am not mocking you or your contemporaries; realism is not necessarily ridicule. After all, the woods (or rather, the bars) are full of my contemporaries with potbellies and too many belongings — men and women who swore when *they* were in college that they would never rest until Spain was free or the Negro was equal.

And so we come back to my question and to your taunt: What *else* is there for you to do today?

I am going to begin my attempt at an answer with another question, addressed to you, and if it in turn leads to yet other questions, I must beg you to bear with me. My query is this: Why are your contemporaries in such a rush to settle down?

Perhaps that is an innocuous question, but isn't it true

that the mad dash of young people nowadays to have not only a home and children, but a job with built-in old-age security — and possessions piled on possessions — is precisely what repels you about your own generation? Isn't it the fear that you too will turn out that way (as I assure you that you will one day, other things being equal in this commercial culture of ours) that drives you to despair? Isn't the fear that you too will turn out that way what causes you to overvalue the idealism and selflessness of the Thirties? How many times have I heard you cry that you didn't want to be stuck in the rut of senseless job, deadly commuting, and monotonous organized-community existence!

If you are going to be honest about it, it seems to me, you must start by conceding that your generation, dissidents and conformists alike, has been sold a bill of goods. The quest for security and personal certitude has been converted by the unremitting pressure of advertising, as well as by the exigencies of a culture which places a premium on the acquisition of goods, into a convulsive rush on the part of people barely out of their teens to live as their parents would rarely have dreamt of living after a decade of marriage.

Hand in hand with this insistent demand for air-conditioned apartments, washer-dryers, stereo-TV, and all the rest of the apparatus which many young people today seem to think they must have in order to begin married life, there goes an absolute, unthinking disregard for the conditions of daily life under which the vast majority of the human race is struggling to exist. For all he knows or cares of the rest of the world, the average American college student today might as well be living in Borneo. If a ragged and half-starved Egyptian schoolboy takes to the streets and, by howling up a demagogue, consigns the rest of the world to hell, we can make allowances, we can understand why he should not understand or care about the consequences of his actions. But what are we to say of the overfed and overdressed American collegian who, exposed to first-rate minds, and with every wonderful facility at his elbow for stretching his horizons, can think only of his creature comforts to the complete exclusion of other matters, and can dream only of creating a cocoon for himself and for his wife and his children – thereby yielding the future of the human race by default to the manipulations of a handful of shrewd ideologues half a world away?

I know you will point out that this absorption with self, this pre-Copernican notion that the world (if there is one) must revolve around the American, is not confined to the college student. That is unfortunately true. Some months ago, the *New York Times* ran a dispatch from Madrid by Benjamin Welles describing the lives of young Americans attached to SAC air bases throughout Spain. Never mind why those bases are there, or what they are costing us. Hear how our compatriots live:

> . . . For newly arrived families, never before out of the United States, lugging baggage and children, speaking no Spanish and worried, the shortage of housing has depressed most of them. . . . To check this morale problem – it spreads like wildfire if unchecked – the United States Government is now building about 1,200 standard, bungalow-type homes. . . . All the houses contain three or four bedrooms; two bathrooms; living room-dinette; central heating; carport; modern kitchens with electric ranges plus washing-drying machines. Each is completely furnished. . . . The overwhelming majority of United States officers, airmen, and their families will live together, eat together, worship together, shop together at the base commissaries and post exchanges and, in short, exist cheek by jowl. Their contacts with the Spanish people will remain at a minimum.

Mr. Welles concludes this obscene forecast with the mild observation that "the military-base program has been an object of hatred among the Spanish left-wing opponents of Generalissimo Francisco Franco. They see it as a device for shoring up an inefficient, paunchy dictatorship. The right-wing 'in,' on the other hand – bankers, industrialists, monarchists, high clerics, machine and bureaucracy bosses and military chiefs – accept, even if they do not like, the presence of the United States forces. It insures peace and order in their time."

Not long after this, the *Times* printed a dispatch from Seoul, Korea, in which Robert Trumbull observed:

> The New American military housing, which the aid mission will also share, will be on more or less secluded military reservations behind barbed wire. Since no unauthorized visitors will be admitted by the guards without a special pass, relatively few ordinary Koreans besides servants are likely to see how the Americans live in these centrally heated, fully electrified duplexes.

While you are pondering the spectacle presented by these barbed-wire oases of togetherness, mindlessness, and gluttony scattered from Spain to Korea across the parched desert of the underdeveloped world, let me at last put to you my concrete proposal. It is very simple: that you and your friends launch an immediate campaign for the establishment of an international volunteer work force of at least 100,000 young people annually. This work force would be recruited from the recent college graduates of universities in the United States, Canada, England, Western Europe, the Scandinavian countries, the U.S.S.R., and the highly developed nations in the Russian orbit such as Czechoslovakia.

Under the auspices of the United Nations, this professional and technical force would place itself at the disposal of underdeveloped lands throughout the world. Instead of imposing itself with missile bases on sullenly reluctant populations, it would come only at the express invitation of the host nation. Instead of living like conquerors, more luxuriously than garrison troops, *it would live on the economy of the host nation:* in temporary pioneer barracks, if necessary, for the single men and women; in simple quarters like those of its opposite numbers among the indigenous population, for the married couples and their babies. Instead of isolating itself from the life around it, it would conceive of a very part of its function as being to participate as widely as possible in that scientific, social, and cultural life for the duration of its stay.

You already know of the existence of such organizations as CARE and the American Friends Service Committee, and of their small staffs working devotedly in many areas distributing food, medical supplies, and other basic necessities to peoples desperately in need of them.

And I am sure that you are familiar, if not from your own summer experiences, then from those of your friends, with the Experiment in International Living, which supervises vacations spent fruitfully in the homes of families in many European, African, and Oriental nations.

But you may possibly be unaware that the UN recently voted into existence the "United Nations Assistance in Public Administration Plan," which will go into effect early in 1960.

This plan, which was viewed very dimly during the debate on it not only by the former big colonial powers such as Belgium, the Netherlands, France, and the United Kingdom, but also by the U.S. and the U.S.S.R., has been outlined by Jane Stolle in an article entitled "Experts for Hire" in *The Nation*. Miss Stolle describes how the scheme to assign experts in public administration to some of the newer nations for at least next year (and hopefully longer) was devised by those nations in conjunction with the UN Secretariat, and how it is in a sense an outgrowth of the United Nations Technical Assistance Administration, which for years has been spotting experts in various countries where their skills can be most helpful. She cites as an example the thirty-seven men who came from thirteen different countries to give India a hand last year. They arrived from the Netherlands, France, the United Kingdom, Denmark, the United States, the U.S.S.R., Belgium, Canada, Norway, Sweden, Switzerland, El Salvador, and Burma: they included statisticians, geologists, demographers, physiotherapists, hydroelectric engineers, chemical and mining engineers, insecticide experts, ceramicists, economists, six computer technicians (all from the U.S.S.R.), and a lighthouse expert from England.

I ask you to imagine what the effect on our moral stature in the Far East would have been if those thirty-seven responsible technicians had been joined by 10,000 young Americans when they came home to take up their careers.

Is there any compelling reason why 50,000 American college graduates cannot postpone – for periods of from one year to three years – the immediate commencement of their careers in this country? If they are eager to marry at once, is there any reason why they cannot spend a truly adventurous honeymoon in a new country, learning something about other people while they are learning about each other?

Is there any compelling reason why a twenty-one-year-old American man has to rush, diploma in hand, to a large corporation which is expected to provide him an old-age pension complementing his social security? Wouldn't the corporation, and the pension, be waiting for him on his return from foreign service in an international volunteer work force? Is there any compelling reason why a twenty-one-year-old American woman must dash from college to a publishing house, museum, or little theater to fill the interval between college and marriage? Isn't it possible that she would find at least as much of an outlet for her admirably selfless idealistic impulses in a year or two spent in the service of a young nation struggling to move up into the twentieth century and achieve its identity?

Let me see if I can anticipate some other possible objections. There may certainly be a very understandable hesitation on the part of people who have barely reached voting age to expose their own lack of experience, or to proclaim that they do in fact have some knowledge worth imparting to others who may be their own age or older. You may remind me, furthermore, that your friends are not all majoring in public administration or hydroelectric engineering, and that those who have been hopefully studying dramatics, English, or education may feel that they really have nothing to offer the youth of a foreign land. To both of these objections, I can only reply that it is hard for me to conceive of a situation in any underdeveloped area in which there could be no benefit from the presence of numbers of recent college graduates. If a girl presumes to have gotten enough out of her college education to teach my children in either primary or secondary school, I should think she would be capable of teaching children in Ghana, Pakistan, or Colombia. It might turn out to be even more satisfying to teach the rudiments of English to the youngsters of Nigeria than to those of Levittown.

It is true that statistically (what a commentary on the realities of our social order behind the flood of cant about raising our educational level!) we have been turning out almost as many college graduates in the areas of commerce and business administration as in all of the sciences, including engineering. Am I wrong in suspecting that our economy might stagger along without the infusion of new blood from five or six hundred of these graduates while they spend several seasons sharing their learning with peoples truly desperately in need of instruction in current commercial and business-administration practices? Indeed, it is even possible that numbers of these budding executives might return from abroad with their sights raised and their inner lives enriched as they commence their climb up the corporate ladder.

I can hear you saying, *But haven't we already exported more than enough Ugly Americans to the far corners of the earth? No matter how noble our motives, won't our do-good invasion be as hotly resented as any other imported pestilence?*

This will be in your hands. If you come in humility to people who need and request your services; if you come with the hope that you may learn as much as you can teach; if you come without trainloads of face creams and footwarmers, but with love and devotion for your new friends and your new job, it is just possible that you will be as well liked abroad as you are when you stay at home. Remember too our insistence from the outset on the *international* character of the volunteer force – you will have to start working for it where you are, but ultimately you will aim for an effort that must override national boundaries and nationalist identifications.

There is already in existence a nonprofit, nonsectarian outfit known as Volunteers for International Development, which is making up a file of people from all over the world "who are willing to serve one or two years in a volunteer service corps at subsistence pay. They will work in international teams in a crusade against hunger, illiteracy, poor health, and misunderstanding." (If you want to know more about VID, which Dean Howard Thurman of Boston University has called "one candle burning against the darkness," you can write to VID File Office, Box 179, Cambridge 38, Massachusetts.)

There remains the question of who would foot the bills for a really large-scale, subsidized international operation – the only kind of operation that would make sense in our world. I honestly do not believe that a people which is quite content to spend some forty billion dollars every year for weapons of mass annihilation (to say nothing of homey accommodations all around the globe for the families of those who man the weapons) can quibble about allocating a minute fraction of that sum for a project which could be considered at worst as a form of mass tourism and at best as renewed evidence of our potential for constructive leadership of the headlong rush to progress of the newly awakening areas of the world. The Hudson River at Tomkins Cove is lined with moth-balled Liberty ships waiting to transport you everywhere in the world, as fifteen years ago they carried me and my friends everywhere in the world; the new nations that have emerged in those years are ready to house you and feed you at least as well as they are attempting to do for the most advanced elements in their own populations.

But with arguments of this nature we move into the realm

of organized agitation and propaganda to gain support from those who would in the last analysis be responsible for the program's success – not only the Congressmen who would vote the funds, not only the administrators and planners of the State Department, not only our delegates to the United Nations, but our gifted and frustrated youth.

You do not, in the new age we are entering, need a set of ideals worth dying for. You do need certain values worth living for, beyond those of cynical nihilism on the one hand and greedy grubbing for gadgets on the other. Those values can only be found, I contend, beyond yourself, beyond your family, beyond your community, beyond your country; they can only be found in a recognition of our common responsibility for what happens to the entire globe in the coming generation as it strains massively to attain the level of human development, indeed to earn the right to face the new problems of a leisured society, which are today uniquely ours here in the United States.

If you do in truth mean business I am suggesting one small avenue along which you and your friends can move, from the morass in which you now confess you are floundering into a future which is as incalculable to me as it is to you, but which you now can help to shape as no other young people could before in human history. All of you, from ambitious graduate students in nineteenth-century French poetry to ambitious graduates of our high schools in printing trades, automotive trades, aviation trades, have it within your grasp to renew the old image of America as a nation of pioneers and freely co-operating men, to demonstrate in action the meaning of responsible democratic endeavor, and to learn with your hands and in your souls what it means to live well by living for others.

Esquire, September 1959

Aftermath

Again the unexpected has happened. In the September 1959 issue of *Esquire* I let fly a shaft at those – particularly among the young – who have been skating along on the congealed American fat of the last decade, instead of exerting themselves to build some moral muscle by participating in the growth of the newer nations of the world. The shaft found its mark, but not quite the one I had expected: apparently it struck an ethical nerve in some hundreds of Americans, young and old, who took the trouble to write, for the most part not to attack me or defend themselves, but to ask if there really was something worth while they could do to prove that they cared enough about their heritage to renew it.

The volume of mail was absolutely without precedent in my own experience as a writer. And the letters did not come from creeps or crackpots; they were written by and large by intelligent, serious, educated men and women who honestly wanted to dedicate themselves for a year or more to an overseas job that would make use of both their skills and their idealism. I got letters from girls at radio stations, advertising executives, wives of Marine Corps officers, young administrators, retired professors; letters from San Francisco, Montreal, Key West, Guam. They all asked about specific opportunities to cut loose if only for a while from a grabby society in order to purge themselves of a feeling of personal waste.

There were letters (and calls and visits too) from friends and former students, and these did not so much ask as tell me what they were doing, and in some cases plead with me for help in publicizing their cause. A young man who has worked these last two years for CARE in Colombia read the article in the middle of the Nechi River jungle, on "an inspection trip to the group of colonists who are clearing land and building a road to a new world in the jungle of Colombia." He was there with a CARE Mission Chief (an American girl) and a Colombian physician, examining new needs for CARE tools and settling a dispute between the social-service association for the area and the leader of the co-operative of colonists. He was excited, as were his Colombian friends, by my article, and here is the nub of his three-page, single-spaced letter:

> I ask for forty-five young American volunteers to work in Colombia, ones who would have volunteered to fight Franco or Hitler in a time lost now. Hate will be lacking as a motive for these young people, unless one can learn to hate the general horrors of starvation and ignorance. But love will come to them as they work and understand. How much have I wanted, and begged, to be given the opportunity to take an ax down from the rack and pitch in with those Pato colonists who have just completed another six kilometers of jungle road. How I have wanted to live with them, to know better their problems, to speak for them when necessary, where their simple words would not be understood. That is one job we would like to offer a young American. . . . In my area alone, the large State of Antioquia, where in the one million rural population (total population two million) sixteen and a half per cent of the people *have* water in their houses and five per cent *have* bathrooms, and 7,000 children under five die annually without ever receiving medical attention, I could cite at least ten places where a young American could work miracles.

A somewhat older American, an educator friend, had just returned from a visit to the educational facilities of some sixteen countries, all around the world, when he read the piece in *Esquire*. He was moved to tell me something about World University Service, the mutual-aid organization sponsored in this country by all the denominational student associations, and praised by Nehru. India, in fact, was one of the countries that hit my friend hardest. He found that 40 per cent of Indian university students came from homes with a monthly income of about fifty dollars, and that it is not surprising that eight of every ten college students suffer from some physical ailment: 84 per cent of them are not getting enough to eat.

Perhaps most significant, and startling, are the hundreds of people who have been impelled by the *Esquire* piece to write to the Volunteers for International Development, the UN-related organization which I mentioned in the article and which has been compiling a register of skilled persons ready to serve at sacrificial pay in international projects. Many of the first three hundred letters "seem to indicate," as Raymond Magee, the Executive Secretary, wrote me, "that the article resulted even in some persons going through an experience which, in the old days, would be called 'repentance.'"

Be that as it may, the correspondence ranged from "letters from professors with experience in technical fields and very qualified for some of our projects, to students who are merely curious."

Within a matter of weeks Mr. Magee was able to tell me that over six hundred letters had come in, with more arriving daily, and to give some detail on the kind of people who were responding. One person sent in four hundred dollars for the fare of an engineer to be sent to Ghana – the engineer may be one of those who volunteered as a result of the article.

Two people with TV experience have written in, and have in consequence been consulted about a current literacy program in Egypt: Three V.I.D. volunteers (an American, a Lebanese, and an Egyptian) in Manoufia, Egypt, have been working with the UNESCO Fundamental Education Center in regard to the plans of the Egyptian government to execute a mass literacy program in 1960 with the aid of TV; in the poor village areas, the government will provide TV sets to coffeehouses and community meeting centers, which will be used for basic reading instruction.

In addition to people like these, several artists have offered their help, a physician has written in, and among the letters from all over the United States (there have also been inquiries from Germany, England, France, Vietnam, South Africa), there have been a good number expressing willingness to query local chambers of commerce, university officials, and the like about the possibility of financing a qualified person from the individual community in a V.I.D. project.

There are a number of reasons why this last is a good idea, beyond the obvious one that it conforms to our tradition of working from the grass roots and involving our friends and neighbors in those public activities we believe worth doing. For one thing, it spreads the idea as well as the responsibility much more widely, and the news of it may even reach those who need the help abroad. For another, it is going to bring home to a lot of Americans what some of us have been learning as a result of the original article.

Surely there is no question now but that there is an enormous reservoir of idealism in young Americans — and in a lot of older ones; surely we know now that they will not call us squares or cornballs if we offer them substantial and practical avenues of action, and that they will not, by and large, flinch or jeer if we use words like "moral" or "ethical" or even "political" to characterize some of the things they can do with their lives. We have found out too that there is work available abroad for many of these people — in some instances their services are desperately needed — but because of a shortage of funds they may have to wait a long time before their offers can be taken up.

It may seem ludicrous, but there it is. The richest nation on earth, which cannot afford new schools, or decent salaries for teachers, or proper housing for all its people, cannot afford either — or so it would seem — to pay the passage and the bare subsistence for all of those who are willing and eager to share their knowledge and technical skills with the people of the newer nations.

But wouldn't there be more occasion for discouragement if there had been no visible response to a piece entitled "Why Resign from the Human Race?" I am confident that Americans who want very badly to do something worth while are going to find the money – or find ways of getting the money – to do it. V.I.D., for example, would very much appreciate suggestions from college people (as well as from the rest of the population – recently retired people are registering, and should register, with V.I.D.) as to how they might help finance a volunteer from their own institution in a V.I.D.-UN-related project, an important step toward a UN Voluntary Service Corps.

Mr. Magee stresses, too, that "some of the people writing would do well to have the experience of working a summer in a college work-camp such as those sponsored by the American Friends Service Committee in Mexico and other lands or by International Civil Service in Europe, Africa, and India. They should, of course, also learn a foreign language. And some might want to take courses in technical assistance at Montana University, Syracuse University, or the American University in Washington, D.C."

This is something that might be borne in mind not only by college students, but by the faculty people who exert such a strong influence on undergraduates. Dean Harlan Cleveland of Syracuse University, who is conducting a world study for the Carnegie Foundation on the question of training Americans for working abroad, has expressed the hope that within the next decade a year's immersion in a foreign culture abroad, perhaps spent during one's college years, would become a requirement for all persons planning to work overseas.

Which brings me to a final suggestion. UNESCO Publication Center (801 Third Avenue, New York 22) puts out a trilingual volume called *Vacations Abroad,* at $1.25. More than simply a listing of vacations, it is a compilation of courses and seminars, hostels and holiday camps, study tours, scholarships, and international voluntary work camps.

Esquire, February 1960

Footnote, 1961: Many people have asked whether I I do not think that President Kennedy's Peace Corps derived from this article, and if so, how I feel about it. The source of such ideas is of no particular importance; this one, like most, was in the air. More interesting is the fact that even when politicians turn ideas into gimmicks, good may come of them. During his first campaign for the Presidency, General Eisenhower was led by one of his writers to promise that he would "go to Korea." In due course, after his election, he did make the promised ceremonial visit; and while the ensuing truce may not have been hastened by the General's ambiguous tour, it was certainly not retarded by it. A net gain for some thousands of soldiers, therefore, from a tricky political ploy.

Just so, Senator Kennedy's discovery, late in his Presidential campaign, that much of American youth was both discontented and idealistic, and ready for an appeal to its altruism, was very likely of the same order as his reiterated appeals to young people to increase their knee-bending and deep breathing. Nonetheless the impact of the program upon the few thousand young men and women who will serve in the Peace Corps can only be salutary. And this despite the fact that the whole scheme was jeopardized at the outset by the idiocy of the Cuban invasion and of the proposal to subject the eager volunteers to a "security" check.

What is disturbing is the possibility that the Peace Corps may ultimately become merely one more element in the whole rickety structure of institutions which serve further to isolate the intellectual and moral elite of American youth from the great mass of self-centered and materialistic adolescents. There is no substantial evidence as yet that the idea of a period of sacrificial foreign service has penetrated to these latter. One gets the impression rather that it is only those who were already idealistic, those who would otherwise have turned to any of a dozen private organizations, who have been galvanized to apply. As for the bulk of American youth, they have not been galvanized by the New Frontier – they are simply hanging around.

One of the most depressing memories of a recent drive across the country is that of the uniformly ugly emptiness of the evening life of young Americans. Whether in Afton, Wyoming, or La Crosse, Wisconsin, the boys are either slopping it up in the juke joints or howling and honking up and down the streets in their convertibles, radios blaring and beer cans sloshing. If you can stand on one corner long enough, you will see the same cars with the same boys cruise past you four, five, six times. They are not tuning in on moral exhortations, not when everything in their daily existence assures them that sacrifice is for the birds and the true national purpose is pleasure.

If the boys in La Crosse had troubled to pick up the paper, as I did that evening when I tired of their hoarse cries, they could have read in the Milwaukee *Journal* an account of the way in which other young Americans were being amused. The youthful wife of their high-minded President was the guest of Paul Mellon at a debutante party for his stepdaughter, Eliza Lloyd, attended by about seven hundred persons, including some two hundred college men who must surely have had their own sense of national purpose.

These young men spent the night "in the tent city which looked like a medieval tournament site with pennants flying from every ridge pole."

> Besides sleeping areas, the tent city included a big cellophane sided plastic tent where snacks and drinks were served around the clock, plus sanitary tents, guard tents and service tents where white dinner jackets could be pressed and evening shoes shined.
>
> The tents were connected by a network of "permanently laid" roads – just in case it should rain and so no man would muddy his shoes. And already this intricate system of hard surfaced roads is being taken up and being replaced with old dirt trails.
>
> The tent city alone cost more than $100,000, it was learned . . .
>
> Those who helped create the tent city and pavilion said they believed there had never before been such a party in the United States. They computed that final bills for this one evening would total more than one million dollars.

Nevertheless, beyond the overstuffed, the blowhard, the bravo, and the prematurely cynical, thousands of young people are reading, writing, arguing, waiting, across the face of a supremely beautiful country, in the kitchens of back-street houses in the small towns, in reading rooms, dormitories, and quiet libraries in the college towns, in coffee houses and crowded hangouts in the big cities – they can be led to do wonderful things. And they will be, not by the phony rhetoric of professional speech-writers and calculating politicians, but by the hard proof which must be forthcoming that we have turned our backs on the pleasure hunt and set our faces to the tasks of the future.